# Law in the Courts of Love

The Politics of Language
Series editors: Tony Crowley, University of Manchester,
Talbot J. Taylor, College of William and Mary,
  Williamsburg, Virginia

*In the lives of individuals and societies, language is a factor of greater importance than any other. For the study of language to remain solely the business of a handful of specialists would be a quite unacceptable state of affairs.*

Saussure

The Politics of Language Series covers the field of language and cultural theory and will publish radical and innovative texts in this area. In recent years the developments and advances in the study of language and cultural criticism have brought to the fore a new set of questions. The shift from purely formal, analytical approaches has created an interest in the role of language in the social, political and ideological realms and the series will seek to address these problems with a clear and informed approach. The intention is to gain recognition for the central role of language in individual and public life.

# Law in the Courts of Love

Literature and other minor jurisprudences

Peter Goodrich

London and New York

First published 1996
by Routledge
11 New Fetter Lane, London EC4P 4EE

Simultaneously published in the USA and Canada
by Routledge
29 West 35th Street, New York, NY 10001

© 1996 Peter Goodrich

Typeset in Palatino by
Ponting–Green Publishing Services, Chesham, Bucks
Printed in Great Britain by T. J. Press Ltd., Padstow, Cornwall

*British Library Cataloguing in Publication Data*
A catalogue record for this book is available from the
British Library

*Library of Congress Cataloguing in Publication Data*
A catalogue record for this book has been requested

ISBN 0–415–06165–2

# Contents

# Preface

These studies trace certain of the boundaries of the modern demon law. They do so in a characteristically rude or personal tone and are imbued with my usual animosity towards the complacency and status or establishment of law. Each study thus pauses and endeavours to stay with a limiting instance, blindspot or addiction of the profession or discipline. In moving from conscience to corporeality, from eating to crying, from forgetting to seducing, or from looking to loving the question is always broadly similar. In critical terms it is that of dwelling upon the weaknesses of law and of analysing the sites of its passage or contact with an 'outside' world, be it that of poetry or the body, of intimacy or ethics, the mouth or the eye. As the physicality or proximity of the metaphors further suggests, the passage of law into everyday life is also a question of existential conditions: the law gets under the skin, it identifies its subjects, it captures the individual, the site or space of its reproduction.

The preface is also a face. It has long been my belief that law is the most disabling or estranged of professions. Such at least is its most radical danger: it inculcates a fear which finds its most prominent expression in the closure of the legal mind, in the lawyers' belief in a norm or rule which speaks as 'the law'. In place of that faith I have tried to argue for a series of minor jurisprudences and specifically for a right to a life – to a literature, a poetry, an ethics, an intimacy or imagination – within law. Specifically in terms of jurisprudence or what is now designated as legal studies the estrangement of law is its greatest injustice. It has been my experience, time and again, that the faith or dogma of law, its distance from subject, person or emotion, is precisely what precludes the dialogue or the attention to singularity which justice or ethics requires. In that sense and only in that sense, to place law in the courts of love is both a nihilistic and a hedonistic undertaking.

The book was written over a period of radical personal transition of which the reader may well not be aware. Started within a space of marginality it was completed after I was appointed Chair of a new law school within the University of London. The shift in institutional role and quite possibly in prominence makes it impossible to hide any longer behind a marginal status or peripheral place. The politics of jurisprudence has never been so immediate or so pressing. Nor have the losses. A close friend and colleague, Ronnie Warrington, died in September 1994. To the extent that this book is for anyone, it is for him.

Peter Goodrich
*Los Angeles,*
*Palm Sunday, 9 May 1995*

# Introduction
## Towards a minor jurisprudence

> I do not know if I should be deemed happy or miserable, because I cannot see the days as I see the nights . . .[1]

On St Valentine's day 1400, Charles VI of France promulgated a statute which established a High Court of Love, or *Cour Amoureuse*, in Paris. The High Court of Love was to have jurisdiction to determine the rules of love and to hear disputes between lovers. It was also, as a court of last instance, to adjudicate appeals from decisions in first instance courts of love. The founding charter suggests that in procedural terms the Court was remarkable for being organised in a non-hierarchical manner: 'no office in the court of love is of greater or lesser dignity than any other, no function is unimportant'.[2] It was instituted as a women's court and the judges were selected by a panel of women on the basis of the recitation or written presentation of poetry. The condition of judgment within the court was collective and similarly poetic. The justice of love was an art of singular and heterogeneous decisions on disputes ranging from violence between lovers to amorous defamation, from breach of erotic confidences to release from unfair contracts of love.

The Court of Love in Paris is but one instance of an alternative jurisdiction or forum of judgment drawn from the diversities of the legal and literary past. There is evidence of many other regional women's courts and of local jurisdictions of love, including those of water and forests, of flowers and gardens, of mourning, of beauty and of the privileges of love.[3] The examples span both literature and law, and their textual records

---

1 [Charles Cotin], *Oeuvres galantes de M. Cotin*, Paris, Estienne Loyson, 1659, 1665 edn, at p. 161.
2 C. Bozzolo and H. Loyau (eds), *La Cour Amoureuse, dite de Charles VI*, Paris, Le Léopard d'or, 1982, at lines 145–150.
3 See particularly Martial d'Auvergne, *Les Arrrets d'amours*, Paris, Picard, 1460, 1951 edn; and for later in the tradition see François Callières, *Nouvelles amoureuses, et galentes*, Paris, G. Quinet, 1678; Jean Donneau de Visé, *Les Nouvelles galantes, comiques et tragiques*, Paris, Estienne Loyson, 1680.

are correspondingly mixed in genre, being variously in the form of poems, narratives, plays, treatises and judicial decisions. They form, I will argue, one of a series of minor jurisprudences or forms of legal knowledge that escape the phantom of a sovereign and unitary law. A minor jurisprudence is one which neither aspires nor pretends to be the only law or universal jurisprudence. Its referent is a law whose jurisdiction is neither jealous of other jurisdictions nor fearful of alternative disciplines. It represents the strangeness of language and so the possibilities of interpretation as also of plural forms of knowledge. A minor jurisprudence, and in the example given a feminine justice, is a challenge to the science of law and a threat to its monopoly of legal knowledge. It challenges the law of masters, the genre and categories of the established institution of doctrine and its artificial and paper rules. The fragmentary and deterritorialised language of minority proceeds upon a different view, it is predicated upon a politics of the literary practice of law and upon the existential commitments of writing: 'where one believed there was the law, there is in fact desire and desire alone. Justice is desire and not law'.[4]

The history of the courts of love is but one instance, although arguably an exemplary one, of a minor jurisprudence. It belongs to a much larger and as yet unwritten history of repressed, forgotten and failed jurisdictions. A history also of lost critical and satirical traditions of jurisprudence, of alternative practices and competing forms of judgment which contemporary legal scholarship either forgets or ignores. Within such a history or pantheon of radical sources and practices of law would be included the rebels, critics, marginals, aliens, women and outsiders who over time repeatedly challenged the dominance of any singular system of legal norms. That the history of such a tradition of radicalism is not written is a failing not of the past but of the contemporary conception of legal scholarship and so also of the possibilities of the history, scholarship and practice of law. A history of radical critiques of law would span a huge array of alternative jurisprudences. It would run from the Roman school of anomalists who challenged the validity of grammatical norms and so the certainty of laws, through those such as Placentinus who challenged the glossatorial reception of Roman law, to Renaissance legal humanism and its reception within common law. It would include also the figures of imagined alternatives to existing legal orders, the daughter of Accursius, for example, who in twelfth-century Montpellier was reported to have carried on her father's practice as a professor of law. It would include the Celtic traditions of women law-givers, as well as troubadour poetry and the tradition of judgments of love.

Alternative or minor jurisprudences are not merely poetic or aesthetic

---

4  Gilles Deleuze and Félix Guattari, *Kafka: Toward a Minor Literature*, Minneapolis, University of Minnesota Press, 1986, at p. 49.

enterprises. Their radicalism and their threat, the reason they are denied or ignored, relates to the history of the practices to which they were tied. The narrative of discarded or failed laws, of jurisdictions denied, repressed or absorbed by the legal tradition includes a vast number of well-documented minor jurisdictions specific to activities, beliefs, ethnicities, localities, trades and representations. Even the briefest of lists would include the ecclesiastical courts, civilian courts, courts of conscience, courts of equity, courts of inquisition as well as laws of the sea, of merchants, of forests, of harvests, of circuses, of fairs, of statuses, of women, of aliens, of Jews, of towns, of hundreds, of tithings, of manors, castles and other localities. Within and between these myriad jurisdictions and sources of law, in their complementarity as in their competition or conflict can be found innumerable alternative principles, fictional rules and radical or wild laws. They form at the very least a glossary of the phantoms which the tradition discarded, a negative representation of its imaginations, a pastiche of its fears and its losses.

The study of minor jurisprudences is hence also a history of law's residues, of imaginary and fictive laws, of 'itinerancy' and fiction as also of contingent and local practices. Most significantly, the theory of minor jurisprudences provides a space within which a radical legal studies can begin to unravel both the history and the resources of alternative legal forms and the practices to which they attached. It promises a history of the legal unconscious. A history of jurisdictions annexed or denied by the phantasm of an all-powerful law, a history of disciplines marginalised by the dream of a common and unitary jurisdiction, a narrative of historical practices denied their reality by a more powerful history, that of the science of law. More than that, the recollection of minor jurisprudences is a history of the dark side of law, of its other scene, of that which it does not know and so cannot control. It is in this sense a history of the desires that survived law. A catalogue of fictions, images and possibilities discarded or repressed by law. A register of imaginary laws which are imaginary for the simple reason that legal science and its history of power denied reality to those jurisdictions, fictions or laws.

The history of the phantasm of a superior law or sovereign jurisprudence can well begin with the narrative of the most peculiar and extreme of jurisdictional annexations or repressions. It is that of the canon or spiritual law and of its courts of conscience which were absorbed into the common law during the first half of the sixteenth century. Although the annexation of the courts of conscience was peculiar to the common law tradition, its essential concerns, those of the separation of law from ethics, of secular law from spiritual law, of the interpretation of rules from questions of conscience, are persistent themes within modern jurisprudence. Chapter 1 briefly traces the history of the two laws, divine and human, canon and common, and elaborates the implications of the demise of the spiritual jurisdiction and of its 'ghostly powers'. The courts of conscience and the interior jurisdiction of spiritual law were absorbed within the common law and only certain residues of the language of conscience remained. In the process of absorption the common law repressed the ethical dimensions and distinct procedural forms of the spiritual law to the end of unifying the system or science of a secular jurisprudence. When contemporary critical legal studies turns to other disciplines or invokes the ethical dimensions of judgment and justice it in many senses returns to the jurisdiction of conscience repressed within common law. The recourse to aesthetics, to literature, to social theory, to philosophy or ethics have in common the desire to reconnect the discipline of law to questions of conscience and more broadly to the politics and casuistic indeterminacies of judgment. Recourse to other disciplines and to minor jurisprudences aspires to reopen questions of jurisdiction and of the plurality of laws, interior and exterior, past and future, imagined and real.

The postmodern use of knowledges external to law is in a curious sense also a premodern phenomenon, a return to the contingencies and hetero-geneities of different jurisdictions and alternative forms of law. In Chapter 2, I pursue one such example, that of the women's courts and judgments of love which are reported by Andreas Capellanus in a late twelfth-century scholastic treatise, *Tractatus amore et de amoris remedio*. The *Treatise* is remarkable for the legal character of its principal themes. It spells out both a set of general principles or precepts of love and also sets out a code of rules for lovers. The twenty-one judgments of love reported in detail in Book 2 of the *Treatise* are casuistic applications of the code and precepts of love to disputes between lovers. My concern in this analysis of a minor jurisprudence of love is to interrupt the idolatry of one law with an alternative historical reality and with the juridical details, the facts, of another jurisdiction. At one level the question which this repressed history of women's courts and judgments of love imposes is that of the rela-tionship between rule and lifestyle, between law and emotion. In dealing with disputes between lovers and so with the most intimate and important of the details or ethics of living, the courts of love transgress the boundaries of positive law and the categories of public reason. They offer a series of legally impossible forms of decision and so challenge in the most concrete and direct of ways the monistic imagination and the unifying logic of positive law. In place of the procedures and the norms of positive law the courts of love suggest a plurality of regimes of regulation dispensing justice according to the ethical dictates of their subject-matter. What is just is what is appropriate to its subject or referent and in matters of intimate relation, what is right or wrong is most usually a question of love.

The example of the courts of love can be used to disturb, parody or deconstruct the sovereign or major jurisprudence of our times. In that the history of women's courts belongs as much to literature as to law, as much to emotion as to reason, as much to empathy as to rule; it is a history that legal historians have chosen to ignore. The absence of the jurisdiction of love from the histories of law is but one example of the fate of minor jurisprudences: they engender fear or jealousy, incomprehension or confusion in the seats of legal power. The recollection of such lost jurisdictions or repressed traditions of jurisprudence can be conceived as a form of scholarly terrorism, a political intervention in law in the manner of interruption. Interruption is rude, wayward and in a sense monstrous. It is in one respect a method of confrontation but it is also at times a hedonistic practice. Interruption heightens pleasure, it prolongs desire by instituting a code of erotic suspension, a seduction by means of deferral. Such at least is one further meaning of interruption as *amor interruptus*, the ritual of distant love in which desire is augmented through separation.

Interruption as it is practised in this book is, however, principally a destabilising technique; it disrupts, breaks, transgresses and moves on. The subsequent chapters endeavour to employ techniques of interruption in interrogating and criticising legal texts and institutions through the use of historical and literary techniques. The interruption of law (*ius interruptum*) thus refers first to a suspension of the strict protocols of legal reading and genre. The analyses presented imply a more hedonistic and subversive rewriting of legal texts and judgments. In this sense the analysis borrows significantly from the traditions of poetic and satirical critiques of law and reintroduces their profane concern not only with pleasure or *eros* but also with the body and its addictions as aspects of law. The stronger sense of interruption thus relates to the etymological meaning of breaking between different orders, as between a fecund and an infertile love (*coitus interruptus*), between desire and satisfaction (*amor interruptus*), between agreement and performance (*contractus interruptus*) or between norm and judgment (*ius interruptum*). In each case the interruption breaks or fragments an existing order and continuity and so troubles the boundaries of an institution, practice or tradition. The interruption is dangerous. It threatens to subvert the genre, to mix the alien and the familiar, to pass without warning between spiritual and profane. In this respect, I will argue, critical legal studies is itself a form of minor jurisprudence. At its best it has interrupted law through a variety of interdisciplinary interventions and has proposed a series of alternative forms of jurisdiction and of practice of law.

Chapters 3 and 4 focus on apparently incidental or marginal features of the legal institution and use these marginalia to analyse aspects of the everyday hold of law upon its subjects. The specific topics drawn upon relate to the history of legal rites and ceremonies, to the banquets, the costumes, the revelries and other masks, the architecture and visual grandeur of courts and laws. Chapter 3 concentrates upon the curious link between law and food and most particularly the continuing requirement in English law that substantial aspects of training to become an advocate and formal qualification as a barrister take place over dinners at the Inns of Court. This seemingly archaic feature of the legal institution is crucial to a legal semiotics that takes seriously the exemplary and tutelary functions of law as the emblem of community. The rites of eating together, of mooting and interpreting law over food, are aspects of instituting a legal form of subjectivity, one of conformity as community, of homosociality as professional persona. The Tables of Justice reflect tablets of law, a community based upon symbols of order, and enacted through the rites of a secular communion, a coming together over flesh and the sacrificial rites of eating meat.

The context of eating law – of the carnivorous jurist – is the separate order and architecture of the Inns of Court. These communities exist through an extraordinary valuation of tradition and an extreme reverence for the symbols and hierarchies of law. Chapter 4 moves from the hermeneutics of law's menus to the aesthetics of law's public face. The aesthetic dimensions of law, its modes of appearance and disappearance, of presence and of judgment, are critically appraised through the extraordinary force or vehemence of the law's protection of its own image. The law of contempt of court has been used on occasion to summarily incarcerate demonstrators outside court, persons who have laughed at seeming absurdities inside court or who have attacked court officials some considerable distance from the courts. The protection of the image of law is part of a much more expansive concern to maintain the symbolic indicia, the signs or outward tokens of the legal institution's spiritual past, its lineage and legitimacy as belonging to an order of judgment that somehow escapes the realm of secular rules or profane and political ends. While the law of contempt claims an extraordinary and sacred origin in a time coeval with the birth of law it is ironic that the claim is made without any awareness of the substantive jurisdiction or alternative forms of spiritual law.

Chapters 5 and 6 move from aesthetics and ethics to literature and re-examine the relationship of law to writing and of justice to genre. Making use of the historical proximity of classical law both to poetics and to literary satire, Chapter 5, 'Of law and forgetting', seeks to remember the literary genre and poetic value of law, its philological and ethical basis in a textuality that was indistinguishable from what antiquity termed virtue and what modernity recast and misrecognised as mere literature or the rhetoric of judgment. In this broadly historical context I argue that literary analysis politicises law, in the academy and in practice, by questioning its values and transgressing its limits as a discipline and so also as a practice. Literature deconstructs law by placing it in the context of what was classically the 'art of life'. Literature suggests other possibilities for law, other means of expression of law and more profoundly conceptions of value and of justice that draw upon a wider variety of experiences of gender, sexuality, ethnicity and lifestyle than are currently available within the closed vision of an embattled legal profession and its mythology of a juristic science. Literature renews law, and in Chapter 6 this claim is spelled out in an analysis of cases relating to mistaken identity in the law of contract. Using a peculiarly literary case, one in which handkerchiefs were stolen during the course of a contract made by post, I argue that attentiveness to the literary and symbolic values of the legal text can provide an expansive method for reinterpretation and revisioning of legal relationships.

The use of literature as an interruption of the modernist project of legality mirrors, at the level of methodology, the history of minor juris-prudences as alternative genres or languages of law. Chapter 7, 'Fate as seduction', directly addresses the problem of law's closure and its correla-tive pretention to mastery. The closure of law, it is argued, is characterised more than anything else by sentiments of jealousy and of fear. The emotional structure of jurisprudence and the existential condition of lawyers has been a priviliged theme within minor jurisprudence. Lawyers take on the mask – the addiction or the terror – of law to the exclusion of all other desires. At the level of jurisprudence the exclusivity of law is reflected in the closure of legal knowledge. Such closure is a form of being towards death, a morbidity which is in turn reflected in inverted form in the lawyer's belief in the phantasm of a sovereign law, a belief in a master or Other who answers in the name of law. At a philosophical level the closure of law is a denial, a negative incorporation, of the substance of the legal tradition: of its history, its violence and its politics. It is the interruptive argument of the minor jurisprudences presented in this book that rather than mastering or by some other means denying the politics and ethics of law, it is precisely these indeterminate and plural features of law that should seduce the lawyer and define the goals of jurisprudence. Using the classical definition of law as the human form of fate the argument is made that the historicality of law, its singular and hetero-geneous practices, inevitably break down its closure. It is the fate of law to act according to principles it cannot know in circumstances of instability and flux. The fate of law is thus its most radical potential; in pursuing the call of justice it is forced to abandon the already known, the prejudiced or predetermined, and to confront a singular destiny that is moved not by rule but by desire.

The concluding chapter returns to the themes of institutional margin-ality and disciplinary politics through addressing issues of jurisdiction and translation. By means of an extended analysis of the history of the critical legal studies movement in America it is argued that sensitivity to dif-ference necessitates recognition of the distinctive and particular character and qualities of specific legal traditions. The mixing of genres and the use of different disciplines to criticise the language and practice of law has its counterparts in phenomena of importation and translation of critical theories and radical agendas from different jurisdictions and across both geographical and linguistic boundaries. The concept of an interruption of law, of the rudeness of criticism, is not a universal and cannot itself avoid the law of interruption. The tendency of critical legal studies to follow fashions, to always keep up with the latest in imported theories and the doctrinaire style of the absolutely current or contemporary has on occasion blurred or obscured the objects of legal critique. The concluding chapter thus attempts to formulate certain cautionary protocols for a legal critique which is sensitive to the geographical and political contexts of theoretical traditions and to the historical contingencies of their development and applications. In this aspect, critical legal studies is a scholastic radicalism, a politics of the institution, an extreme rhetoric which promises a rewriting of the disciplines of law. To perform such a task requires a critical recognition of the displacement of the disciplines that can radicalise law, as well as a sensitivity to the peculiar displacement of academic writing.

At its best, at its most subversive, critical legal studies interrupts law in both its rhetorical and its judgmental functions, in both its tutelary and its legislative roles. In breaking between the norm and its expression, between doctrine and writing, critique opens the possibility of using the literary genre of law to reinstate the uncertainty and the undecidability of the writing of law. The reason and the value of such suspension or aporia in relation to judgment is a question of justice, of attention to the particular. In this aspect suspension of judgment offers the opportunity to recognise and in some sense account the desires of the subject that writes and of the subject judged. That subjectivities motivate both judgment and the writing of law is a theme closer to literature than to legal doctrine within the contemporary order of disciplines. It implies a recognition of the phantasmatic character of legal practice, of the bridging of the unbridgeable gap between norm and judgment, rule and application. The phantasmatic structure of legal practice is the theme which runs across all the studies in this collection. They follow the path of the law from the imaginary to the symbolic, from the icon to the body and from community to exile. They follow that itinerary in the mode of interruption and in the hope that interruption moves the law on, that it forces the institution to recognise the racial, sexual and cultural limitations of its phantasms, of its laws.

# Chapter 1

# Salem and Bizance
## A short history of the two laws

The study of law or jurisprudence, according to one of the earliest definitions recorded in the *Digest*, is 'the knowledge of things divine and human, and the science of what is just or unjust'.[1] Equivalent definitions elaborated legal study as 'true philosophy' and as the 'art of the good and the equal'.[2] Law, in other words, was never a merely temporal or secular study, nor was the substance of law ever to be conceived as divorced from its spiritual essence. The positive forms of law, in short, were inevitably and inexorably bound to the methods of an art and the criteria of justice and truth. The Renaissance reception of Roman law reiterated a classical tradition which consistently subordinated municipal or local rules to the image of a universal and theocratic source of law. The order of legal method was thus one which for obvious reasons gave priority to the divine origins of law and ordered the means of temporal justice according to a hierarchy of differing titles of legality. It was not simply that the art of law aspired to wisdom, but rather that the discipline and practice of legal judgment were predicated upon a series of higher orders of knowledge. Even in a late sixteenth-century primer or preparative to legal study, the depiction of law as embedded in the concerns of justice dictated that the law student be familiar with the substance of legal rules only after acquiring a knowledge of and respect for those disciplines which came in advance of law, namely, the rules of divinity, nature, moral philosophy, logic and grammar.[3]

Insofar as the claims of other disciplines and the dictates of other laws

---

1 *Digest* 1.1.10.2. (Ulpian) 'Iuris prudentia est divinarum atque humanarum rerum notitia, iusti atque iniusti scientia.'
2 *Digest* 1.1.1. (Celsus) 'ius est ars boni et aequi ... veram nisi fallor philosophiam, non simulatam affectantes'.
3 Fulbecke, *Direction or Preparative to the Study of the Law*, London, J. and W.T. Clarke 1599, 1829 edn, ch. 1. Interesting and comparable delineations of the discipline can be found as early as Sir John Fortescue, *De Laudibus Legum Angliae*, London, Gosling, 1466, 1737 edn; and subsequently in St German, *Doctor and Student*, London, Selden Society, 1528, 1974 edn; John Doderidge, *The English Lawyer*, London, I. More, 1631 edn; Sir Henry Finch, *Law or a Discourse Thereof in Foure Books*, London, Society of Stationers, 1628.

sound strangely in the context of contemporary jurisprudence, which conceives itself to be a modernist science subject to distinct and autonomous rules of legal method, it is worth spelling out this initial historical observation somewhat further. In philosophical terms, law was subject to a variety of other laws, and most notably those of theology, conscience and history. In institutional terms, the profession of secular law or in England of common law, was simply one of numerous legal jurisdictions, a pluralism of laws which reflected the hierarchy and diversity of the sources of knowledge and representations of truth. The courts spiritual, the courts of conscience and of the church, courts of honour and of equity as well as of specific localities and activities, of cities and forests, of trade and matrimony, of war and of the seas all subsisted under different laws, forms of knowledge or sources of justice. Far from being 'pure' or based upon the exclusion or repression of other disciplines, the classical tradition incorporated law into a complex and plural epistemological frame in which the diverse disciplines of particular courts and laws were subject ultimately to the dictates or criteria of an absolute knowledge only in part accessible to humanity and its fragile perspectives of reason and faith. In which pluralistic sense it might be noted finally that in hermeneutic terms the truth of law or of judgment was in each instance to be determined ultimately by reference to ontological rather than epistemological criteria. A text, a tradition or a reported rule might provide access to some aspect of nature or truth, but the criteria and methods of human law were only ever forms of return or of partial apprehension of a truth which belonged in its entirety to another order and to the being or essence of the divinity. The text was thus secondary to the meaning (*mens legis*), the word to the spirit (*anima legis*), the language of law to the force, power or virtue that underlies its enunciation.[4]

The argument of the present chapter will be that modern jurisprudence, and most specifically the doctrinal tradition of common law which developed in the first half of the seventeenth century, was predicated upon an indicative and historically significant repression of precisely those disciplines, knowledges and jurisdictions that constituted not only the plurality of laws but equally the spirit, virtue and meaning of legal judgment. In that it will not be possible to trace the full history of this displacement of jurisprudence from divine to human, from art to science and from justice to law, the argument will be based around the example of the polemic between spirituality and temporality and will suggest that the defeat or annexation of the spiritual jurisdiction was significantly

---

4   See, classically, *Digest* 1.3.17 (Celsus); *Digest* 1.3.29 (Paulus); *Digest* 50.16.6.1 (Ulpian). For a remarkable discussion of these texts in their Renaissance context, see Ian Maclean, *Interpretation and Meaning in the Renaissance: The Case of Law*, Cambridge, Cambridge University Press, 1992, at pp. 142–158.

constitutive of what might in more general terms be elaborated as a positive unconscious of legal science. In the concluding portion of the chapter it will be argued that the repressed returns and that the contemporary crisis of the legal form, its modern history of positivisation, irrationality and injustice are symptoms of the return of a distant and traumatic past, that of the repression of the spiritual jurisdiction and the exclusion or closure of law to those other knowledges which were inherent in its classical designation as being also a form of justice, an art which mixed spirituality and temporality, body and soul.

It is, finally, to the effects of the relationship between knowledge and power or jurisdictions that this chapter is addressed. The history of *utrumque ius*,[5] of what can be termed the enfolding of laws, not only effectively repressed the trauma of the dissolution of the spiritual jurisdiction but it also reproduced the social subject, a symbolic or dogmatic subjectivity which could neither know nor directly address the law of its own subjectivity. In this sense, it is the institution which, to borrow the classical formulation of Roman law, institutes life, which functions *vitam instituere* in its specific forms.[6] The study of the two laws thus offers elements of a prehistory of the modern subject of law and of its disciplines, a subject whose identity and contours were so copiously and evocatively drawn by Foucault in *The Order of Things* and in *Discipline and Punish*.[7] It should also, however, be said that the period examined, principally that of post-Reformation law, both elaborates and undermines Foucault's thesis of the specifically modern character of discipline. The institution of a disciplined subject and its apparatus of conscience, the fascination or fixation of the body or surface to or by panoptic visibilities already had a history within spiritual law and its successor, the doctrine of common or Anglican jurisprudence.

## THE MAN WHO MISTOOK THE LAW FOR A HAT

The conflict of jurisdictions and more specifically the relation between canon, civil and common law was an integral theme of the earliest common law treatises although it gained its most vehement expressions during the Reformation. Rather than review the polemical and apologetic literature

---

5  For an analysis of this theme, see P. Legendre, 'Le droit romain, modèle et langage: De la signification de l'*Utrumque Ius*', in P. Legendre, *Ecrits juridiques du moyen age occidental*, London, Variorum, 1988. For a more extensive and technical discussion, see P. Legendre, *La Pénétration du droit romain dans le droit canonique classique*, Paris, Imprimerie Jouve, 1964. For a critical commentary, see Y. Hachamovitch, 'One Law on the Other' (1990) 8 *International Journal for the Semiotics of Law* 187.

6  *Digest* 1.3.2 (Marcian). For discussion P. Legendre, *L'Inestimable objet de la transmission: étude sur le principe généalogique en Occident*, Paris, Fayard, 1985, pp. 349–375.

7  M. Foucault, *The Order of Things*, London, Tavistock, 1974; *idem*, *Discipline and Punish*, London, Allen Lane, 1979.

in any detail, an indicative sense of the levels and the issues of the division between the different laws can be gained through reconstructing an example from an era somewhat after the re-establishment of the Anglican constitution. It is taken from an exchange between the Anglican Bishop Dr Edward Stillingfleet and the recusant divine Thomas Godden. In *A Discourse concerning the Idolatry practised in the Church of Rome*, Stillingfleet had defended the Anglican prohibition on the worship (*latria*) of images, but distinguished civil worship, and gave as an instance of permissible civil reverence the example of honour given to the State.[8] It is against this example of civil worship that Godden reacts and towards the end of his treatise, entitled *Catholicks no Idolaters or a full Refutation of Dr Stillingfleet's unjust charge of Idolatry against the Church of Rome*, inverts the Anglican arguments against images by using them to ridicule those engaged in accepted forms of civil reverence.

Godden tells an anecdote of a countryman or peasant before the law. A gentleman passing the Royal Court observes a countryman being apprehended at the entrance to the Court by the 'yeoman guards' because 'the clown, it seems, would have gone into the Presence covered. They pulled him back, and told him when he went into that room he must pull off his Hat'.[9] He challenged that demand on the ground that he saw nothing in the Court but a chair and a canopy. On being informed that it was the king's Chair of State and that 'he must do it to the chair out of respect for the King' the countryman demands to know 'whether any worship at all were due to the Chair or no?' Mimicking the scholastic argument against St Basil,[10] the peasant reasons that the reverence or worship shown to the chair has either to be the same as that given to the king or distinct from it. If the same, then proper regal worhip would be given to something beside the king, 'which were treason'. If distinct, then the chair would be worshipped 'with regal honour for itself, and not relatively, which were for a man to submit himself to a piece of wood'.

Aside from more general arguments as to the inconsistency of the Anglican position, for example, that it allowed people to bow at the name of Jesus or to kneel at the altar, Godden's argument is that the countryman's objections arise from a peculiarly English empiricism or indeed stupidity. The argument that a chair is a chair is a chair and no more, denies

8   E. Stillingfleet, *A Discourse concerning the Idolatry practised in the Church of Rome*, London, H. Mortlock, 1671, at pp. 91–92. The same position and example can be found in William Perkins, *A Warning against the Idolatrie of the Last Times*, Cambridge, Legat, 1601, at pp. 96–97. For discussion of the latter text and its context, see Margaret Aston, *England's Iconoclasts I: Laws against Images*, Oxford, Oxford University Press, 1988, at pp. 408–415.

9   Thomas Godden, *Catholicks no Idolaters or a full Refutation of Dr Stillingfleet's unjust charge of Idolatry against the Church of Rome*, London, 1672, at p. 179.

10 The often cited iconophilic *topos* attributed to St Basil is the maxim *honos qui eis exhibetur, refertur ad prototypa*.

all sense of aesthetics, of history and of the symbolic. It also indicates an extreme inability to distinguish, or radical resistance to, the division between the visible world or 'spectacle of things' and the invisibility or force of which it is the spectacle.[11] The Protestant position against the image is presented by Godden both as repressive and as denigrating the subject that worships: civil worship simply implies, as does the use of images, an ability or intelligence capable of distinguishing 'like proportionable reverence' from the honour due divinity. In scholastic terms, *honor est in honorante*, honour resides in the mind which gives it. More than that, the image is simply writing, a mark of memory, a trace that can touch or depict or reflect the colours of the soul:

> if one thing hath connexion with, or analogy to another, although invisible, when the former is represented to a person that understands the analogy or connexion there is between them, it is apt to bring to his remembrance the latter. Hence it is, that although the soul of man cannot be drawn in colours, yet when the body to which it is united, is represented in picture, the representation serves as a means to bring to our minds the perfections or graces of the soul which informs it; and not to draw them down to the figure and lineaments of a body drawn upon a Table, or carved in an image.[12]

Within this perspective *latria* and *dulia* can be distinguished by virtue of the difference of their object, one ending in or terminated upon the divine substance, the other relative to the signs or marks of divine governance or dominion.[13] The idol, upon the same principle of reference, is distinct by virtue of transparency: *idolum nihil representat*, it is nothing, a simulation, *rei mortua*.

For the sake of completeness, Stillingfleet's response to Godden requires brief advertisement. The original claim had simply been that there was a category distinction to be made between Divine worship and civil worship and that 'bowing towards the Chair of State' or the king's picture or garments was 'of the same nature with putting off of our Hats' while in court or church; it was a relative or inferior honour and should be conceived as a natural act of reverence, similar to 'that way which the ancient Christians did use to direct their worship'.[14] At a more fundamental doctrinal level, the argument in relation to the Chair of State was

---

11 James Calfhill, *An Answere to the Treatise of the Cross*, London, H. Denham, 1565, at sig. 169ᵛ: 'The world itself is a certain spectacle of things invisible, for that the order and frame of it, is a glass to behold the secret working and hidden grace of God.'

12 Godden, *Catholicks no Idolaters*, at p. 84.

13 For discussion of the distinction between *latria* and *dulia*, see, for example, N. Sander, *A Treatise of the Images of Christ and his Saints: and that it is unlawful to breake them, and lawful to honour them*, Omers, J. Heigham, 1624, at pp. 78–90.

14 Stillingfleet, *A Discourse concerning Idolatry*, at pp. 91–94.

linked to a distinction between two forms of law. Divine worship was to proceed without the use of either external or 'inward images' for the reason that God had so prescribed: the law, the second commandment, dictated that it was forbidden to worship by means of images. In the case of the reverence shown to the Chair of State, a separate and more secular source of law operated: 'all expressions of respect depend on custom and the Prince's pleasure, or the Rules of the Court, the only question a man is to ask, is, whether it be custom of the Court, or the will of the Prince to have men uncovered.'[15] It is the law of custom or the common practice of the court which determines the material or secular issue of reverence and while it entails an element of symbolism and of indirect representation, the knowledge of civil matters and common laws was, at least for Stillingfleet, distinct from those images that purported to relate to a God whose essence was invisibility and whose substance was a self-presence which denied the possibility of any further representation: divinity could neither be painted, nor through any 'creature, nor phantasm of God in our minds' be portrayed.[16]

The references to different orders of knowledge and to separate species of law are not unconnected. The various visibilities which the two laws jointly yet distinctly endeavour to regulate belong to separate epistemic fields and constitute distinct positivities. The object of perception, either external or internal, only exists by virtue of a law which defines not only its visibility but also the scopic regime within which the subject's gaze (*honorariam adorationem*) terminates upon an object which is neither present nor visible to the naked eye. The joint orders of visibility and of law, of iconicity and idolatry have their own histories or discursive archaeologies which will here be ignored. It is my intention rather to reread Godden's story of the peasant before the law in more legalistic terms. What is at stake in this story is also a question of a juridical transition and closure, of an unacknowledged transmission or succession from one law to another. It is a question of inheritance which might be termed an enfolding of laws and it is within that enfolding that a specific jurisdiction and imaginary unity of law, a fictively distinct juridical reason, is constituted and elaborated for the modern tradition of common or Anglican law.

## GHOSTLY POWERS

The brief relation of the story of the peasant before the law can be reconstructed in detail as a dispute over the concept of presence within two separate orders or jurisdictions of law. What is significant about the

15 Stillingfleet, *A Defence of the Discourse concerning the Idolatry practised in the Church of Rome in answer to a Book entitled Catholics no Idolaters*, London, Robert White, 1676, at 849–850.
16 Stillingfleet, *A Discourse concerning Idolatry*, at p. 79.

debate, however, is not the distinction between the respective theological positions but rather their similarity. The most forceful feature of the Anglican defence of civil honour as being in accordance with custom or local law (*ius commune*) is not the distinctiveness of the locality or institution but rather its adaptation, its borrowing or reception of the principle of interior law or inward court, from the very position which it apparently excluded. There is, in short, an identity forged through negation, an identity which takes up what has been denied in the form of repression or, at the very least, in the form of displacement. It is this curious transmission of the spiritual into the secular law which will now be addressed more directly.

The rhetoric of common law, of an Anglican constitution and English custom has always paid a certain respect towards higher orders or sources of justice and law. Such recognition, however, has tended to be in terms of the very specific and direct relation of common law or indigenous custom and the *leges terrae* to some art, divinity, justice or other 'higher' source of law. Thus, in its classical formulation, *regnum Angliae est regnum Dei*, to which it is immediately added that common law is the appropriate measure of all issues tried in England and should be kept free of canon and civil law which are 'but beggarly baggage, and arguments of brawling braines'.[17] Even in a late and moderate institutional treatise the point is made at some length that 'the law of England in particular, is an Art to know what is Justice in England' and concludes that 'the common law is the absolute perfection of reason'.[18] What is important about such statements, or more accurately denials, is not the formulaic exaggeration of a tenuous identity, but rather the repression of the genealogy or more simply the diversity of knowledges and practices which make up the common law. The anecdote of the countryman refusing to show reverence in the Royal Court is to be understood initially precisely as a narrative of the plurality of laws and of practices. It is to be interpreted in this sense as a struggle over jurisdiction and correlatively over the site of enunciation of law. It is a question of geography to be sure, but this resistance which the peasant showed towards the site and the pretention of secular law can be taken further and understood as a species of irreverence or nascent critique of law's presence as such. In this respect the solid and simple peasant is an

17 John Leslie, *A Defence of the Honour of the Right Highe, Mightye and Noble Princesse Marie Queene of Scotlande and Dowager of France*, London, Eusebius Dicaeophile, 1569, at sig. 97ᵛ and 120ʳ. The other exemplary expression of this argument is to be found in Aylmer, *An Harborowe for Faithfull and Trewe Subjectes against the late blowne blaste, concerning the governement of women*, Strasborowe, 1559, at fol. P i b–P iv a. For a review of the literature on nationalism and common law, see Goodrich, 'History, Nationalism and Common Law' (1992) 1 *Social and Legal Studies* 7. See also J.G.A. Pocock, *The Ancient Constitution and the Feudal Law*, Cambridge, Cambridge University Press, 1987.
18 Thomas Wood, *An Institute of the Laws of England*, Savoy, Sare, 1720 edn, at pp. 6–7.

emblem not only of scepticism as to the place of law but also a figure or omen of the future positivisation of the secular form and institution of law.

The peasant, in ridiculing the claim of the Royal Court to be honoured in precisely the same terms as the Protestants had used to debunk the Roman Catholic defence of the image, provides an interesting clue as to a further feature of the debate between the two laws. The attack on the image and the correlative movement towards a law without images was predicated upon the power and hence the danger of the image and of circumscription. In refusing the claim of the image to represent truth or inward virtue, the reform of the law had simultaneously to replace the image, the terrain of nothing and non-representation, with licit figures of law and of direction or perception. The result was, on the surface at least, an order of vision predicated upon the text and hostile to both plastic figures and textual images. The figures of truth and the rules of law were to have an identical and unitary expression in demonstrable and literal forms. One order of figuration was to be succeeded by another, but this succession was also a denial of what was inherited, acquired or taken on with the form and the power of law itself. It inherited the jurisdiction of the spirituality but in the form of negation. It instituted an internal law but in the form of repression. It established an order, constitution and reason but it did so in the form of passivity.

In synoptic style a contrast may be drawn between two separate but comparable laws. On one side of the transition from spiritual to temporal supremacy lay the shattered and increasingly subordinate jurisdiction of spiritual law. The distinction is signalled most powerfully in the debate between Sir Thomas More and Christopher St German in the early sixteenth century, and it is the barrister St German who first opposes Salem and Bizance, spiritual and temporal law. As against the Lord Chancellor More, German argued strenuously for the restriction of the powers of the ordinaries (the spiritual judges) and for increasing use of writs of prohibition which would take temporal matters out of the discretionary *arbitrium* of the church courts. The argument against the spiritual jurisdiction was against the excessive authority of the ecclesiastical courts and against the illiberal character of their procedures. Actions ex officio for heresy under the statute *De Haeretico Comburendo* were exemplary of all that was wrong in the process and the substance of the spirituality and St German lengthily lists the details of such excess of power and the forms of its abuse.[19] The significant issue, however, is not the tabling of abuses nor the justification of the increasingly absolutist

19 See St German, *A Treatise Concerning the Division between the Spirituality and the Temporality*, London, R. Redman, 1533; and St German, *Salem and Bizance*, London, Berthelti, 1533. For Thomas More's responses, see More, *The Apologye*, London, W. Rastell, 1533, and *The Deballacyon of Salem and Bizance*, London, W. Rastell, 1533.

jurisdiction of the common law courts, but rather the subsistence of the spiritual jurisdiction in ever new places and forms.

With regard to St German, the polemic against the spirituality is reformist in the precise sense that he believed that the common law was a safer guardian of the nation's soul than arbitrary and excessive Roman legal practices. In particular it may be noted that the principal effect of his arguments was to insist upon the right of the common law to incorporate or to subsume the spirituality. It is not that the spiritual jurisdiction should be removed or abandoned but rather that it be transferred so as better to reflect the 'true state of English law'.[20] In his classic dialogue on the virtue of common law, *Doctor and Student*, it is plain in the extreme that St German supports fully the spiritual power of law and the divine character of all judgment. The law is always subject to equity and to conscience, a point which can be elaborated through St German's complex explanation of judgment:

> conscience, which derives from *cum scientia*, with knowledge, imports both knowledge of itself and knowledge with another thing. As knowledge by itself it is a natural act and is both cognitive and also motive and inclines the soul to pursue good and eschew evil. Thus its place is superior to reason and is conjoined with that higher light of reason called sinderesis. As knowledge with another thing it imports knowledge with some particular act[21]

and in this lesser form it subordinates the application of knowledge or law to the desire or equity that governs the function of judgment. The spiritual in short is and always was a part of the temporal law; it was its source and its authority[22] and if any should doubt that conjunction of source and spirit Sir John Fortescue early on had observed that the very word law (*ius*) was but an abbreviation of the figure and term of justice (*iustitia*).[23]

The complaint of the canon lawyers and the polemical virulence of recusants and Catholics had little to do with the substance of the jurisdiction, nor did it relate directly to the application of law but rather to the

---

20 Thus, St German, *A Treatise*, at sig. 28ᵛ: 'Another cause of the division has been by reason of divers laws and constitutions which have been made by the church . . . wherein they have many times exceeded their authority, and attempted in many things against the laws of the realm.'

21 St German, *Doctor and Student*, at pp. 87–89.

22 See, for example, John Poynet, *A Short Treatise of Politike power, and of the obedience which subjectes owe to kynges and other civile Governours*, London, 1556, at fol. B iii b:

> Rulers in the world have sometimes wished to be taken for Gods, that is, the ministers and images of God here on earth, the examples and mirrors of all godliness, justice, equity and other virtues, and claim and exercise an absolute power . . . with *sic volo, sic iubeo* . . . . Such power is laughable. God instituted civil and political power to maintain justice.

23 Sir John Fortescue, *De Natura Legis Naturae*, London, private distribution, *c.* 1466, at p. 231.

politics of institutional place. Richard Cosin, in an important defence of the ecclesiastical courts, argues that the 'mean spirited and unchristian' gibes and attacks upon ecclesiastical courts were both unnecessary and self-contradictory. In terms of self-contradiction, he points precisely to the irony that

> these professed dealers for an innovation in the Church doe most greedily take holde of these exceptions from the common lawe, against jurisdiction ecclesiastical, and doe alledge also sundry others, yet pretending to ground themselves for both, not alonely upon the lawes of the realme . . . but upon Gods lawe also, the civill, the Canon, or Ecclesiasticall law, and upon equitie and reason . . .[24]

The issue was not therefore the abandonment or loss of a jursidiction or type of action but simply a question of its transmission to new institutional sites. Thus, somewhat later, John Godolphin in a classic compilation of ecclesiastical law remarks, by way of preface to the abridgement, that 'all that follows would be but insignificant and disfigured cyphers' without an understanding of the implications of the Act of Supremacy, for 'When Henry VIII was both Parliamentrarily and Synodically invested herewith, although it were with all the privileges and preheminences incident thereto, yet no more accrues to the Crown thereby, than was legally inherent in it before'.[25]

Where canon and civilian lawyers argued in favour of a plurality of laws, not least on the ground that the 'exorbitant licentiousness'[26] of the age would justify any number of laws, however manifold in source and procedure, the Anglican defence of the English constitution asserted both the priority and the particularity of common law. This defence of an imaginary past, of an immemorial law tied indissolubly to the body politic of England in spite of all foreign incursions, was no more than a thinly veiled transposition of Catholic arguments into the new polity. Hooker's 'love of things ancient' and belief in the 'ripeness of understanding . . . and virtue of old age' referred to principles of establishment, of tradition and conservation with which the Romans would have been equally at home.[27] It is indeed tradition as unwritten law and as perfected knowledge which Stillingfleet praises as the genuine source of common law and its various

---

24 Richard Cosin, *An Apologie for Sundrie Proceedings by Jurisdiction Ecclesiastical, of Late Times by some Challenged and also Diversely by them Impugned*, n.p., 1591, at fol. A 2 a.

25 John Godolphin, *Repertorium Canonicum or, an abridgement of the Ecclesiastical laws of this Realm consistent with the Temporal*, London, R. Atkins, 1678, at pp. 1–2. This argument was a common one. See, for further examples, Dr W. Fulke, *T. Stapleton and Martiall (two Popish Heretics) Confuted and of their Particular Heresies Detected*, London, H. Middleton, 1580; Dr John Favour, *Antiquitie Triumphing over Noveltie: whereby it is proved that Antiquitie is a true and certaine note of the Christian Catholike Church*, London, Richard Field, 1619.

26 H. Consett, *The Practice of the Spiritual or Ecclesiastical Courts*, London, T. Bassett, 1685, at fol. A 2 b.

constitutions. Turning to the discussion of the obligatory force of ecclesiastical law and canons within the constitution he therefore propounds
the view that time and uninterrupted usage are the real foundations of the
force of law: *longa possessio parit ius possindendi*, long possession transfers
dominion. Custom gains the authority of law by virtue of the affirmation
of time and the consent, the practice and reception of the populace.[28]
Antiquity was foundation and tradition was both the form of its legitimacy, its approval and also the means of its transmission.

The notion that time would write the law and further that uninterrupted usage took the form of prescription are both broadly phenomenological conceptions of legality. What distinguishes the Anglican catholic
sense of tradition and customary law from later and less artistic or less
dynamic forms of legal positivisation is precisely the sense of interiority
which accompanies tradition as law. The classical conception of ecclesiastical jurisdiction was of a law which regulated the manifestations
or manners and good order of the public sphere but as incidents and
expressions of interior states. The authority of the ordinary was a ghostly
power; it was determined as a control of the spirit and as an ordering of
inward sense because it was subjectivity, the soul, which was the object
or termination of law's rule. The constitution was that of both an
ecclesiastical and a civil polity and the person was likewise an impossible
duality, both substance and soul. The struggle over images and the
correlative growth in the power and extent of common law was not a
dispute over the object of law's power but rather over the means or
institutions through which to achieve an appropriate discipline. The
natural image, in one apologetic definition, was an 'inward image, an
inward imagination. An image is of past tidings and affections, it repeats
and calls to remembrance . . . [for] the mind reads backwards, as it were
in its inward book, the whole order of its history'.[29] In an exemplary
polemic against the image, the same relationship of reference is referred
to but in disparaging terms, the phantasm or inward imagination distracts, it is *esse vestitum imagine*, being clothed with an image.[30]

The position of a secular law which was founded in the midst of the war
over images and which was nominally iconomach and for a time quite
actively iconoclastic was somewhat ambivalent and frequently less than

---

27 Richard Hooker, *Of the Lawes of Ecclesiastical Politie*, London, R. Scott, 1676 edn, at pp.
   195–196. For an extended discussion of this theme see Goodrich, *Languages of Law; From
   Logics of Memory to Nomadic Masks*, London, Weidenfeld and Nicolson, 1990, chs. 2 and
   3.
28 Edward Stillingfleet, *Ecclesiastical Cases relating to the duties and rights of the parochial Clergy,
   stated and resolved according to Principles of Conscience and Law*, London, Henry Mortlock,
   1698, at pp. 329 and 349.
29 Sander, *A Treatise*, at p. 159.
30 Robert Parker, *A Scholasticall Discourse against Symbolizing with Antichrist in Ceremonies:
   especially in the signe of the Crosse*, n.p., 1607, at sig. 2$^r$.

explicit. For the principal authors of the settlement and the modern discourse of constitution and law, the interplay of tradition and text, of ghostly power and positive law, of unwritten truth and visible word, in short, of spirit and meaning, was a complex inheritance of a law of images and their inward sense, of spiritual laws and their pastoral implementation. The ecclesiastical eye or *speculum pastoralis*,[31] the watch-tower that surveyed the soul, became an element in a combined or dual polity in which common law was to take on the custody of the *corpus mysticum* of state. As Stillingfleet made clear in justifying the civil honour to be shown to the Chair of State, the mystical antiquity of common law custom, the essential legality of the unwritten tradition as expressive of the soul of the people and the spirit of the land was never to be understood as the only source of law. It was to be joined with the sacral character of the sovereign and its legislation and indeed whether a specific custom or practice were to be observed at any instance was in the end a matter of legislation, the question being, did it please the prince and so take on the force of law?

The relation between these sources of law, custom and sovereignty need not be rehearsed here save to observe that in its own particular way the common law accepted in a somewhat interpolated form the Roman principle that all the laws were inscribed in the sovereign's breast.[32] As early as Glanvill and Fleta, common law had also observed the principle of absolute royal power and simply transferred the domain of its application and the extent of its jurisdiction in recognising the common lawyers as the principal directors and interpreters of this pleasure or volition which would always have the power or *potestas* of father and law.[33] In unifying polity and law, the sovereign and everything which such sovereignty implied in terms of custom, constitution and law was taken into or enfolded within the positivity of common law. In becoming a science, common law became mystical. Sir Edward Coke's *vocabula artis* and professional knowledge, his self-evident antiquity was beyond record as connatural to the people and in need of no proof, an initiate science whose trauma of inauguration instituted a pattern of repetition which is arguably still repeated today.[34] The law embraced both *patria potestas* and *regia*

---

31 T. Stapleton, *A Returne of Untruthes upon M. Jewell*, Antwerp, Ihon Laet, 1566, at sig. 57ʳ: '*specula pastoralis* the pastoral watch-tower is common to all that bear the office of Bishop'.
32 The classical maxim is usually given as *omnia iura habet in scrinio pectoris sui*. For commentary on this theme see Pierre Legendre, *Le Désir politique de Dieu: études sur les montage de l'état el du droit*, Paris, Fayard, 1990, pp. 221–35.
33 See H.G. Richardson and G.O. Sayles (eds), *Fleta*, London, Selden Society, 1955 edn, p. 36: 'quod principi placuit legis habet vigorem'. All right belonged to the crown – *sua iura est*.
34 See Coke, *The first part of the Institutes of the lawes of England, or a commentarie upon Littleton, not the name of a lawyer onely, but of law iself*, London, Atkins, 1629, sig. 6ʳ. See, for comparable analysis, Sir John Davies, *A Discourse of Law and Lawyers*, Dublin, Franckton, 1615. See Goodrich, 'Critical Legal Studies in England: Prospective Histories' (1992) 12 *Oxford Journal of Legal Studies* 195.

*potestas*, it instituted an incommunicable and supreme power or *iura sublimia*, a law which joined in one jurisdiction both *iure positivo pontificio* and *iure divino Apostolico*.[35]

The crown, in one peculiarly striking definition, was a 'Nursing Father' whose ghostly power was to be used to the end of nurturing the inner subjection or spiritual obedience of both institutions and individuals within the commonwealth.[36] The function of law, deriving from this seizure or paternity and dominion over all subjects, was to order the external laws of the commonwealth so as to abide by and contribute towards both knowledge and its spiritual objects: *misera servitus, ubi jus est vagum aut incognitum*, it is a miserable servitude where law is both wandering and unknown.[37] The final end or *ratio finalis* of law was not that of maintaining external security but an internal cause, that of establishing 'peace inwardly' and governing *in ordine ad bonum spirituale*.[38] In short, human laws, concerned as they are with the external positivities of the public sphere, were mere accidents or effects of a superior and anterior cause, of that essence or being that formed the inner nature and supreme law of the subject. Human law was simply indicative. It pointed to causes and virtues that would bind the conscience, it was no more than the image or legitimate representation of an invisible nature and its divine cause, and in that sense or role common law was in substance and effect an aspect of the law of nature and a reflection of an a-temporal and inalterable essence, given *ex institutione naturae*. Subjection was thus similarly derived from the law and virtue of nature and the regulation of such subjectivity was in the same sense a feature of bonds or obligations which belonged to conscience and to the order of nature and of causes and not only or simply to that of positive law.

## THE ENGLISH JANUS

The order of sources of law reflected a hierarchy of forms of subjection. One law depended on the other and took its meaning and its justification from its higher source. In practical terms it would thus be possible to trace the orders of subjection in direct parallel to the historical hierarchy of sources of law. While the orders and jurisdictions were soon fused in a unitary concept of a system of law, a genealogical reading of one law in the other, of *utrumque ius*, can offer considerable insight into the past and possibilities of plural legal jurisdictions and the various implications and

---

35 Calybute Downing, *A Discourse of the State Ecclesiastical of this Kingdome, in Relation to the Civill*, Oxford, W. Turner, 1632, pp. 66–68.
36 Roger Coke, *Elements of Power and Subjection or the Causes of all Humane, Christian and Legal Society*, London, T. Newcomb, 1660, pp. 98–99.
37 Ibid., p. 42.
38 Ibid., pp. 33–34.

residues of a diversity of laws.[39] In the first instance it is important to trace again the subject of spiritual law and to indicate the features of a law that addressed directly the inner sense, the conscience and imagination of the hidden citizen or invisible subject, nursed though not always directly acknowledged, by both state, sovereign and law.

The most direct expression of the role of law within the ecclesiastical constitution can be found in some of the earliest defences of the Anglican polity. The subject of law was not external obedience, nor was it a mere conformity to the text, but rather an internalisation of the word and a 'keeping of the tradition' in its unwritten and lived form. The order of governance is in a sense unexceptionable: 'carry not images but the law in your heart', to which it is added that such law, transmitted by print and by speech, is no mere text or Apostolic preaching, but rather 'those things which are spoken . . . are images of their souls' and should be heard and incorporated as such.[40] In Bishop Jewel's words, even literal interpretation of the law by the text was a species of 'ostentation and sophistry' to which it was necessary to oppose an unwritten law 'graven not in stone but in the heart', or, in a classical maxim, *corde creditur ad iustitiam*, he who believes with the heart will do justice.[41] The law was to be understood as an allegory for the direction and protection of conscience, its basis being virtue and an ethics of custom which would lead the internal subject of the realm, the undying body or *corpus mysticum* of state and subject, to truth.

The logic of internalisation is spelled out through metaphors of the mouth and the eye. The law can never be seen nor read in itself, it is not touched with the body nor seen with the eye, but rather 'there is a spiritual mouth of the inner man which is nourished by receiving the word of life (*verbum vitae*)' as also there are eyes of the spirit (*oculi spiritus*) 'which are able to see things that are not seen, and have no being . . . for *oculi anima*, the eyes of the soul, will pass through all obstacles whereas *oculi corporales*, that see visible things, cannot do so much'.[42] The inward spiritual eyes saw through imagining and through mystery, through substance and faith, and not through any merely apparent phenomena or manifest forms. Thus for St German, 'man received of God a double eye, that is to say, an outward and an inward eye . . . that is the eye of reason, whereby he knows things invisible and divine'.[43] It is in this inventive sense that the reference to ethics and to conscience should be understood; they are references to

39 On the concept of *utrumque ius*, see P. Legendre, 'Le droit romain, modèle et langage'.
40 Calfhill, *An Answere*, sig. 65ᵛ.
41 John Jewel, *An Apologie or Answere in Defence of the Churche of Englande*, London, 1562, fol. A viii b. For the maxim, see Thomas Stapleton, *A Fortresse of the Faith first planted amonge us Englishmen*, Antwerp, Ihon Laet, 1565, sig. 162ʳ.
42 J. Jewel, *A Defence of the Apologie of the Churche of England*, London, Fleet Street, 1567, at pp. 272–273.
43 St German, *Doctor and Student*, p. 83.

the substance of subjectivity, to an unconscious discipline or juristic soul. It is indeed equally in this sense that the division of laws and of courts should also be comprehended. The positive law existed to adjudicate and rule *in foro exteriori et contentioso*, in the forum of external conflicts, but such conflict and its resolution was only a living metaphor or allegory for the courts of conscience and of the spirit wherein outward obligation was subjected to interior substance. The cure of the soul belonged not only to that authority and law which adjudicated *in foro exteriori*, but equally and also to judgment *in foro interiori*, and on occasion to both, *in utroque simul*.[44]

Such a concept of the depth of law may be contemporarily opaque, as also is the language of ethics and of laws of the soul, but the order of progression or enfolding of exterior law and interior subjection, the movement from one visibility to another, spells out much of the power that is at stake in law. It is a question again of the potentially dynamic[45] or creative character of law, a question well understood in certain of the more incidental debates over the law of images. In one such, the relation between the different courts and their corresponding regimes of visibility is beautifully elaborated in terms of vanishing or 'aereall signs'. The debate in question concerned whether or not an 'aereall' sign, which is 'transient and presently vanishing', such as the sign of the cross made in air or with water on the forehead, should be deemed idolatry at law. The response was that

the image is, and always was, a vanishing aereall shadow, like the ghost or shade (*umbra*) of one dead, which being true, the vanishing airiness (ayrenes) of the cross furthereth and stayeth not the idolizing of it. The cross aereall is if anything more dangerous [than the material] because *in similitudinem umbrarum, transeunt et intereunt*, they vanish and pass away like shadows.[46]

In a stronger formulation, the danger of the transient or vanishing sign is precisely the inversion of the relation between and significance of the transient and the substance to which it refers. The danger of the contingent or impermanent sign was its fluidity, its momentary and uncircumscribed excitation of the mind: the less material the sign, so much the quicker is the passage *ab imagine ad rem significatam*, from the image to the thing signified.[47]

The vanishing sign is not least threatening by virtue of its recollection of the immateriality of law and the transience of the text or *litera* of

44 Stillingfleet, *Ecclesiastical Cases*, pp. 24–25.
45 The author of the concept of dynamic jurisprudence is the irrepressible Arthur Jacobson, 'The Idolatry of Rules: Writing Law according to Moses, with Reference to other Jurisprudences' (1990) 11 *Cardozo Law Review*, 1079.
46 Parker, *Scholasticall Discourse against Symbolizing*, pp. 17–18.
47 Ibid., p. 48.

regulation. The fluidity of the discipline and the contingency of the art of law is evidenced quite clearly in the sign which disappears in the moment of its signification. More than that, however, the transience of the sign diminishes the status of positive law or recollects an order and plurality of jurisdictions which directly challenges the shallow and conformist belief in the unity of the system of positive law. Common law, as Selden most vividly pronounced it, was two-faced, its emblem being Janus and its sign that of Mercury. The Janus face of common law was a reference not only to the repressed history of the spiritual jurisdiction, but more than that it was a recollection of the plurality of laws which subsisted within the tradition and which, in their fragmentary and partial forms, made up the commonality of English law.[48] It was justice, in Selden's argument, which lay hidden by the positivisation of law and it was against that very local, contemporary and oblivious sense of legal rule that he counterposed the 'reverse or back face' of English law, its plural histories, its fragments or scraps of forgotten rule, its lost customs and its myths and other remainders of neglected laws and injured subjectivities that convention, desuetude and blindness had obscured from view. The other faces of English law were, for Selden, those of plurality and of the diversity of its jurisdictions, times and peoples. His work indeed constantly returned to the history of laws that had been excluded or ignored by the unscholarly breed of lawyers at the Inns of Court.[49] In the broader and more synoptic terms of the present argument, the Janus face of English law may be taken to refer quite simply to its dual character and to the repression or duplicity whereby it shows only one face and simulates a science of dogmatics pertaining to a singular law.

## CONCLUSION

The brief recollection of a jurisdiction historically and substantively hidden or lost within the common law offers a number of lessons or at least allows certain observations of contemporary forms of legal governance. The first is simply topographic. To the side or on the margins of common law there subsists the jurisdiction, the residue and certain vestiges of the spiritual jurisdiction and the functions of conscience. The art of judgment, in other words, might be deemed to include, if only in the most displaced forms, the inward court or imaginary *regulae* of ethical subjection. The discipline that governed the soul or tutored and bound the citizen of the ecclesiastical polity *iure divino* as well as by positive law taught the subject a species of fatalism. Providence dictated the order of law and it also marked the place and the purpose, the fate or destiny of

48 John Selden, *Jani Anglorum facies altera*, London, T. Bassett, 1610, preface.
49 See most particularly Selden, *The Historie of Tithes*, London, private circulation, 1618.

the subject. It was against this background of the Christian version of *amor fati* or of fortune's decree that the order of spiritual law and the ruling of the spiritual courts had their place.

The courts of conscience bound in conscience alone and so took their place and their rule through the word and through the spirit. This dependence upon conscience did not preclude causes nor did it divorce the reason of spirituality from the practice of law. While the spiritual courts gradually lost their powers of enforcement to the expansive jurisdiction of common law, the scope of this speculative justice should not be underestimated. The spiritual courts not only preceded the common law in ethical and hierarchical terms but also had the power to take cognisance of a wide range of speculative and institutional causes. Many such actions, as, for example, for perjury, blasphemy, sacrilege, apostasy, heresy and schism, simony, tithes, excommunication, commutation of penance and the like were public forms of offence against the establishment, while rules governing slander, spousals, matrimony, divorce, bastardy, testaments, incests, fornications (incontinencies), adulteries, solicitation of chastity, drunkenness and filthy talking came much closer to the application of rules governing personal ethics and care of the self. Much more so, the rules of 'Christian oeconomy' or domestic governance which spelt out the duties of the members of the smallest Christian community or polity, the family.[50] What is genuinely interesting about the application of rules within the domain of conscience, or within the internal sphere of the 'other kingdom', the scene of a judgment that did not belong to this world, is not the detail of actual application but rather the rules and procedures of a distinct form of law.

The court of conscience would archetypically proceed according to rules of conscience and would apply the norms of a justice that transcended the temporal law and its positive procedures. More than that, however, the courts of spiritual justice existed alongside the community and process of common law, not simply to apply a separate law to the community of the ecclesiastical estate in its institutional sense, the clerics and all who could plead the privilege of the clergy, but also to provide a parallel set of rules for those who would seek some other justice than that available at common law. A simple though perhaps slightly technical example could be taken from the judgment of contractual obligations in the spiritual courts. To prove a contract at common law required not simply evidence of a promise but also proof of a temporal bargain in the sense of consideration for the

50 See William Perkins, *Christian Oeconomie or a Short Survey of the Right Manner of Erecting and Ordering a Family,* Cambridge, Cantrell Legge, 1609. The most interesting works in this genre include John Dod and Robert Cleaver, *A Godlie Form of Householde Government,* London, Thomas Man, 1612; William Gouge, *Of Domesticall Duties Eight Treatises,* London, William Bladen, 1622; M. Griffith, *Bethel or, A Forme for Families,* London, Jacob Bloome, 1633; D. Rogers, *Matrimoniall Honour,* London, 1642.

promise made. Without such proof, the exchange of bare promises created no obligation but was and indeed is viewed as *nudum pactum*. The court Christian, however, would hear any action based upon a 'faith' or promise and would try an action for breach of faith or *pro laesione fidei* according to spiritual rules and spiritual punishments. A voluntary oath was a matter of conscience and upon a suit before the ecclesiastical judges the breach of the promise would be followed by injunction to corporal penance without prejudice to any action for recovery of debt at common law.[51]

In more technical terms, parties to a contract would often, for greater security, make faith or oath of performance in private or before ordinaries. In either case the promise was termed *fidei praestatio* and if either party failed to perform, they would be called by ecclesiastical process before the ordinary and made to answer. If proved against them, 'the offender was enjoined grievous penance, and compelled by censures to keep his faith or oath, by satisfying the other party ... the observation of an oath is *praeceptum iuris divini* and therefore indispensable'.[52] In later law, the secular courts made various attempts to recognise these types of spiritual duty in the form of what were termed moral obligations or simply through the equitable diversion of positive norms. Increasingly, however, the source, the logic and the domain of spiritual rules and their application was lost through an increasingly insular, positivised and closed conception of common law system. The tie between law and a knowledge of things divine and human, the repressed and so merely residual and intellectually passive jurisdiction over the spirituality of the subject as well as the subordination of all rules of positive law to the criteria of an artistic justice recollect a fecund set of possibilities for the deconstruction of the positivity of common law.

The Anglican law required the peasant, whose story began this chapter, to remove his hat before entering the Court. That norm of civil honour or secular reverence was not an accident of custom or of local practice, it was a recognition, although perhaps only a partial one, of the historical transmission of spirituality and of 'ghostly power' from natural to positive law. It was a recognition or an acting out of the displacement of social paternity or of *regia potestas* from ecclesiastical to civil sources, a displacement which was self-consciously represented as a continuity of the *longue durée* of common law: 'we have overthrown no kingdom, we have decayed no men's power or right, we have disordered no commonwealth. There continue in their own accustomed state and ancient dignity the Kings of our country England'.[53] Among the jurisdictions and the courts

51 Cosin, *An Apologie for Sundrie Proceedings*, pp. 25–26.
52 Ibid., p. 51.
53 Jewel, *An Apologie*, fol. G i b. See also Cosin, *An Apologie for Sundrie Proceedings*, p. 40: 'all jurisdiction Ecclesiastical being now in fact and Lawe united to the Crowne and from thence derived'.

that were so transmitted must be included not only the residues of divine or natural justice, the rules of conscience and of spiritual action but also the manners and norms of domestic relation, bodily function and moral integrity. Both language and desire, belief and subjective place were subject now to the governance of common law. What had to be assumed and passed on within this other unwritten tradition was what Fortescue had much earlier termed a 'filial fear of God' and of law.[54] The institution, in short, had always to nurture and the law to nurse the subjects, the children, which governance created. It is in this sense, at the level of structure or of law's indefinite time, that Foucault observed that if there really is an Oedipus complex within western culture,

> it does not concern our unconscious and our desire . . . it does not play at the level of the individual, but at that of the collective; and not in relation to desire and the unconscious but in relation to power and knowledge.[55]

The unconscious, as Legendre has frequently remarked, is a jurist and it is precisely the complex legal form of subjective place that the history of the two laws can help recollect in the modern terms of theories of judgment and of the discipline of law. It is helpful to recall that the function of common law, after its absorption of the jurisdiction of conscience, was explicitly that of a 'nursing father'; it was to watch over and to care for the well-being of the ghostly realm; it was to take on the task of registering the visibility of the spiritual territory of its subjects.[56] That the common law could absorb or embrace this domain of conscience with relative ease refers in its turn to a tradition which was historically and explicitly that of a written law which defined itself not only in terms of its texts but also in terms of an unwritten tradition, of interpretation or classically *traditio* and of the corresponding *corpus mysticum* of a dual realm.[57] The function of *specula pastoralis* or of inner jursidiction and regulation was already a feature of the secular legal concern with governance of the internal subjects of the crown and of control of their words and of the images through which legal power was represented and thought. As 'nursing father' the secular law took over the governance of conduct and it entered a jurisdiction which included the specification and regulation of subjective space not

54 Fortescue, *De Laudibus Legum Angliae*, p. 3.
55 M. Foucault, 'La vérité et les formes juridiques' (1990) 10 *Chimères* 11.
56 On the common law conception of the nursing parent, see Roger Coke, *Justice Vindicated, from the false fucus put upon it, by Thomas White Gent., Mr Thomas Hobbs, and Hugo Grotius. As also Elements of Power and Subjection; wherein is demonstrated the cause of all Humane, Christian and Legal Society,* London, T. Newcomb, 1660.
57 In historical terms, the classic elaboration of this theme is to be found in Ernst Kantorowicz, *The King's Two Bodies*, Princeton, Princeton University Press, 1958. See also M. Foucault, 'On Governmentality', in G. Burchell, C. Gordon and P. Miller (eds), *The Foucault Effect*, Hemel Hempstead, Harvester Wheatsheaf, 1991.

only as 'oikonomia' or domesticity and relation but also as the site of education, ethics, conduct and civic virtue. Where the contemporary legal form has endeavoured to present law as an autonomous domain of positivised and merely written texts, the repression of the unwritten jurisdiction and of the invisible subject and its ghostly powers has merely rendered the subject of judgment and the governance of the soul un-conscious. It is in that darkness, in the unlit territory of attachment to and dissemination of law, that the irrationality of the legal form and the injustice of legal decision has come to be most strikingly felt as the legality of a contingency which law can never either fully know or directly address.

# Chapter 2

# Law in the Courts of Love
## Andreas Capellanus and the Judgments of love

A man, a potential lover, seeks the love of a woman who already has a lover. She declares herself bound to the love of another but offers her suitor a certain hope. If she were ever to be deprived of, or more literally disappointed or frustrated by her present lover (*sui coamantis amore frustrari*) then she promises that she would undoubtedly take the suitor as her lover. A short while later she marries her lover and the suitor demands that she keep her word. The woman denies this claim on the ground that she has not lost her lover. The dispute is presented to the Court of Queen Eleanor of France where it is decided in favour of the suitor. The ostensible ground of the decision is a precedent judgment delivered by the Court of the Countess of Champagne, a court composed of some thirty women who collectively debated the distinct principles of love and marriage. In the precedent decision, handed down on the 1 May 1174, the Court of the Countess of Champagne had stated that love and marriage were mutually exclusive: 'Lovers give all they have to each other freely, and without any consideration of necessity, whereas married partners are forced to comply with each others desires as an obligation, and under no circumstances can they refuse each other.'[1] Principally on that ground, the Court found that the promise of love should be kept for the simple reason that when her lover became her husband, the woman lost her lover, and thus fulfilled the condition of her promise.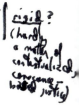

The decision, Judgment xvii of *De iudiciis amoris*, reported in Book 2 of Andreas Capellanus, *Tractatus de amore*, evinces a curious and compelling conjunction of casuistry and of lifestyle, of the art of law and the rules of love, of the juridical and the personal. The reasoning of Judgment xvii is strikingly casuistic. The precedent referred to from the Court of Champagne is a reference to an extensively argued decision and it in turn makes reference indirectly to a number of further grounds of decision. One

1 Andreas Capellanus, *Tractatus de amore et de amoris remedio*, Havaniae, Gadiana, 1176, 1892 edn, 397–398; trans. P.G. Walsh, *Andreas Capellanus on Love*, London, Duckworth, 1982, p. 157.

is in effect statutory: the first rule of the code of love, the *regulae amoris* reported in Book 3 of the *Tractatus*, states that 'marriage does not constitute a valid (*recta*) excuse for not loving'.[2] Another is in the form of further precedents. In Judgment viii of *De iudiciis amoris*, the Court of the Viscountess of Narbonne had upheld the plea of a lover who had been spurned when his beloved had married. It was held that 'a marriage alliance does not properly replace an earlier love-liaison unless the woman ceases to devote herself to love entirely, and is in no way disposed to further loves'.[3] In Judgment ix, the same Court was asked to determine whether the greater affection lay between lovers or spouses. Judgment took the form of stating that the two emotions were completely distinct, marital affection and true love were different in species and had their origin in radically distinct movements of the soul. They could not, in consequence, be compared.[4] Finally, custom and precepts of love or *amoris praecepta* allowed for further justifications, discussions and reasonings in relation to the character and institutions of relationships of desire.

The sources of such discursive reasoning are too numerous and entangled to be unravelled here, but it should nonetheless briefly be observed that the court of love enforced a most intimate promise on what must be taken to be grounds of amorous conscience. An ethical dispute or differentiation of right and wrong was decided as a question of love. Such a relation of desire to faith, of love to fidelity, or of body to contract clearly borrows from the spiritual jurisdiction and its courts of conscience. The Judgment is concerned with matters of spiritual law and reiterates in a novel context that promises of love be kept and that desire be channelled in an ethical direction. Although the doctrine and rules of the courts of love were eventually to be defined as a heresy by the medieval church and as a phantasm by later literary and legal historians, the ethical character of the rules of love and the parallel yet illicit nature of their juristic procedures and feminine personnel cannot be so easily ignored or denied. The reasoning of the decision evidences a sense not only of fidelity to a lover's words but also a combination of spiritual and temporal conceptions of relationship, of attachment and of its ends. In substantive terms Judgment xvii drew upon precedent and law that existed outside of the ordinary jurisdiction of regal law or *ius commune*, a law that was neither of the established monarchical state nor of the church but of a feminine public sphere and concerned exclusively with disputes relating to the art of love and relationships between lovers.

Women's courts spoke to a law of emotion and a corresponding jurisdiction concerned not with individual rights or passions but rather

---

2   Ibid., Bk 2, pp. 44–45; trans., p. 283.
3   Ibid., Bk 2, pp. 20–21; trans., p. 259.
4   Ibid., Bk 2, pp. 21–23; trans., p. 259.

with a space in between lovers and independent of any recognised right, property or established propriety. The extensive logic of Judgment xvii was that love and marriage are combinations of different species of love. The Christian institution of marriage was a form of *amor purus* or of an essentially spiritual love, of Augustine's *vera caritas* or inner love of a life beyond the body and other to the apparent and merely temporal world of things. The faith or *caritas* to which Augustine and the patristic texts spoke was that of a subjection to another order of spiritual affectation. The early fathers defined faith in terms of an other-worldly love, a love invariably attached to an eternal being, a pure love. The secular institution of marriage was to be the temporal shadow or emulation of its spiritual exemplar and was to be based upon an imitative obedience to an earthly father and conjugal hierarchy. The relationship of lovers adjudicated by women in the courts of love was, by contrast, an *amor mixtus*, both spiritual and profane, both *agape* and *eros*, an investment of the soul inscribed, often elliptically, in mundane and corporeal rules.

While the subject-matter of the particular decision described may be somewhat arcane to contemporary understanding – the code of love has shifted ever so slightly[5] – the casuistic basis of the report, the recourse to precedent and to reasoning drawn from the code of love, reference to Christian conceptions of marriage and to poetic notions of love and its various duties, all offer a royal road to questions of the place of law in intimate relationships, of the public in the private, of the juridical as well as the political in the personal. It is in terms of that casuistry of conscience, in terms further of the relationship between conscience and regulation, amorous intent and the determinations of law, that the present chapter will address the history and law of the courts of love as systematised in the scholastic classic *Tractatus de amore*.[6] It will be argued that the courts of love place law face to face with an ethics of emotion and a phenomenology of relationship and it is in that sense that the history and law of such courts can be used as a way to think through certain strictly contemporary concerns with the rights of sexuality as well as the sexuality of rights. Not only are women's courts a striking model of feminine justice, of 'the lady

---

5  Such is, of course, the thesis developed in Niklas Luhmann, *Love as Passion*, Cambridge, Polity Press, 1986.

6  The work of Capellanus represents the first systematic treatise reporting of 'Judgments of love'. As will be observed later in the chapter, there is plenty of extrinsic evidence in literature and particularly in troubadour poetry of other decisions and judgments of love contemporary with Capellanus. My concern here has been to focus on the legal dimension of this tradition and hence to restrict analysis to Judgments of love. As regards later decisions, the other major source is the treatise of Martial d'Auvergne, *Les arrêts d'amour*, Paris, Picard, 1460, 1951 edn. See further, for legal commentaries contemporary with Martial d'Auvergne, Stephano Forcatulo Bliterensi (iurisconsulto autore), *Cupido iusperitus*, Lugduni: Ioan Tornaesium, 1553; see also Benoit de Court (jurisconsulte), *Commentaires juridiques*, Paris, P. Gandouin, 1731 edn.

common law', of *Justitia* or *domina Jurisprudentia*, but they also spell out in great detail the terms of an art of love or *ars amatoria* that addresses precisely those questions of lifestyle, of trust, relationship, care and sexual exchange which contemporary feminist jurisprudence, both on the continent and in America, has laboured to formulate and address. In the strangest of paradoxes, the tradition of *amour lointain*, its women's courts, its judgments of love and the principles of law which they elaborated can act as an emblem for rethinking the laws of love in an age of object-choice.[7] The analysis will move from certain preliminary historical observations on love of the past as well as the past of love, to the substantive issues raised by the judgments, the principles and the casuistic rules of *amor mixtus* and the art of love.

## HISTORICISM'S *AMOUR LOINTAIN*

It may seem ... a curious and unusual detour', remarks the French psychoanalyst Jacques Lacan in his seminar on *The Psychoses*, 'to resort to a medieval theory of love in order to introduce the question of psychosis. It is, however, impossible to conceive the nature of madness otherwise.'[8] To understand psychosis or madness we need, according to Lacan, to understand everything that belongs to the order of the imaginary, both *animus* and *anima*, and particularly the phantasmatic structure of the relationship of self to other and of one sex to another. To understand the imaginary is therefore to trace the schemata and places of desire and to recognise the potential absolutism or madness of love, the phantasm of *amour fou* or 'objective chance' as it is addressed within the judgments of love.[9] So also Lacan's most successful contemporary interpreter, Slavoj Zizek, states that

> The impression that courtly love is something out of date, long super-seded by modern manners, is a lure which blinds us to the fact that the logic of courtly love still defines the parameters within which the two sexes relate to each other.[10]

The problematic of courtly love to which Lacan and Zizek jointly refer is

---

7  On object-choice, see S. Freud, 'A Special Type of Object Choice made by Men', in *Collected Papers IV*, London, Hogarth Press, 1925. For further discussion, see Klaus Theweleit, *Object-Choice*, London, Verso, 1994. In more literary terms see also Giorgio Agamben, 'The Phantasms of Eros', in *idem, Stanzas: Word and Phantasm in Western Culture*, Minneapolis, University of Minnesota Press, 1993.
8  Jacques Lacan, *The Psychoses*, London, Routledge, 1993, at p. 253.
9  Lacan, 'Courtly love as anamorphosis', in *idem, The Ethics of Psychoanalysis*, New York: Norton, 1992 at p. 154, referring to André Breton.
10 Slavoj Zizek, 'Courtly Love, or, Woman as Thing', in *idem, The Metastases of Enjoyment*, London, Verso, 1994, at p. 89. For a series of recent perspectives, see Renata Salecl (ed.), *Lacan and Love*, London: Lawrence & Wishart, 1994, (special issue of *New Formations*).

that of the inaccessibility of the object of love, the experience of love being, in neo-Freudian terms, the recognition of the otherness of the object of love. That recognition is depicted in the literature of courtly love in terms of distance and of obstacles in the path of love, in terms of augmenting love through economies of jealousy, of scarcity and of the geography of separation. Thus *amour lointain*, love from elsewhere, impossible love or love indefinitely postponed, is the exemplary metaphor of a law of distance and of the structure of love as passion in the real world.

Such economies of relationship and of delayed, interrupted or postponed sexual exchange are explained in Freudian terms by reference to boundaries, limits and distance, as well as by reference to the more familiar and morbid ecclesiastical terms of fidelity and of waiting, faith and death. It is a distance or waiting that not only characterises the historical relationship of courtly lovers but equally marks the relationship of the historian, and on occasion the psychoanalyst, to love. While I will return to that relationship of historical distance I am more concerned here simply to indicate the legitimate contemporaneity of the topic of courtly love, its repetition in and restraint by the modern imagination. The subject and the subjectivity of the courts of love must remain an open question. The boundaries and the practices of this mixed love and its sexuate justice will also offer a resource and jurisdiction that is both literary and legal, both real and phantasmatic, both long past and disturbingly contemporary. That there are records of women's courts and cases of love cannot be disputed, but the interpretation of their existence or non-existence – their real or fictive character – and the elaboration of their principles or rules are, like all textual attentions, indefinite and infinitely expansive undertakings.[11] It should be noted also in this context of text, body and love, of law and the real, that both the judgments and their surrounding literature are deeply allegorical and so play many additional games with the language and the *personae* of love. Although the rules and literature of love often appear to concern a strictly heterosexual norm, closer attention to or openness towards the literature and records of courts of love and feminine justice provides many examples of love between woman and woman and between man and man. The allegorical character of the literature and of the judgments also suggests that men often took on the names or *personae*

11 For a general account of the arguments for and against, see Paul Remy, 'Les "cours d'amour": légende et réalité' (1954–1955) 7 *Revue de l'Université de Bruxelles* 179 (arguing that at best the courts of love had a literary and didactic existence). See also Jacques Lafitte-Houssat, *Troubadours et cours d'amour*, Paris, Presses Universitaires de France, 1971 (arguing that the courts of love undoubtedly did exist but that they were a social diversion or amusement rather than genuine tribunals); M. Lazar, *Amour courtois et fin'amors*, Paris: Seuil, 1964.

of women and women frequently took on the guise or mask of men.[12] Such a complication of the rules and their referent has been taken to suggest strongly gay and lesbian themes within the rules of love and such a norm again suggests not only a sexual politics of love but equally a sexual politics of the history of passion and other intimate emotions, one which still burdens and distances contemporary historicism from the 'reality' of this sexual past.[13] In the present context I will limit my discussion to suggesting two preliminary hypotheses of a loosely historiographic nature.

The first thesis takes the form of the argument that if, following Lacan, we can understand both madness and love through the poetics and the rules of *amour lointain* – distant love or love of distance – it may equally be possible to understand important features of law, and particularly of justice, through the history of the courts of love. It is possible to argue that just as an historically distant conception of love structures contemporary relationships – even if such are extraordinary relationships, those of love and of other psychoses – so too an historically distant practice of law in the courts of love can be taken to structure our conceptions of equity and of the casuistry of justice, as well as helping to explain the opaque role of desire in relation to legality. The second thesis is more complicated. The history of love has not been a feminist or even a feminine enterprise; to the extent that there is such a history it has been concerned pre-eminently with the proprietorial institutions of relationship even if its subject-matter has in some senses been associated with feminine attributes, with the characteristics of the *gynaeceum*, of the discourses, practices and relationships which fall outside the public or external realm. The narrative of the courts of love can offer one salutary and corrective instance of the necessarily plural quality of historical writing. There are at least two histories of the judgments of love, for the simple reason that there are at least two places, two persons or two sexes, two subjectivities involved in the art of amorous or sexual relationship and so also in the forms in which it is marked and recovered, through which it becomes a structure or is repeated as historical and juridical knowledge. In the terms used by

12 The most interesting evidence of love between woman and woman comes from the *trobairitz*, the poetry and judgments of a small group of women troubadours. For exemplary texts of this kind, see Reni Nelli (ed.), *Ecrivains anticonformistes du moyen-age occitan: la femme et l'amour*, Paris, Phébus, 1977, vol. II, at pp. 247–255, 261–269, 301–305. See further Meg Bogin, *The Woman Troubadours*, New York, Norton, 1976. For the inevitable argument that the *trobairitz* did not exist, see the admirable Jean-Charles Huchet, 'Les femmes troubadours ou la voix critique' (1983) 51 *Littérature*, p. 59.

13 On the homosexual or better homosocial character of courtly love, see J.-C. Huchet, *L'Amour discourtois*, Toulouse, Privat, 1987. See also Reni Nelli, *L'Erotique des troubadours*, Toulouse, Union Générale des Editions, 1974, vol. 2, at p. 140: 'At the very least it had to be recognised that courtly society generally practised sodomy so as to avoid the normal carnal fact of procreation; one cannot but acknowledge that courtly love was in its essence, love "against nature"'.

Capellanus, we can refer to a double signification (*duplicem sententiam*),[14] a Janus face or dual meaning. If love is defined, for example, in its Protestant form, then the courts of love will appear to be fantasies or simple distractions from the history of marriage and of succession according to masculine legal norms. If love is defined in more ambitious and psychoanalytical terms, the courts of love will be likely to be interpreted in terms of a masculine unconscious in which the woman is metaphor or sign for a communication, an exchange of value, between two men. In this analysis *amour lointain* spells out an imaginary and forbidden copulation between two men. The woman here takes the place of the other in the sense of being extrinsic to a homosexual desire:

> [t]he woman offers herself as the site of an imaginary and impossible copulation between two men. The woman circulates from one man to an other, but in the sole title of signifier of a desire which does not concern her, the unavowable homosexual desire.[15]

The Janus or 'backface' of legal history refers, in other words, to the necessarily ambiguous relation of contemporary conceptions of desire to the plurality of historical norms of erotic sensibility.

A brief survey of the various histories of the courts of love can provide an interesting illustration and elaboration of the latter point. For Lacan, whatever the insight that can be drawn from this history of a 'juridical power exercised by women' and irrespective of a certain 'strangeness' that for him 'cannot fail to excite a thrill', the courts of love are condemned to failure, to the status of a structural fiction or necessary but nevertheless merely rhetorical metaphor.[16] More than that, courtly love was created 'more or less as you see the fantasm emerge from the syringe', while its concept of love 'is commonly called, quite rightly, a form of madness', in Freudian terms a mirage or delusion.[17] From such inauspicious beginnings it is unsurprising that the more politically motivated Zizek sees courtly love as 'a semblance which conceals the actuality of male domination'; it is image, fantasy, a lure to servitude.[18] In the more conventional histories of canon law and of law and sexuality, the *Tractatus* is honoured only in its absence, it does not measure up to the real and is therefore ignored.[19]

---

14 *Tractatus*, Bk III, at p. 117; trans., p. 223. For discussion of this reference, see D.W. Robertson, 'The Subject of the *De amore* of Andreas Capellanus' (1953) 50 *Modern Philology* 145.
15 Huchet, *L'Amour discourtois*, at p. 25. Huchet further suggests that the woman is, within this discourse, the means of a forbidden communication between (*inter*) two men (*dit*), the 'inter-dit' or interdicted.
16 Lacan, *Ethics*, at pp. 146 and 149.
17 Lacan, *Psychoses*, at p. 254.
18 Zizek, 'Courtly Love', at pp. 108–109.
19 James Brundage, *Law, Sex and Christian Society in Medieval Europe*, Chicago, Chicago University Press, 1987, at p. 309. See, even more strikingly, Henry Ansgar Kelly, *Love and Marriage in the Age of Chaucer*, Ithaca, NY, Cornell University Press, 1975.

Thus we are informed that there is neither 'hard evidence' for the existence of courts of love before 1400,[20] nor could courtly love as a practice be viewed as 'remotely credible' in the scheme of historical ontology.[21] Although historians are agreed on the dates and the forms of invention of the courts of love, they are ironically equally unanimous that measured against the demands of the real, the courts of love could not be said to have existed.

The concern of literary historians has been biographical but largely comparable.[22] As if it were a significant feature of the art of love, immense philological and archival energy has been expended on searching for the identity of the cleric who wrote the *Tractatus* and even for his venerable interlocutor, the friend Walter, to whom the didactically formulated treatise was addressed.[23] From the perspective of literary historicism, the courts of love are quite simply erased, they did not exist or, in the well chosen words of John Benton, 'the *De Amore* is . . . a work of imagination, and . . . the decisions of the Courts of love are, in my opinion, amusing fantasies'.[24] Such a view is positively liberal in comparison with the more acerbic historicism which sees the continuance of these fantasies as an offence to the reality of the past, as a transgression of the rules of historical evidence and as an obstacle to the understanding of related literature.[25]

20 The date of promulgation of the statute of love which established the 'cour amoureuse' in Paris. See C. Bozzolo and H. Loyau (eds), *La Cour Amoureuse dite de Charles VI*, Paris, Le Léopard d'or, 1982.

21 John Benton, 'Clio and Venus: an Historical View of Medieval Love', in F.X. Newman (ed.), *The Meaning of Courtly Love*, Albany, NY, State University of New York Press, 1968, at pp. 19ff.

22 I should at this point advert to a particular further biographical irony. Capellanus was fairly certainly a male cleric and although there are texts by women, and most notably Christine de Pisan, which discuss the courts of love, the only record of these early judgments in women's courts comes in the work of a male cleric. More than that, my own recuperation of this history is that of a white man. I cannot apologise for that circumstance but I can recognise certain of the limitations as well as the privileges which it places upon my interpretation or imagination of these texts. To the extent that women's courts were concerned specifically with the space in between lovers and between or within the sexes, it is possible to appropriate one of Irigaray's metaphors, that of a 'sex which is not one', as a species of self-reflection. I have tried, in short, to reflect upon or interpret the judgments of love from within a space of relation and in a dialogue across the boundaries of my sex. As to the privileges of masculinity, it seems ironic that the fact that it is a man who writes this history of women still lends the narrative a status or credibility (and publicity) which would probably be lacking from an account which belonged by both sex and inclination to feminist legal history.

23 For a recent summary of the state of the scholarship, see John Baldwin, *The Language of Sex: Five Voices from Northern France around 1200*, Chicago, Chicago University Press, 1994, at pp. 16–26.

24 John Benton, 'Collaborative Approaches to Fantasy and Reality in the Literature of Champagne', in G. Burgess (ed.), *Court and Poet*, Liverpool, Francis Cairns, 1981, at p. 46.

25 D.W. Robertson, 'The Concept of Courtly Love as an Impediment to the Understanding of Medieval Texts', in Newman (ed.), *The Meaning of Courtly Love*, at ch. 1. Robertson, *A Preface to Chaucer*, Princeton, Princeton University Press, 1962. See also P.S. Noble, *Love and Marriage in Chrétien de Troyes*, Cardiff, University of Wales Press, 1982, introduction.

The rules and courts of love were the products of romantic fiction, and as such were to be deemed trivial affectations, ironic and theatrical diversions from truth. They were, in short, the stuff of women's literature, they were ephemera or chimera, fantastical products of the fickle attention of the feminine mind. In the stronger terms of the disciplines, their genre was literature and not law, their substance was imagination and not reality, their being was no more than symptomatic of a madness that historians and analysts could alike condemn to non-existence. In short, the normative order of historicism could neither imagine nor perceive the relevance of women's courts or of laws of love.

That women, who were defined early on in the patristic tradition as lack or as nothing, should produce nothing as their law, that their courts and their rules should be perceived as madness or depicted as taking the form of fantasies regulating imaginary relationships, fits all too well within the historiographical tradition. There is certainly room, even within the terms of the old historicism and of claims to a verifiable past, to challenge the historian's denial of the reality of the courts of love and of the amorous art to which they relate, but a more plausible and relevant line of analysis would simply be to recollect that the courts undoubtedly 'existed' for those contemporary with them. Thus I would note the inclusion of the *Tractatus* on a list of condemned books published by Bishop Stephen Tempier in 1277 and which incidentally also banned the works of Thomas Aquinas. The *De amore* was condemned for its 'vanity and insane falsity' as well as for its 'many manifest and execrable errors'.[26] Other reactions included attempts to censor the *Treatise* by means of rewriting it, as well as less dramatic criticism of its threat to the stability of marriage.[27] On the ground that one does not deny or condemn, censor or exclude, a purely imaginary or simply fantastical spectre, it seems plausible to suppose a certain reality, be it corporeal substance, political practice or textual remnant, to this mere – or merely feminine – literature and its reporting of judgments in the courts of love.

The other side or second signification of this history, however, does not depend upon proving some school or person or text to be wrong. Let them have their reality, let them enjoy their presence in the past, the *fort–da* of objective histories. The more radical strand of genealogical thinking is concerned precisely with the imaginary domain, with the symbolic space of difference and its implication of a politics that takes place across

26 See A.J. Denomy, 'The *De amore* of Andreas Capellanus and the Condemnation' (1946) VIII *Mediaeval Studies* 107; and more extensively Denomy, *The Heresy of Courtly Love*, (1965) Gloucester, Mass., P. Smith, 1965. For commentary, see Pierre Legendre, 'Protocole de la lettre de l'amour', in Legendre, *Paroles poétiques échappées du texte*, Paris, Seuil, 1982, at pp. 91–120.

27 See R. Bossuat (ed.), *Li livres d'amours de Drouart la Vache*, Paris, Librarie Ancienne Honoré Champion, 1926. See also Cannon Willard, 'Christine de Pizan's *Cent Ballades d'Amant et de Dame*: Criticism of Courtly Love', in Burgess (ed.), *Court and Poet*, at p. 357.

boundaries and the established limits of genre. Genealogy connotes what Irigaray has termed 'a political militancy of the impossible',[28] a militancy which desires to achieve the most radical and foundational of all cultural transformations, that of changing the relationship between the sexes, 'between man and woman, women and men'.[29] In other vocabularies such militancy concerns the will to rupture established patterns of political relation or legal rule, the will to express desire in institutional life or to find a space for the imaginary domain, for intimacy or the uniqueness of love within the symbolic forms of social life.[30] Militancy concerns, in other words, the specification of impossible rights or utopian demands on the basis that nothing less is worth fighting for or giving up.

The earliest recorded case of love can illustrate the nature of this political militancy of alternative history in graphic terms. It is a case which comes not from the era of the courtly lyric and troubadour poem but from the first century and the histories of the Greek biographer Plutarch. The case is reported and interpreted not by Capellanus but by Jacques Ferrand in a sixteenth-century treatise on lovesickness or erotic mania, De la maladie d'amour ou melancholie érotique.[31] The case is discussed in the context of a chapter concerned with remedies for erotic melancholy. The first remedy recommended is that of sleeping with the object of desire on the ground that the wounds of love are best cured by those that caused them.[32] The case concerns an oneiric variation on this cure. A young Egyptian was lost in love for a woman of the Athenian court. He pursued her relentlessly and tried by innumerable means to persuade her to take him as her lover. She refused emphatically and consistently and his obsession with her became all-consuming. He decided eventually to offer her a very large sum of money if she would sleep with him once, in the hope that this would cure him of his erotic madness. She agreed. The night before the contract was to be fulfilled the young man had a dream in which he slept with the woman and made love to her at great length and in vivid detail – avec tous les délices. Upon waking the next day he realised that he was cured of his

28 Luce Irigaray, J'aime à toi. Esquisse d'une félicité dans l'histoire, Paris, Grasset, 1992, at p. 26.
29 Ibid., at p. 202. For a loosely comparable position, see Francine Demichel, 'Concepts juridiques et différence sexuelle', in Mara Négron (ed.), Lectures de la différence sexuelle, Paris, des femmes, 1994.
30 On the question of rupture and the 'imaginary domain', see Drucilla Cornell, The Imaginary Domain: Abortion, Pornography and Sexual Harassment, New York, Routledge, 1995. Her earlier work, Cornell, Beyond Accommodation: Ethical Feminism, Deconstruction and the Law, New York, Routledge, 1991, also addresses this issue.
31 Jacques Ferrand, De la maladie d'amour ou melancholie érotique, Paris 1575/1640 edn, translated as Ferrand, A Treatise on Lovesickness, Syracuse, NY, Syracuse University Press, 1990, at pp. 233–234, citing Plutarch, Lives, vol. ix, p. 67.
32 The second recommendation was a cold enema with hemp seeds on top, taken first thing in the morning.

mania, 'that the ardor threatening to consume him had been allayed'.[33] When word of this dream cure came to the woman she filed a suit for payment of the agreed amount.

The suit argued by the woman was that it was her image that had cured the young man and therefore, having performed her part of the contract, albeit by different means, she was entitled to the price promised. The judge commanded the young man to appear before the court with the money. In the presence of both parties, the judge took the money and poured it into a brass bowl. It was then returned to the young man and judgment pronounced for the woman: just as the young man had been satisfied by the woman's image and an imaginary pleasure, so the woman had been paid by the sight and sound of the gold. The decision was received with approval by all present, except for the woman who appealed unsuccessfully on the ground that while her image had cured the young man, the sight and sound of the gold had whetted her desires rather than satisfying them. The judge's decision had been just in the most classical of senses of justice. It had taken the parties exactly as they were, face to face, image to image, and had determined the dispute in light of and according to the order of causes of love to which it belonged. The judgment was appropriate to the complaint and radical in the extreme both in recognising the imaginary as grounds for a cause of action and in resolving the dispute by doing justice to the image. The decision was exemplary, and as Ferrand's use of it suggests, it became a precedent for those concerned with the rules and remedies of love. What is significant for the immediate discussion, however, is a slightly separate point. The decision dealt with the conjunction of two laws, the law of the body and the law of the soul. In doing so it recognised or accorded reality to both love and faith, emotion and promise. More than that, the decision mixed the genres of law and the interpretation of dreams and in doing so accorded reality to the phantasm while equally treating the real as being also phantasmatic. To a normative historicism the judgment in this case would belong to a jurisdiction outside that of law, to a non-history of the phantasm and merely imaginary things. For a genealogy of law and of its many jurisdictions, however, the question is one of another form of judgment, of a minor jurisprudence and of a law appropriate to love.

To return to Irigaray's formulation, the militant or unthinkable question concerns what it means to deny reality to the history and (paradoxical) rules of passion, to withold being from literature, to be as blind or as empty as lawyers in the face of love.[34] At the very least it might be suspected that

---

33 Ferrand, *Treatise*, at p. 333.
34 For a recent version of this *topos*, see B. Sells, 'Lawyers in Love', in *idem*, *The Soul of the Law*, Rockport, MA: Element 1994. Other contemporary studies of this issue include Peter Gabel, 'The Phenomenology of Rights Consciousness and the Pact of Withdrawn Selves' (1984) 62 *Texas Law Review*, 1563. For a brief survey of the theme in historical perspective, see P. Goodrich, 'Gynaetopia: Feminine Genealogies of Common Law' (1993) 20 *Journal of Law and Society* 276, at pp. 276–278.

such an historiographical procedure and evaluation reflects a very contemporary or modern division of virtues and values. The real in this
historical schema belongs to the sphere of objects and not that of subjects,
truth belongs to reference and not to sense, while law relates to what is
recognised and not what is strange. The historian's *amour lointain*, or love
of the past, is in this instance seemingly an *amour propre*, a narcissism
concerned to deny the blandishments of time or the change which distance
brings. To reconstruct such change or to attend to what is communicated
across such distance actively requires a blurring of boundaries, a re-
investment of myth, a narrative or fiction of truth. This is in part a simple
question of ethics, a requirement that a history of the other, here of women,
attend to the other in her own terms. It is also, however, a question of law
in that what is also at issue is the legitimacy of a particular historical
character and correspondingly the reality of a specific past, that of
feminine identities, constitutional rights and women's law.

The French Renaissance historian Le Moyne, in a work devoted to the
history of women, *La Gallerie des femmes fortes*, placed an unusual emphasis
upon the significance of what he termed 'imaginary historical spaces –
*espaces imaginaires de l'histoire*'.[35] Within such imaginary spaces Le Moyne
discovered and expounded a history of feminine power and of women's
law. He elaborated, in this space of imagination, an alternative history, a
genealogy of another gender and of its law, remarking significantly in the
preface that the theme of a history of powerful women: 'is not as limited
as it might seem to those who do not know the virtues, or to those who
. . . do not believe that there is another power to that which prejudice most
usually perceives'.[36] In more contemporary terms, Luce Irigaray and
Hélène Cixous have undertaken a very similar work of reconstructing
'other spaces' of the history, literature and law of sexual exchange. Thus
Irigaray begins a recent polemical statement of the project of feminine
genealogy precisely with a challenge to the denial of imagination and the
impoverishment of our conceptions of relationship and of love:

> the best minds of our epoch maintain that eros is chaos, night, bestiality,
> lack, annihilation, but that we should submit ourselves to eros so as to
> relieve ourselves, so as to discharge – 'to empty' – ourselves and so to
> return to repose

---

35 Le Moyne, *La Gallerie des femmes fortes*, Paris, Cockart, 1663 edn, at p. 13. The theme is not
   that unusual in the histories of strong or erudite or powerful women. Further examples
   can be found, for example, in John Leslie, *De illustrium foeminarum*, Rheims, Fognaeus,
   1580, at fol. 19b; also Thomas Heywood, *Gunaikeion or Nine Bookes of Various History
   concerninge Women*, London, Islip, 1624, at p. 2 (referring to 'the apprehension of an
   imaginarie thing'). In specifically juristic terms the major study is that of John Selden, *Jani
   Anglorum facies altera*, London, Bassett, 1610/1683 edn.
36 Le Moyne, *Gallerie des femmes*, preface.

or all too often to sleep. If love is 'une petite mort', a drug, a loss of self, and sex no more than need combined with relief of tension, then, as Irigaray puts it, 'Pauvre Eros! Pauvre Amour!'[37] More than that, however, the negation of eros and of relationship, the displacement of desire and of love to a space outside of serious social speech or law, raises questions of social justice as well as of justice in and of history.

The first question of justice arises from historicism's denial of the relevance of proximity, or the subjectivity of love's law. It is possible to trace what may legitimately be termed the historian's fear of relationship.[38] Fear negates and fear of relationship, of corporeality and in this instance of women, of love, sexual desire or simply imagination negates those persons, qualities or forces and particularly as they are apprehended in us. The first moment of feminist genealogy is thus caught up in understanding such fear and its tendency to destroy or to silence both the body and the speech, the values and the cultures, of the feminine in the contemporary and so also in the past. The 'destruction of feminine genealogy' is a facet of the definition and demarcation of sexual relationship as an indifferent, chaotic and destructive force. In these terms woman is still, both historically and epistemologically, as inexplicable and as irrational as passion.[39] From the perspective of academic and legal reason, such passion – such lack of control – negatively marks the feminine from very early on within the parallel traditions of history and law. Without reiterating the theme of early legal representations of femininity as pretence, as confusion, insatiability and excess,[40] it is enough to point to the forgetting of feminine genealogies and the denial of feminine myths as active and positive features of the history of legal reason, features which require extended interpretation.[41] At the very least justice requires an account of the values and the possibilities which are repressed through

37 L. Irigaray, *Le Temps de la différence*, Paris, Livre de Poche, 1987, at p. 103. Without suggesting any directly comparable position, see also H. Cixous, 'Writing and the Law' in, *idem*, *Readings. The Poetics of Blanchot, Joyce, Kafka, Kleist, Lispector and Tsvetayeva*, Minneapolis, University of Minnesota Press, 1991; also, H. Cixous, *Coming to Writing and Other Essays*, Cambridge, Mass., Harvard University Press, 1991.

38 For some comments on this theme in one specific case, see P. Goodrich, 'Doctor Duxbury's Cure: Or, a Note on Legal Historiography' (1994) 15 *Cardozo Law Review* 1567. See further, L. Irigaray, *Marine Lover*, New York, Columbia University Press, 1991, especially pp. 30–33, 104ff.

39 Such an understanding – or rather non-understanding – of *amour passion* is well elaborated in Luhmann, *Love as Passion*, at pp. 58–75.

40 As for example in Andreas Alciatus, *De notitia dignitatem*, Paris, Cramoisy, 1651 edn, at p. 190: 'Quid est mulier? ... Hominis confusio, insaturabilis bestia, continua solicitudo, indefineus purgna.' (What is a woman? ... A confused man, an insatiable beast, continuous disquiet and excuse.) For an extended discussion of this topic, see P. Goodrich, *Oedipus Lex: Psychoanalysis, History, Law*, Berkeley and Los Angeles, California University Press, 1995.

41 See Irigaray, *Temps de la différence*, at pp. 121–123. For commentary, see Rosi Braidotti, *Patterns of Dissonance*, (1991) Cambridge, Polity, 1991, at pp. 248–263.

the denial of the history and literature of feminine culture as a species of reason or as form of legitimacy and so of law. It is necessary, in one felicitous formulation, 'to insist upon the necessity of an illusion. The illusion consists in believing that people who have been hostages, from time immemorial, of the world of calculation and the world of law are capable of leaving it'.[42]

The positive revaluation of historical and mythical feminine cultures forms a significant aspect of the politics of contemporary feminist jurisprudence. Thus Cixous has elaborated her project as that of having pursued an 'untamed' writing and the 'tablets of another law . . . a law of the order of the living'.[43] Irigaray has followed what, in terms of academic rhetoric, is an equally extreme or militant path. For Irigaray the positive goal of historical understanding is that of recuperating the allegories and mythologies as well as the plastic and literary artifacts of feminine cultures and feminine myths. Such leads her to write of love and to experiment with a poetics or prose of love[44] and it also leads her to reintroduce ignored texts and forgotten or derided mythologies – Aphrodite and Antigone, Eve and Mary, water, air and birds – into her genealogy of contemporary civic culture. Thus she writes of rebellious feminine gods, of ethical resistances to law, of plural and polytheistic social relations as well as of the body, energy, breath and writing, 'for in fact we still exist in the absence of a culture of sexuality, of the flesh, of the identity or style of genres'.[45] Throughout this project the purpose is everywhere similar, it is that of lending a certain political force and social presence to the literature and the language of this imaginary domain, in this instance that of the feminine which she terms, in our culture, that of the other, of difference, of the space of an alienated desire. Her project is to give symbolic status to what has been defined and devalued as subjectivity, privacy or intimacy and within which desire acts itself out according to predictable if socially unconscious laws. She thus writes in a style or genre which is both analytical and allegorical, philosophical and poetic, of introducing a series of ignored or

42 To borrow this time from Cixous, *Readings*, at pp. 72–76. She continues:

> Here, I am not sending a pessimistic message. I think that nothing can destroy in us the part made for happiness and love, happiness or love. But I also think that nothing can transform the part that is not made for it. A politically just procedure would be to look for and regroup forces capable of the same happiness and to not let oneself be altered by the bad, the other, part.

43 Ibid., at p. 26.

44 Most notably in Irigaray, *Marine Lover*; and L. Irigaray, *Elemental Passions*, London, Athlone Press, 1992. See also H. Cixous, *Three Steps on the Ladder of Writing*, New York, Columbia University Press, 1993.

45 Irigaray, *J'aime à toi*, at p. 214. For a different expression of a similar view, see Irigaray, *Marine Lover*, at p. 51: 'To think of the sea from afar, to eye her from a distance, to use her to fashion his highest reveries, to weave his dreams of her, and spread his sails while remaining safe in port, that is the delirium of the sea lover.'

excluded or 'private' values into the public sphere, into the symbolic. In a dual sense the logic of such a discovery of other values and possibilities raises questions of law.

First, it argues for a law of value, an ethics which suspends and judges law, a justice derived from a history of other relations and other loves. The literary and genealogical recovery of another law based upon a certain reversal, upon the nature and proximity of the feminine, is not only of symbolic value. In conventional genealogical terms it traces a maternal lineage, another origin or source of laws, a legitimacy which is not that of the established secular order. The designation of such an historical project as imaginary thus raises a further and quite direct question of positive law. Resorting to Celtic and other mythologies of feminine deities, Irigaray has frequently made the claim that genealogy can relay a sense of earlier and different – or simply displaced – cultures of relationship and of love. In a generic meaning, the question of sources, of origin and creativity is necessarily linked to femininity. In a broader historical sense, she also argues that

> a return to the origins of our culture reveals that it was once otherwise, that there was an epoch when it was women who initiated relations of love. In that time, woman was goddess and not servant, and she guarded both the spiritual and the carnal dimensions of love.[46]

That woman was goddess means in essence that she was not limited, but also that the relationship of desire or of sexual exchange was accorded both respect and a species of juridical value.

The other history of feminine gods, feminine values, women's justice and laws is recuperated so as to inject a novel and powerful presence into contemporary culture. The value of such recollection of alternative traditions is not simply that of providing further possible identities or places and jurisdictions of the feminine. It is more strongly that of empowering a politics of the feminine, of symbolic and civic spaces appropriate to what has hitherto been devalued as unreal or dismissed as merely subjective. Such may be an aesthetic, poetic and amorous good, but so long as it remains at the level of such 'subjective' (or simply imaginary) presences, it lacks political force or symbolic value and for that reason will only have genuine transformative potential if introduced into law and so given what in contemporary terms is perceived to be the objectivity, the visibility and enforcement, the full status of serious social speech, of law. What is at issue is a law of relationship, of what passes between the sexes and within the sexes, an objective space of sexual and amorous transmission.[47] Such a

---

46 J'aime à toi, at pp. 210–211. See further L. Irigaray, Sexes and Genealogies, New York, Columbia University Press, 1993, at pp. 55–73.

47 The term is borrowed from Pierre Legendre, L'Inestimable objet de la transmission, Paris, Fayard, 1984; Luhmann, Love as Passion, develops the notion of 'interpenetration'.

juridical space or object of legal knowledge would itself have further significant functions. In one sense it would act to connect law to its temporality, to the subjectivity and the corporeality upon which both relationships and laws are inscribed, for *in corporibus est sexum*. It would equally create the possibility of removing the feminine from the space of male projection, from a space of otherness or alienation, a distance across which femininity is ultimately silenced. The feminine other has been the object of a discourse not its subject. The feminine has been conceived as the space of lack, the site of a masculine desire without being in itself: that subsequent legal history should deny reality to the place, response or language of women, to *trobairitz*, women's courts or 'lesbian rule' adds a further subjection to a history already replete with the silencing of 'the other sex'.

Woman as veil or distance, transcendence or absence, woman as goddess or idol, woman as care or contingency are all alike historical categories or places projected and introjected within orders of sociality and law which were not those of feminine subjects, so much as they were products of a dark and masculine unconscious and its homosocial desire. Ironically one could well argue that the legal historian acts out the dominant fantasy of the courtly lyric and so re-establishes the hierarchical relation of distant love within the troubadour literature: the historian projects

> a silent, pure regard, which lives in the hope of a return of its gaze. The curve (*courbe*) of the gaze returns to its source, it images the trajectory of speech addressed to the woman, whose silence sends back to the troubadour his own song as the discourse of the other. The woman is a place where desire is called upon to bind itself to language.[48]

To follow or reconstruct the narrative of the courts of love is to suggest that it may well be possible to specify spaces of subjective self-definition that have social value; or, in terms of Renaissance iconography, and of the *Confessio Amantis*, that *Justitia* be joined with *Eros*, that love have its laws, and the soul its jurisdiction.

## THE JURISDICTION OF LOVE

Insofar as legal history has recorded a jurisdiction of love it has been an object of canon law and a negative incident of the regulation of marriage. Without embarking upon the outlines of a history of ecclesiastical law's governance of sexuality, a history which has already been well covered in

---

48 Huchet, *L'Amour discourtois*, at p. 36.

both technical and theological detail,[49] it may nonetheless be necessary to point briefly to certain characteristics of the legal space of relationship. The history of spiritualised love, of *agape* or *amor purus*, and of its attachment to an eternal object has at the very least the status of a parallel or competing jurisdiction to the numerous orders of earthly love or heresies of carnal desire. It is after all the failure or at least the limitation of ecclesiastical regulation that initially created the space for the courts of love.

The classical jurisdiction of ecclesiastical law was that of governance of the soul. The maxim that traditionally depicted the site or space of such regulation, by way of distinguishing spiritual from temporal rule, simply refers to laws and pleas *quae ad regimen animarum pertinent*, and which should be decided in the ecclesiastical courts.[50] Such a site of regulation principally concerned the maintenance of the conditions of faith, of a spiritual love of God which was constantly threatened by the concupiscence, the lure or insatiability of the carnal realm. Isidore of Seville in his *Etymologies* revealed a clear sense of the threat of feminine sensuality, of lust and its excess, in defining the word *femina* as coming 'from the Greek derived from the force of fire, because her concupiscence is very passionate: women are more libidinous than men'.[51] The regulation of sexuality thus played itself out within an opposition between spiritual love and carnal threat or perpetual lust represented by the temptation and seduction of the feminine: 'woman's love is accused of ever being insatiable; put it out, it bursts into flame; give it plenty, it is again in need; it enervates a man's mind, and engrosses all thought except for the passion which it feeds.'[52] The ideal of femininity was thus virginity and most particularly for Tertullian it was to be veiled or, in later terms, shame-faced.[53] The feminine should look down or look away so as neither to

49 See Brundage, *Law, Sex and Christian Society*; and Peter Brown, *The Body and Society. Men, Women, and Sexual Renunciation in Early Christianity*, New York, Columbia University Press, 1988. In terms of philosophical critique Nietzsche provides the strongest or most antagonistic account of Christian repression. See F. Nietzsche, *The Genealogy of Morals*, Edinburgh, Foulis, 1913; also Nietzsche, 'Morality as the Enemy of Nature', in *idem Twilight of the Idols*, Edinburgh, Foulis, 1915. This theme is brought out in Irigaray, *Marine Lover*.

50 John Godolphin, *Reportorium Canonicum or, an Abridgement of the Ecclesiastical Laws of this Realm Consistent with the Temporal: Wherein the most material points relating to such persons and things as come within the cognizance thereof, are succinctly treated*, London, Atkins, 1678, 1687 edn, at p. 96 (which relate to the regulation of the soul). See also, J.-F. Senault, *De l'usage des passions*, Paris, Fayard, 1641, 1987 edn, on the uses of love.

51 Isidore of Seville, *Isidori Hispalensis episcopi origium sive etymologiarum*, in *Auctores latinae linguae*, n.p., Guillielmum Leimarium, 1685. For a later discussion of the same theme, see Jacques Ferrand, *Treatise*, at ch. XII (whether uterine fury is a species of lovesickness).

52 St Jerome, 'Against Jovinian', in *A Select Library of Nicene and Post-Nicene Fathers*, New York, Christian Literature Co., 1893, at p. 367. For an excellent discussion of this theme, see Joyce Salisbury, *Church Fathers, Independent Virgins*, London, Verso, 1991.

53 Tertullian, 'On the Veiling of Virgins', in A. Roberts and J. Donaldson (eds), *Ante-Nicene Christian Library*, Edinburgh, Clark, 1989, vol. XVIII. On shamefacedness, see Jan Luis Vives, *A very Fruteful and Plesant Boke Called the Instruction of Christen Woman*, London, Wykes, 1583, at fol. J v a.

tempt nor to fascinate the eyes of men. The self-effacement of the virgin was the paradigm of the spiritualisation of love and it took its place within the laws of faith in the negative form of all those heresies which preached freedom of sexual relationship or the power of women. The single most common tenet of heretical doctrines listed in the *Black Catalogue of Heretics* was the belief that 'concupiscence and lust', which according to the Pelagians, for example, 'is naturally in us . . . is good, and there is nothing in it of which we need be shamed'.[54]

It is equally in this context of the condemnation of a sexuality which interferes with both faith and thought, with law and reason, that the ecclesiastical jurisdiction and law spelled out the necessity of distance and of masks, of asceticism, to the relationship between and within the sexes. That asceticism, that veiling or blindness to the body and sensuality becomes an important figure within the law. The patristic limitation of sexuality to reproduction gains a varied and expansive expression in both ecclesiastical and secular law. In relation to ecclesiastical law and its *forum internum* or inner court of conscience, the principal rules governing lust or impurity of thought relate to the dual offences of adultery and idolatry, in which the latter is the internal manifestation of the former. Other rules and principally those of defamation regulated the reputation of women and maintained the symbolic as well as the proprietary value of sexual continence:

> if a woman is called a whore by a man, the suit for such slander lies in the ecclesiastical courts. If a woman be slandered in her reputation, whereby she is hindered in her marriage, she may sue either at the common law or in the spiritual courts.[55]

In either case, the regulation of sexual relations was a matter of the law of images: the veiling of the *imago*, mask or face, was designed to introduce an indifference of appearance and an asexuality of bodies.

The more detailed regulation of the specific offences relating to other forms of sexual incontinency – fornication, lechery, incest, *stuprum*, polygamy and 'all unlawful company of man and woman'[56] – all share a classical theme of denigrating and punishing the sin of lust, whether real or imagined. And it is broadly speaking that tradition of asceticism which has made its way into secular law in the form of the desire of justice to be blind, in the hostility to anything more figurative or expressive than the cold dead letters or *littera mortua* of the text, in the desire to keep law separate from the domestic sphere and to define all non-marital sexual

---

54 Godolphin, *Reportorium Canonicum*, at p. 576.
55 Ibid., at p. 517.
56 Richard Cosin, *An Apologie for Sundrie Proceedings by Jurisdiction Ecclesiastical, of late time by some challenged*, London, 1591, at pp. 30–31.

relations if not in terms of incontinency then in terms of perversion or abnormality. If law is the principal form of serious social speech, if it represents to a culture those things which it values or those transgressions which threaten its criteria of civility, then the sphere of relationships and of sexual exchanges, inside and outside of marriage, inhabit an opaque zone of cultural neglect: they exist in law only in the form of offences or as indications of proprietary relation. Where the Renaissance was fond of debating the indifference of the feminine soul, namely that it could not be distinguished from that of the male, it should also be recalled that the indifference of the soul further made it impossible to distinguish the bodies of male and female in legal terms. Personality was an indifferent feature of a unitary conception, of an abstract corporeality, sex no more than an appearance, an image: it was either an attribute or a lack, an icon or an idol, a status or simple absence from the symbolic realm.

The laws governing the image lie at the base of the modern legal tradition and require interpretation not simply as forms of governance of the appropriate forms of worship but also as specifying the imitative place and mimetic role of the image, of appearance and of woman within the social. The other context and jurisdiction of love is that of ecclesiastical and secular regulation of the 'iconomy' or domesticity, the domain of private law and of the circulation of images, of women, between father and husband. In this context again the definition of relationship and of affectivity is not in terms of subjectivity or desire but in terms of possession, prohibition and power. If we take just one early instance, that of the literature concerned with what William Perkins dubs the 'christian oeconomie',[57] the only direct advice relating to sexuality was the warning against choosing a woman as wife by virtue of her beauty. The eyes were to express the 'inward chastity of the mind' and so were not to rest upon the surface of things, nor to be attracted to any idolisation of the body or face:

> thou may'st not trust too much to thine eyes (which are many times but a false pair of spectacles). . . . Some women are like painted cloth; look on one side, and thou seest Virgins, Virtues, Queens; but on the other, nothing but patches and rags: And then what match has thou made, when thou has gotten a *picture* to thine eye; and a poison to thine Heart? Golden chains and silken snares.[58]

Inner affinity should govern external relation, and unity of the soul should take precedence over bodily pleasure. To this it may be added that the wife

---

57 William Perkins, *Christian Oeconomie: Or a Short Survey of the Right Manner of Erecting and Ordering a Family, according to the Scriptures*, Cambridge, Cantrell Legge, 1609.

58 M. Griffith, *Bethel or, a Forme for Families: In which all sorts, of both sexes, are so squared, and framed by the word of God, as they may best serve in their severall places, for useful pieces in God's Building*, London, Bloome, 1633, at pp. 256–257 (emphasis in original).

was to give up her name, that she was bound to stay at home and not to travel abroad, that her duty was to be silent. Silence, indeed, is depicted by Vives 'as the noblest ornament of woman', to which he adds curiously: 'thou art no attorny at law . . . nor plead in court, hold thou thy peace as boldly as others speak in court'.[59] The reason for which advice no doubt related quite directly to the subordinate or accessory status of the woman as an adjunct and subject of her father or husband.

The jurisdiction of love traditionally concerned the hierarchical relation between sovereign and subject and was predicated upon the identity of all such relationships. The rules briefly outlined, delimited and confined relationships of love to their function of reproduction. Faith, fidelity and desire were alike to be directed to the goal of reproducing the church, the ecclesiastical commonwealth and the male line. Similarly, where the secular law talks of love, it does so in the context of political love and a 'ghostly power' by means of which the sovereign should nurture his or her subjects. The crown was depicted thus as having an internal juris-diction, it was *specula pastoralis*, and was to be 'nursing father' or 'nursing mother' to the polity and to care for the souls, the 'inward peace' of the subjects or members of the realm.[60] The final attribute of such love or political desire can be elicited from the fact that this jurisdiction and function of attachment is divine and so depicted as 'incommunicable or inalienable'.[61] While the roles and places of political love may be internal, they are subject to a law of distance, of non-disclosure, of dissimulation. Being formulated in negative terms and directed in silence beyond the body or the image towards an invisible and eternal object, the most striking feature of such attachment is its emptiness: what is kept at a distance is so kept for a reason; it cannot be loved but only worshipped.

The jurisdiction of love thus defines the amorous relation either as a sin or as something which cannot be communicated or directly addressed. It is love of an object and insofar as that object is reflected in its creation, the love involved is not only an objectification, but strongly narcissistic, a self-marriage, an escape both from the body and from its temporality. It is indeed this feature of Christian patristic love which is most relevant to the jurisdiction of the courts of love and merits brief commentary. The jurisdiction of love is most remarkable for being strongly hostile both to the body and to love in its temporal forms. Love is an illusion induced by the false surfaces of mundane things, including women:

---

59 Jan Luis Vives, *A very Fruteful and Pleasant Boke Called the Instruction of a Christian Woman*, London, Wykes, 1557 edn, at fol. M iii a. For more extensive discussion of feminine silence, see George Fox, *The Woman Learning in Silence or, the Mysterie of the Woman's subjection to her Husband*, London, Simmonds, 1655.

60 The term 'nursing father' comes from Roger Coke, *Elements of Power and Subjection or the Causes of all Humane, Christian and Legal Society*, London: Newcomb, 1660, at p. 43.

61 Ibid., p. 99.

for if someone wears a mask, is he not trying to hide the total absence of a face? To cover over the desertion of his body? To lure into the abyss one who is deceived by the mere appearance of life?[62]

The mask, the appearance, the subject of Christian love directs love to an object external to the world and to time and in so doing makes love an unconscious and irrational thing:

but if your love is for eternity, why stay on this earth? If pleasures and mortifications, for you, are perpetually bound together, why don't you give up living? If birth amounts to a beginning of death, why drag out the agony?[63]

The tradition of courtly love, which forms the context of the courts of love, certainly relates love to death in the species of fidelity and infidelity. In one celebrated judgment of the Court of the King of Behaigne the question was whether a lady whose lover had died suffered more than a knight whose lover had been unfaithful and had taken a new *ami*. The judgment of the Court is that the knight has suffered more, 'that his soul is in greater anxiety (*souxi*)' and that he is farther from consolation, than the lady.[64] The grounds offered for this judgment are framed explicitly in terms of reason and of justice and are formulated precisely in terms of the continuing emotions and relations that the thwarted lovers experience. Such indeed are the proper concerns of justice and they allow the position of the lady whose lover has died to be strongly distinguished from the knight whose lover has been unfaithful. For her, the fact that she will not see her lover again distinguishes her position:

since she will not see him again, it will happen that . . . [she will] forget him; for the heart will never love anything so much that it won't forget it after separation . . . there's no woman or man alive whose love is so blameless, if he's caught by the amorous flame, who does not love the body much better than the soul . . . Why is that? Because love comes from carnal affection.[65]

For the knight, by contrast, separation or forgetting are not possible; he is constantly reminded of her because of her continued presence: 'and he who is nearest the fire burns the most'.[66] It is added finally to this that his soul and life are the most endangered and that beyond the folly, grief and delirium in which he exists, he is subject to the most stringent jealousy.

---

62 Irigaray, *Marine Lover*, at p. 59.
63 Ibid., at p. 23.
64 See Guillaume de Machaut, *Le Jugement du roy de Behaigne*, Athens, Ga., University of Georgia Press, *c.* 1358, 1988 edn, at pp. 148 and 152.
65 Ibid., at pp. 145–146.
66 Ibid., at pp. 146–147.

The judgment illustrates a number of most significant features of the law of love. Many of these aspects of amorous relationship are codified in the *regulae* and the *praecepta amoris* and offer a striking contrast, though not simply an inversion of the ecclesiastical jurisdiction. The principal feature of the tradition of judgments of love is that although they are codified by a cleric and although the tradition and its codifications have their immediate origin in the monasteries, their concern is with human love, with passion and its bodily effects.[67] The difference may be formulated most easily in terms of a series of substitutions. Most obviously the eternity of the ecclesiastical jurisdiction is replaced by the temporality of the worldly relationship and carnal love. The judgment is explicitly concerned with the anguish of the living and not with the fear of death. More than that, the ecclesiastical concern with the sublimation of love to an other-worldly end was generally expressed in terms of the illusory character of temporal love, its place being that of mere appearance, of image or semblance, whereas the judgments of love and the *regulae amoris* are directed precisely at the worldly and bodily qualities of the art of love as a species of *amor mixtus*.

The physical character of the rules of love is both evident and not without certain precedents: it was Bernard of Clairvaux who most clearly stated that 'we are carnal, and born of the concupiscence of the flesh, so is it also necessary that our love begins with the flesh'.[68] The significant feature of the tradition of the art of love was that profane love was mixed with sacred affection, passion with everyday life. Whatever the theological interpretation of this mixing of spiritual and temporal, and whatever its relation to the patristic conception of the role of the feminine and of the soul in the direction of love, the *regulae amoris* offer strikingly temporal and physical guides to emotional states.[69] Some of these take the form of descriptions. By rule 15 we are told that 'a lover tends to grow pale (*pallescere*) when their lover (*coamantis*) looks at them'. By rule 16 it is stated that 'the heart of a lover beats faster at the sudden sight of the beloved'. By rule 23 we learn that those in the throes of love find it hard to eat or sleep. The blush or the palpitation, emotional conditions of attenuation or disturbance, excitation and fear, signify spiritual states, and are complemented by rules that indicate a sense of the practical as well as the ethical import of such physical responses. The code of love is also a phenomenology or latterly symptomology of the physical expressions of

67 On the historical and theological background to the tradition, see C.S. Jaeger, *The Origins of Courtliness: Civilizing Trends and the Formation of the Courtly Ideals 939–1210*, Philadelphia, University of Pennsylvania Press, 1985. See also Jean Markale, *L'Amour courtois ou le couple infernale*, Paris, Imago, 1987.

68 Bernard of Clairvaux, cited in Markale, *L'Amour courtois*, at p. 20.

69 The *regulae* discussed in what follows are listed at the end of Book 2 of the *Tractatus*, Bk 2, pp. 44–49; trans., pp. 283–285.

what the Renaissance was variously to term erotic mania, lovesickness or love melancholy. The law, it must be remembered, concerned remedies for love as well as establishing the space or imaginary domain within which that sweet sickness could develop and be expressed in sighs and pallor, tears and words, letter-writing, dreams and other contracts.

Love, in short, is both fascinating and obsessive, and by rule 30 a true lover (*verus amans*) is said to always have the image of the loved one without interruption before their eyes, while rule 24 dictates that 'every and any (*quilibet*) act of a lover is bounded by the thought of the beloved'. Similarly by rule 25 the true lover regards nothing as good but that which will please their lover. Such obsession or fascination does not only concern the definition or corporeal recognition of the state of love but also indicates a fidelity that belongs to the flesh. By rule 12 it is stated that a 'true lover does not desire the embrace of any other than that of their lover' and similarly by rule 17 'a new love puts the old love to flight'. Love waxes and wanes (rule 4), should always be true to itself – 'a lover can only extract bitter love from an unwilling partner' (rule 5) – and should be entered into with caution and with attention to the ethical character of the partner. By rule 18 it is stated that 'honesty of character (*probitas*) alone makes a man worthy of love', while by rule 29 'the man affected by excessive sensuality' and so by infidelity or promiscuity 'is usually not in love'. While much of Book 2 of the *Tractatus* is concerned with entering into relationships of love and with maintaining love, rule 19 recognises that 'if love diminishes, it soon fades and hardly ever gains strength'.

The final feature of the *regulae* to be noted at this juncture is that they recognise the strict temporality of love and impose duties that accord with that recognition. The concern of the tradition of judgment is the reality and hence the contingency of love. The lover, by rule 2, is always and necessarily jealous, and by rule 21 'true jealousy (*vera zelotypia*) makes the feeling of love grow'. Love exists within an economy of fear and of jealousy and one consequence of such emotional context is that love ends. The *regulae* state clearly that love should only end for good reason (rule 8), that is by virtue of another love or the extinction of passion. In such circumstance, the rules further state that the lover should remain bound to their former lover for two years and refrain from other relationships. In such a manner the rules endeavour to govern the beginning, the maintenance and the ending of relations of love and to do so with a degree of ethical as well as pragmatic concern. Love ends, but it cannot simply be abandoned; love moves on, but even within this epic form of love, it does so for a reason and, insofar as is possible, it pays its debts to sorrow and to lust.

The point about the jurisdiction of love is not that the rules are consistent, nor that they are applied as a code. The issue is rather that the *regulae*, and the judgments from which they are collated, create an ethical casuistry of relationship and of sexual exchange. Rather than denying the orthodoxy, morality or reality of passion and love, the code addresses the kinds of practical and ethical problems that are faced by lovers and indeed by every remotely emotionally invested relationship. It is not therefore the contents of the code that is of significance but it is rather the willingness to accept and address, in the form of principles and rules, the demands of intimacy, the ethics of relationship and the beginning and ending of love. What is looked for in the casuistry of love is a certain justice in relationships, a justice that requires at the very least that the relation between lovers be the object of serious social speech, that in its power and its passion it be deemed worthy of something more and other than the simple designation of irrationality or sin. In this sense, the *regulae amoris* work towards the notion of a jurisdiction which does justice to intimacy, that in some measure fulfils expectations and recognises that relationship is always predicated upon the difference of the subjects and subjectivities engaged in exchange. In that respect, although much of the tradition of courts of love and of *fin' amors* concern the distance and the non-consummation of love, the tradition of judgments not only opens up the possibility of laws that govern affectivity but also addresses and judges disputes that are much more concerned with proximity, the body and the power as well as the devastation of amorous engagement.

## JUDGMENTS IN THE CAUSES OF LOVE

The *regulae amoris* and *Le Jugement du roy du Behaigne*, adverted to above, both suggest an important justification for the jurisdiction of love. It is that of the immediacy, intensity and psychic as well as physical charge of relationships of love. The rules and the judgments both indicate that the severity of the anguish and the reality of the physical effects of such relationships require not only consolation but some species of justice adequate to the nature and the metaphysics of such disputes. Cupid, like Justice, is often depicted iconographically as blind.[70] Although the usual interpretation of such blindness is that it parodies the blindfolding of *Justitia* and is a blindness which ignores both reason and the scales of *Fortuna*, a more interesting interpretation would acknowledge the blindness of Cupid or *Eros* as a species of the aporia of justice, namely that in the affairs of the heart or in relation to the laws of love it is impossible to know in advance the causes or the resolutions of specific wrongs, disappointments, frustrations or simple disputes. The blindness of love, of what Selden termed the 'laws of the first Venus', the law of nature, as

---

70 E. Panofsky, *Studies in Iconology: Humanistic Themes in the Art of the Renaissance*, New York, 1939. For discussion, see Marie Collins, 'Love, Nature and Law', in Burgess (ed.), *Court and Poet*, at p. 113.

opposed to the prudential rules of 'the second Venus', namely positive law,[71] would here be taken to relate to the nature and contingency, the force and violence of love, as well as to that of a justice which recognises the difference of the other that comes to be judged.

The aporia of justice refers to the suspension of judgment and the undecidability of law. It refers in this regard to the incalculable moment in which interpretation of the circumstances and persons to be judged, the singularity of the object of judgment, suspends the rules and makes new law.[72] More important, however, than the hermeneutic character of justice is the classical link between justice and love in which the laws of the first Venus are a species of natural law, of what the *Confessio Amantis* terms the 'law of kind'.[73] The laws of love belong to a nature that is only in part accessible to humanity but is visible as a movement of the sensitive soul and as a law of physical being. The aporia of justice in relation to love, in figurative terms the relation of *Justitia* to Cupid, is that of the gap which separates two distinct orders of law. In scholastic terms love is the greater law – *maior lex amor est*[74] – and it lays down its own rules, it suspends the criteria or the foundations of justice through judging each case anew and yet the rules of love and their courts or schools also recognise that some of what passes within love's own law can be taught, inculcated or judged as an ethics of relationship and as a way of life. The blindness of Cupid and of *Justitia* can in this sense be understood to represent the reciprocal distance between two laws, the subjectivity and singularity of their respective judgments. Their casuistry endeavours to fold the laws of one Venus into those of the other; it attempts to transcend the unseeing or phantasmatic character of the relation of love and to bridge the abyss that separates two hitherto unconjoinable jurisdictions.[75]

The aporia of the justice of love is the aporia intrinsic to parallel jurisdictions or orders of law. It is an aporetic structure which returns in many contemporary analyses of passion. Their conjuction is their blindness, their union is their difference, a theme which finds ample expression in the literature of love in the maxim that nothing is further from love than duty, or that law and the following of rules or observing of limits is the antithesis of love which 'is without contract and without hope of return'.[76]

---

71 John Selden, *Jani Anglorum facies altera*, London, Bassett, 1610/1683 edn, at p. 11.
72 This is the theme of J. Derrida, 'Force of Law: The Mystical Foundation of Authority' (1990) 11 *Cardozo Law Review* 919, particularly at pp. 961–973. It is a theme which borrows much from E. Levinas, *Totality and Infinity*, Holland, Kluwer, 1991.
73 Reference to John Gower, *Confessio Amantis*, is in G.C. Macaulay (ed.), *The English Works of John Gower*, London, 1900–1901. For discussion of this theme, see Frances McNeely Leonard, *Laughter in the Courts of Love*, Norman, Okla., Pilgrim Books, 1981.
74 Boethius, *Consolation of Philosophy*, London, Stock, 1897, at 160 (III, m12, 47–48)
75 See Jean-Claude Milner, *For the Love of Language*, London, Macmillan, 1990, pp. at 120–122 for an analysis of the relation of language to love as 'an impossible conjunction'.
76 See, for example, P. Le Boulanger, *Morale galante ou l'art de bien aimer*, Paris, Jean Le Blanc, 1969, vol. I, at p. 97, discussed in Luhmann, *Love as Passion*, at pp. 67–73.

It is the paradoxical character of love and the improbability of its communication which Luhmann rightly stresses in his study of *Love as Passion*; it is the militancy and the impossibility which Irigaray stresses in *J'aime à toi*; the hedonistic law of the living, of 'another reason, another logic' or 'other scene' which Cixous addresses in 'Writing and the Law'. The question remains, however, of how we are to understand the jurisdiction and judgments of love as something more than illusions that are banned from the city or distant and veiled sites of the other, of the feminine, beyond the apprehension of any manifest or positive law.[77] The answer to such a questioning lies in a reading of the judgments themselves.

The first and most obvious theme of the judgments of love is that of distance, of *amour lointain*, as a metaphor for the secrecy and the hiddenness of relations of love in both literal and metaphorical senses. According to *regula* 13, 'a love which is made public (*vulgatus*) rarely lasts'. The requirement that love be hidden, that the lovers have only a few confidantes, is also spelled out in precept 6 which dictates that the lovers 'do not take too many as confidantes' in their love.[78] Such rules pervade the *Tractatus* and constantly reiterate that the secrecy of passion must always be maintained, that communications between lovers must be indirect and through intermediaries or letters, that trysts be at night or the language of lovers obscure or sufficiently encrypted to be opaque to the world. Such are rules that relate only on their surface to the extramarital character of the relationship of love. The secrecy of the relationship of love can be understood better by reference to the homosocial economy of jealousy, the uniqueness of love and the contingent and often unconscious object of its choices. That love be hidden, secret, dark or distant is thus best taken to refer to the fate, nature or law that governs love but which is treated either as illusion, unconsciousness or excess by the orders of men and of laws that govern the polity. The hiddenness of love is a radical metaphor for the externality of love to the public domain, its character being that of threat or transgression, and so dark or distant only in the sense of the exile or the alien, the party expelled or the subject on the border who wants to come in from the space or distance, the other place or scene inhabited by the lover. Thus most famously in the words of Bernard de Ventadour: 'Là est mon désir', there where my love is, a sentiment of alienation that refers both to the separation of lover and beloved and more significantly to a desire which is other to the subject who loves, an internal alienation,

---

77 Irigaray, *Marine Lover*, at p. 99, puts it thus:

> Illusion no longer has the freedom of the city. It is no longer the companion, the adornment of life. It fascinates like something beyond good living that must be expelled, wiped out of everyday life. That illusion, in the final analysis, determines the laws of society cannot and must not be seen.

78 *Tractatus*, Bk 1, pp. 268–270; trans., at pp. 116–117: *amoris tui secretarios noli plures habere.*

something unheard within.[79] Such in more positive terms is the destiny or fate of the lover who is bound no longer to a unity or *persona* but to another space or intensity of relation that exists and endures between two persons but cannot be defined by either one.

Judgment xiv of *De iudiciis amoris* concerned a lady who had a lover who had gone abroad on an expedition, in a worthy cause (in all probability a Crusade).[80] She had not heard from her lover for some three years and had no expectation of his return – 'in fact everyone despaired of his presence or arrival (*adventus*)'. The lady therefore sought another lover. A confidant (*secretarius*) of the first lover objected to the woman's infidelity (*fide mutata*) and spoke against her new love. The woman offered two defences of her decision. The first was by analogy with the rules relating to widowhood, namely that if a husband died a woman was entitled to remarry after two years; this concession, she argued, should be granted all the more to a woman who had been bereft of a living lover for more than two years. Her second argument was that throughout his extended absence, her lover had sent not a single message, letter or other sign, despite the availability of messengers and the relative ease of communication. The dispute was argued lengthily on both sides before the Court of the Countess of Champagne. The Countess gave judgment against the woman on two principal grounds. The first, pursuant to *regula* 8 that 'no-one should be deprived of love except for a most compelling reason', was that the woman could not desert her lover simply on the ground of his absence. She would have to clearly ascertain that he had been deficient in his love or had been unfaithful. As to the failure of the lover to write letters or send messengers, this was to be accounted an act of great wisdom:

> he cannot entrust this secret of his to any stranger (*extraneo*). If he had sent a letter with the contents hidden from the bearer, the secrets of his love (*amoris arcana*) could still easily have been spread abroad either by the wickedness of the messenger or by virtue of his death *en route*.

In Judgment xxi the same point is made in a ruling that if lovers write letters they should never write their names nor should they stamp letters to each other with their own seals unless they have secret seals unknown to anyone else 'by such action their love will be kept intact and un-damaged'.[81]

The envelope might be opened, the letter purloined or the message might simply not arrive at its destination. It would be a case in the domain of communication of what Lacan terms *amor interruptus* or suspension of

---

79 Cited in Huchet, *L'Amour discourtois*, at p. 35.
80 *Tractatus*, Bk 2, pp. 31–35; trans., pp. 262–263.
81 Ibid., Bk 2, p. 51; trans., p. 271.

the message.[82] It is a species of *fatum epistolarum* or non-arrival, of 'the law that a letter can always – and therefore must – never arrive at its destination. And this is not negative', Derrida continues, 'it is good, and is the condition (the tragic condition, certainly, and we know something about that) that something does arrive – and that I love you. Who would I have loved, otherwise? My family perhaps, starting with my father'.[83] The non-arrival is connected to waiting, to delay, to the desire to determine an addressee who might also 'always, *by chance*, not arrive'.[84] This uncertainty is not fortuitous or merely playful; the structure of forgetting and of going astray, of the possibility of multiple destinations, and of destinerrancy are all conditions of secrecy and of the probability of successfully hiding an amorous or intimate letter in the public hands of the post.[85] Such also, of course, is the structure of the relationship and of love. It must recognise that the unconscious – be it *eros* or *libido* – is not fully determinable nor capable of being entirely known.

Let us take the matter a step further by reference to Judgment xviii: a certain man, from the worst (*turpiter*) of motives, publicised (*vulgavit*) the most intimate secrets of his love. A specially convened Court of the ladies (*dominarum*) of Gascony unanimously laid down by perpetual decree that the knight should be denied all hope of love thereafter, 'and should continue to be the object of derision and contempt in the whole court . . . And if any lady should defy the statute of the Court, she should be forever subject to the same punishment".[86] His betrayal of the *arcana amoris* or secret of love was subject to what can be described best as the amorous equivalent of excommunication. To this it might be added that the courts themselves were approached anonymously and were, by Judgment xxi, specifically to be held *in camera*. Secrecy of procedure added to secrecy of process and privacy of communication clearly do not intimate any literal inaccessibility to the gynocratic jurisdiction. It is predicated, after all, upon the communication of its decisions and observance of its codes. The secrecy, I will therefore repeat, is better understood as belonging to a psychic order in which the object of desire is always obscure and scarcity or lack determine the value of love within an economy of jealousies. The secrecy of the distant love does not, however, only express the value of the object of love or *fin' amors*. It also encodes the limits of relationship and marks the inevitable indeterminacy of the choices of love.

In a more Freudian terminology, the secrecy of love quite possibly

---

82 Lacan, *Ethics*, at p. 152.
83 Jacques Derrida, *The Post Card. From Socrates to Freud and Beyond*, Chicago, Chicago University Press, 1987, at p. 121.
84 Ibid., at p. 191 (emphasis in original).
85 On the notion of 'destinerrancy', see Jacques Derrida, 'For the Love of Lacan' (1995) 16 *Cardozo Law Review* 967.
86 *Tractatus*, at pp. 266–267.

repeats the trauma of the bedroom scene and the child's discovery of its parents' sexuality, the primal scene. Secrecy as repetition would here represent a repression or an inability to return to that scene of trauma but rather incorporates it in a practice of love that institutes a fear of losing love, a jealousy which is quite explicit in the *regulae amoris*, as by rule 28 where it is stated that 'the smallest suspicion forces a lover to entertain dark thoughts about the beloved'. To this, rule 21 adds that 'true jealousy makes the feeling of love grow'.[87] What is significant is not so much the simple repetition but rather the unconscious character of love which the *regulae* both recognise and transgress. While *amour lointain* is on the surface a form of object-choice, a falling in love which unconsciously repeats the early structure of love – 'the desire to have something *back*, which had once existed'[88] – the crucial feature of such love is its unconscious character. Whether based on the attachment model or the narcissistic model, the theory of object-choice offers a conception of the unconscious and so secret character of love as a limit within which the courts of love can be used to rethink or recuperate the ethics of such repetition or the laws that determine the dual loss of self and subjectivity in the process of falling in and out of love.

Whatever the epistemology of love secreted in the code of distance and its affects, the courts of love offer a means of treating such love according to a less cryptic regulation. The secrecy of the relationship is to be placed side by side with the visibility of judgment. If such a procedure of openness is possible then it offers a striking homology between the determinations of twelfth-century women's courts and contemporary feminist concerns. For inadmissible yet necessary reasons, it is best to begin with the concerns of the contemporary. It is the argument of recent French feminist jurisprudence, as also of some francophile Anglo-American feminist legal theory, that social justice demands the legislation of a civic personality and correspondingly sexuate rights for the feminine. The argument is predicated upon a demand for recognition of feminine difference and more specifically upon the necessity of a much delayed political and juridical acknowledgement of the existential force and personal importance of intimate relationship, of 'l'amour entre nous'[89] as both a public and private phenomenon. There is an urgent need, Irigaray has argued recently, for 'objective laws that will organise the relationships between women, and between women and men . . . in the absence of civil laws which positively define their real rights and duties, women only have subjective criteria by which to refer to themselves', mere speech or opinion

---

87 Ibid., at pp. 282–283 (translation modified).
88 Theweleit, *Object-Choice*, at p. 9.
89 Irigaray, *J'aime à toi*, at p. 29. For an excellent discussion of this text, see Alain Pottage, 'Recreating Difference' (1993) 5 *Law and Critique* at 131.

or conscience without either authority, objective force or social truth.[90] Her argument is both that the personal is juridical, the unconscious a jurist, and also that the instantiation of legal rights could directly and objectively establish the feminine within the symbolic.

The delineation of the project of a code of feminine rights begins with the demand for the bifurcation of the traditional conception of legal personality so as to recognise both the duality of the sexes and the fact that (heterosexual) relationship takes place between the spheres of sexual difference. It is this space of exchange which becomes the focus of radical legal theory in that this site and duration of relationship, this imaginary domain, is irreducible to existing legal categories, it is unbound to any extant unity, identity or singularity but rather takes place between two lovers, between man and man, woman and woman or man and woman. In prosaic terms the argument is that

> we do not have a civil law concerning actual persons, and first and foremost men and women . . . there is no definition of woman as woman in the *Code Civil*, nor is there anywhere else any definition of man as man. Man and woman are nowhere defined as sexual identities . . . but as neutral individuals.[91]

The elaboration of rights appropriate to the feminine genre and so also to the relationship between the sexes is variously spelled out by Irigaray in terms of rights of speech, of aesthetic expression, of public representation, institutional space, maternity and welfare provision as well as in terms of freedom from exploitative images and sexual commodification.[92] Such codification would provide symbolic value or political substance to the rights of the feminine and would build into law a conception, as yet lacking, of the temporality and the subjectivity of relationship. Through the symbolic affirmation of feminine difference, Irigaray proposes not only to revalue the feminine within public space but equally to introduce law into the socially unconscious terrain of sexual relationship. In this latter respect, Irigaray is most radical where she formulates demands for impossible or utopian rights, where she insists upon the radically transformative character of this rewriting of both literature and law. Aesthetic rights, rights to histories, philosophies, literatures and sciences in a feminine genre, the right to positive public representations, the right to spirituality and further to half of institutional space all constitute the beginnings of a very serious challenge to a jurisdiction and order of law which is predicated upon the unity of a system and the singularity of its sources.

90 Irigaray, *J'aime à toi*, at p. 12.
91 Ibid., at pp. 43 and 205.
92 These are listed in *J'aime à toi*, at pp. 18–36, 202–220; in *Temps de la différence*, at pp. 74–78, 82–90; and Irigaray, *Je, tu, nous*, Paris, Grasset, 1990, at pp. 101–113.

Where Irigaray offers a surprisingly expansive and legally somewhat extraordinary, if at times indeterminate, set of specific proposals, other feminist lawyers have added comparable and on occasion more concrete delineations of the requirements of sexually explicit rights. Another French jurist, Francine Demichel, reiterates a very similar path of argument to that used by Irigaray in offering a powerful critique of the asexual and disembodied rights of established laws. In her terms, law needs to reintroduce subjectivity into legality in the form of sexuate and temporalised legal concepts and offers a pluralistic model of rights appropriate to 'lived time, to actual time, to the time of life'.[93] Her particular concern is with laws that can apprehend rupture and passage rather than simple power:

> Law already knows the concepts of identity, system and unity. But the space in between (*l'entre deux*), movement, mixing or crossing, that which evolves and changes, the complex agency of things, lie outside of the legal understanding. . . . Nomadic, mobile, inhibited, women have not yet constructed a legal symbolism

nor instituted any sphere of rights with significant social force.[94] To change the law so as to account for the domain of relationships and to express the social significance of desire and of sexuality, to give symbolic value to sexual relationships, would rewrite the hierarchical yet socially unconscious terms of the *gynaeceum*, the contingency of the private sphere.

Anglo-American feminist jurisprudence has followed a somewhat different route and in early efforts to legislate, sexuate rights or recognition of the feminine has tended to rely upon pre-existing models of state law and its proprietary rights. Rather than developing any concept of distinct jurisdictions or radically distinctive procedures the tendency has been to adapt extant rights and claims to novel subjectivities. One contemporary example can be taken from a recent work proposing the introduction of a tort of sexual deceit.[95] The argument again concerns the question of symbolic value or the political and juridical thought which a culture is prepared to address towards sexual relationships. The new cause of action proposed develops the historic tort of seduction into the equivalent of an action for misrepresentation inducing sexual contact or exchange. While the law of contract and of tort have long recognised a right of action where a party fraudulently or negligently induces consent to a commercial transaction by means of misrepresentation, the new tort would allow recovery where consent to sexual intercourse was induced by deception. Thus misrepresentation of physical condition, the failure to disclose a

---

93 Francine Demichel, 'Concepts juridiques et différence sexuelle', in Mara Négron (ed.), *Lectures de la différence sexuelle*, Paris, des femmes, 1994, at p. 164.
94 Ibid., at pp. 166–167.
95 Jane Larson, '"Women Understand so Little, they Call my Good Nature Deceit": A Feminist Rethinking of Seduction' (1993) 93 *Columbia Law Review* 375.

sexually transmitted disease, the misrepresentation of infertility or health, the abuse of a therapeutic relationship to gain consent to sex, would all form the basis of an action. More borderline cases[96] concern factual representations of intention with regard to other relationships or to marriage, past or future, but the borderlines of the tort of sexual fraud are nonetheless fairly easily drawn: where a party fraudulently makes a misrepresentation of fact, opinion, intention or law, for the purpose of inducing another to consent to sexual relations in reliance upon it, an action will lie. The tort requires proof of two key elements, namely deceit and reliance and so incorporates a measure of inherent restraint upon the availability of the action.[97]

The significance of Larson's proposal does not, however, lie in the details of the tort but rather in the application of the law of tort to a new area of human relationship. It is true of course that the proposal comes on the back of a series of limited reforms of the law's relation to the private realm, but such reforms fall far short of any principled or even reasoned remapping of the *gynaeceum*, that sphere which the courts have traditionally labelled an Alsatia or domain 'into which the King's writ does not seek to run'.[98] The issue which Larson's proposal raises, and which is elsewhere raised most clearly in relation to the regulation of pornography, is that of the contingency of the distinction between public and private and the inevitable mixing of the boundaries by means of which an established legal hierarchy or political culture demarcates these spheres or draws the *Carte du Tendre*.[99] What is at issue is precisely the justice of relationships and the ethics of sexual expression. To the extent that cultural norms or legal arguments drawn from concepts of privacy or domesticity preclude law from considering, evaluating or judging sexual relationships it leaves the power in such relationships as it stands: the paterfamilias, husband or father, is in such circumstances likely to be 'advocate, judge, Court, sheriff's officer and reporter'.[100] In Larson's words, such scepticism

---

96 See *Perry v Atkinson* 240 Cal. Rptr. 402 (Ct. App. 1987), discussed in Larson, 'Women Understand So Little', at pp. 464–465.

97 Larson, 'Women Understand So Little', at p. 455.

98 Most famously in *Balfour v Balfour* [1919] 2 KB 571, at 579.

99 On the legal distinction between public and private, see Nicola Lacey, 'Theory into Practice? Pornography and the Public/Private Dichotomy' (1993) 20 *Journal of Law and Society* 93, at 99: 'Different meanings and possibilities can be glimpsed or imagined which may gradually allow us to transcend the oppressive social relations expressed in the current dichotomies.'

100 This conception of the domestic sphere is taken directly from Lord Atkin in *Balfour v Balfour*, at 579. For a critique of this view by a late seventeenth-century feminist critic of the common law, see Mary Astell, *Some Reflections upon Marriage Occasioned by the Duke and Dutchess of Mazarine's Case*, London, J. Nutt, 1700, at p. 38:

For covenants between husband and wife, like laws in an arbitrary government, are of little force, the will of the sovereign is all in all ... thus men happily sign articles (relating to property and goods) but then retract them, because being absolute master, she and all the grants he makes her are in his power . . . .

of legal power 'is paralyzing; worse, it consigns women to an existence outside of civil society, cut off from the system of public justice. . . . The argument that sexual matters are private carries with it the implication that sexual relations are *not* political', a conclusion which in turn cedes 'the governance of that sphere to private regimes of power'.[101]

Larson's argument incorporates the feminine into the structure of the existing legal jurisdiction and proposes feasibly reformist legal resolutions to a specific species of misrepresentation. While the argument for a new tort can be framed in terms of an additional symbolic value for sexuate rights and powers, it does not address the structural character of the legal inability to address the domain of intimacy or of relationship in its own terms. It is only if the space of relationship and of sexuality is conceived as an independent temporality, space or site, that it is possible to embark upon rethinking the plurality of sexual difference and the diverse jurisdictions which might displace 'the law' in expressing and determining disputes that arise at the level of the ethics and aesthetics of the art of life. It is the radicalism of relationship, the devastation of desire and the politics of love which draw the attention of a psychoanalytically informed jurisprudence and allow Drucilla Cornell, to mention one further American example, to develop the conception of sexuate rights in a novel and philosophically sensitive manner. Her argument in *The Imaginary Domain* is precisely that sexuate rights must be predicated upon the recognition of a novel jurisdiction and object of law. The concept of a civic identity and symbolic space for sexual persons is only possible if the jurisdiction of law is broken up and new forms of identity and of desire are allowed to develop within separate jurisdictions and diverse political forms. Law is only one imperfect instrument for the project of free development of sexual personality but it does provide the possibility of creating and protecting a space for such development:

> it is under my definition a project that demands the space for the renewal of the imagination and the concomitant re-imagining of who one is and who one seeks to become. Hence, my insistence on the imaginary domain as crucial to the very possibility of freedom . . . to transform oneself. . .[102]

To facilitate this possibility of transformation, to provide the symbolic space within which the sexuate person can dream, imagine or fantasise new forms of relationship and of expression is only marginally a legal task. Insofar as it depends upon a space guaranteed or supervised by legal means it requires new procedures, novel jurisdictions and diverse and distinct forms of judgment and of rule.

Such contemporary justifications for the jurisdiction and judgments of

---

101 Larson, 'Women Understand So Little', at pp. 435, 438–439.
102 Cornell, *The Imaginary Domain*, at p. 5.

what was for Capellanus the domain of the courts of love suggests that a juridical discourse on the politics of sexuality can yet learn something from the history of those judgments. At the very least the women's courts allow us to imagine a certain "feminisation"[103] of law. The art of love which was the subject-matter of the judgments of love is in essence an art of living and hence a political art, and so, even by classical criteria, it is legitimately an object of social and legal knowledge while at the same time representing an alternative in procedure, judgment and substantive rules to the existing legal hierarchy. The *regulae amoris* were concerned to bring ethics to love, justice to relationships, the laws of the 'second Venus' or '*legitimam Venerem*' to both sexual relationships and to the bonds of friendship. The tradition fused literature and law, but also betrayed its theological derivation in insisting that love *was* justice, a natural law, a marking of the soul with divine love – *vestigium divinae caritatis*.[104] That such were the terms of twelfth-century doctrine need not, however, predetermine the afterlife of those courts. There are indeed surprising substantive similarities between their judgments and contemporary concerns with amorous deceit and the exploitation of femininity.

Returning to the *Tractatus* it is necessary to preface further discussion of the judgments by reference to one other feature of the principles or precepts of love which form the doctrinal background to the decisions. The jurisdiction of love concerns the governance of souls or *regimen animarum* and is consequently and immediately bound to questions of faith and infidelity, honesty and lying, sincerity and misrepresentation.[105] The precepts of love make the condition of love depend upon honesty. Thus by precept 5 it is ordained that the lover should avoid all lying (*mendacia*). This is evidently a principle of morality in the form of law and is on the surface difficult to reconcile with the requirement of the secrecy of love. More importantly, however, it connotes a dictate of good faith in relationships, of sincerity in sexual interactions and makes the pretence of love, false love, the most heinous of the crimes before the courts of love.[106] In addition to this, it should be noted that the requirement of fidelity is

---

103 A notion taken from Cornell, *Beyond Accommodation*, at p. 95.
104 Discussed in Robertson, 'The Subject of the *De Amore*', at pp. 148–149. See also Danielle Régnier, 'Postface', in *idem, Coeur mangé*, Paris: Stock, 1979, at pp. 330ff.; also Markale, *L'Amour courtois*, at pp. 57ff.
105 One of the most common titles under which manuscripts of the *Tractatus* circulated was *De arte honeste amandi et de reprobatione inhonesti amoris*.
106 For discussion of this point, see Markale, *L'Amour courtois*, at pp. 34–35. Consider also Irigaray, *Marine Lover*, at p. 12:

> Too long have I been held back by the thread of compassion. I wanted a destiny for you – and me. How is it possible, from the weight of his destiny, to unburden the man who submits to it? . . . Moving on is surely the road to take when love takes such a road. And surely this farewell is the sign of love. Opening your horizon again to a more distant coming.

more of a requirement of speaking the truth about love than it is a rule of absolute faithfulness in a modern sense. Capellanus, in the dialogue which immediately precedes the judgments, is asked the question

> what if a man breaks faith with his lover, not with the intention of winning a new love, but under the impulse of pleasure (*voluptas*) which will not keep its distance? Supposing a convenient place offers him an unknown woman, or a courtesan ... in the mood for love (*Veneris incitatantis*) ... should he be deprived of his partner's love?

The answer given is that 'a lover should not be judged unworthy of love on this account, unless he chances to commit such excesses frequently and with many women, to such a degree that he be judged excessively licentious (*voluptas abundantia*)'.[107] To this it should be added that such hedonism is ethically qualified by the third principle of the precepts, namely that 'when a woman is properly (*idonee*) joined to another in love, do not knowingly try to seduce her'.[108]

Before returning to judgments concerned with that theme of fidelity and of sincerity in relationships, more general principles of neither slandering (precept 9) nor exposing love (precept 10) are also set out. That one should never speak ill (*maledicus*) of other lovers is also, in effect, a requirement that suitors do not lie. More than that, however, it concerns the maintenance of the civility of relationships, and requires that the representation of women in the public sphere, even if such was then predominantly a domain of oral representations, be positive, that the images of women, or interpreted more broadly of lovers of either sex, be valued symbolically but also subject to ethical or courtly restraints. Such restraints, it should be stressed, do not relate to the individual right or property in reputation or image, but rather to the protection or more appropriately the respect needed for amorous communication or the symbolic valuation and space of imagination required for the transformation and development intrinsic to love. The same themes of respect for the other and of fidelity or sincerity in relationship underpin Judgment xii.

A certain individual, who was already joined in a suitable love affair, persistently sought the love of a second lady (*dominae*), claiming throughout that he was destitute of the love of any other woman (*mulieris*) whatsoever. His persistent and urgent pleading was successful and he obtained absolutely everything that he desired. Having obtained the love of the second lady, he then deceived his second lover and returned and sought the love of his original lover. The Court of the Countess of Flanders judged as follows:

---

107 *Tractatus*, Bk 2, pp. 10–11; trans., p. 241 (translation modified).
108 Ibid., Bk 1, pp. 268–269; trans., p. 117.

this man, who has employed such fraudulent schemes (*fraudis . . . machinatione*), deserves to be deprived of the love of both ladies, and he ought never to receive the love of any other woman of worth. We believe he is ruled by an uncontrolled licentiousness (*impetuosa . . . voluptas*), and this is wholly inimical to love.

It is noteworthy that the Court goes on to add that lovers should take every precaution not to be deceived by the amorous fraudulence of men, but that where someone is genuinely deceived then they are not to be blamed:

> however devoted a woman is to the cause of love, [it must be recognised] that no one finds it easy to test the inner fidelity of men, or the intricate secrets of the heart, even great prudence often finds itself deceived by heavily veiled words (*palliatione sermonis*).[109]

Far from consigning the question of deceit to the ruses of love or to the war of the sexes, the judgment of the fraudulent lover indicates a direct perception not only of the ethical limits of seduction but also of the public need to judge the acts of those who gain consent by illicit means. The questions posed to the courts of love belonged not simply to the internal realm of the *libido*, nor could they be hidden either behind the veil of object-choice – of unconscious patterns of repetition – or protected from comment by doctrines of privacy, domesticity or family values. The ethics of love, like the morality of behaviour within relationships, was a question of the art of living, of the propagation of a civilised lifestyle and of respect for persons of both sexes. The development of sexuate rights entailed treating persons/of whatever gender according to the reasoned principles of love and according to the spaces of desire or imagination which such rights made possible. It is worth recalling that within the tradition of *fin' amors*, of the ends of love, desire and relationship were perceived to dominate much of social life and the aesthetic as well as the ethic of relationship was always present within human social proximity. The interactions of the sexes and the interactions within the sexes thus occupied a vast territory of public space as well as of emotional life and as such were deemed to deserve a degree of judgment, discrimination or political and legal analysis comparable to that accorded to the other institutions and relationships which law governed.[110] In short, it is the trivialisation of relationship and the denigration of desire as a social force which is the first and appropriately subversive object of the art of love and of its courts. The courts of

---

109 Ibid., Bk 2, pp. 25–26 and 27–28; trans., p. 261 (translation modified).
110 For a sympathetic analysis along these lines, which focuses upon the *trobairitz* – a small group of women troubadours – see Laurie Finke, 'The Rhetoric of Desire in the Courtly Lyric', in *idem, Feminist Theory, Women's Writing*, Ithaca, NY, Cornell University Press, 1992. See also Marianne Shapiro, 'The Provençal *Trobairitz* and the Limits of Courtly Love' (1978) 3 *Signs* 560.

love existed to instantiate and legitimate the space of the imaginary and the value of desire. A further, remarkably feministic, judgment can usefully illustrate this point.

In Judgment xiii, the Court of the Countess of Flanders heard the following plea. A certain man was utterly without moral worth (*probitate*) or human value, and was accordingly refused love by all women. He nonetheless sought the love of a certain woman with such importunity (*improbitate*) that she granted him the hope of love. This lady by her moral teaching so improved this man's style and manners that through her affections and counsel in the art of love and of lovemaking he attained 'the highest moral character' and became the object of general praise for his honesty. Now trained to be honourable and to live according to the precepts of love another lady seduced him. The man succumbed to the seduction and became her lover, paradoxically quite forgetting the generosity and the pains of the previous woman. The issue before the Court would thus seem to be very similar to the more contemporary debate concerning implied or explicit contracts for domestic labour or for the recompense of emotional services. The Court held that

> everyone would surely see and approve the claim of the first lover to be able to recall her lover from the love of any other woman, for by her industry and labour she has raised him from the depths of immorality to the highest levels of civility and morality. The law thus holds that the woman has a reasonable right to this man, for by her wisdom and labour she has transformed a man devoid of moral character into someone honest, a man adorned with thought and manners.[111]

What is intriguing about the decision is not simply its fine and improbable casuistry but rather the degree of value which is accorded to the labour of the woman. To teach a man to love is an extraordinary achievement. To teach him to think or to adorn him with an awareness of the needs of others is so precious an exercise and so unlikely an outcome that the law had no doubt that it should be rewarded, that society should symbolise its sense of the value of what the woman had done by giving her judgment in her claim. While the decision is not without a certain element of irony and of paradox – the education had not in the event been entirely successful – the doctrine of the art of love required fidelity or honesty of the man and so imposed a temporality or duration upon the relationship. In one sense the man is made to pay for the time and the love which he took, but that payment is not of the order of possession or of some other existential proprietary right. It insists upon a recognition of the other, a justice of proximity, a species of art made into law. It also comes

111 *Tractatus*, Bk 2, pp. 28–31; trans., pp. 261–263.

some way towards addressing the question not of individual right but of a right between two parties or *entre deux*. The problems faced by the courts of love have not changed very greatly in this respect, namely how can the rules of love bring justice to relationship when love is a relationship constituted within a time and intentionality of its own? The fact that it was not simply chance or fate (the operation of more distant causes) but also labour that instituted the relationship in Judgment xiii allows a clearer sense of that problem. What is at issue is the construction and application of rules which recognise the problem of duration and within it the subjectivities – the intentionalities[112] – of the parties to love. What is crucial and specific to the justice of love is a recognition of a subjectivity that does not belong to either of the parties but which exists between them as an event, as a temporality and as a libidinal and so juristic exchange. Love in the time of object-choice is always potentially love in the time of law.

It is in terms of a justice appropriate to the time and intentionality of love as a radical emotion, as a desire which moves and changes the prior identities or purposes of its subjects, that judgment must recognise a space of relationship between parties rather than conceiving rights as the property of an individual. The difference of such a justice resides in a fluidity or contingency that can only judge according to the sudden and future orientated acts of a subjectivity created between two subjects, a mixing of subjectivities or 'interpenetration', a space between, a space – a touch, caress, body or bond – that is not of itself but rather for the other. What is judged is not judged according to the past but rather according to an event and according to its future: what is ethically essential and juridically distinctive is that it is not even the present of the relationship or bond that is at issue, but in a fuller and more radical sense it is a question of what comes after and so within the time of relationship. While such may appear not to be that radically different from certain of the problems that faced the classical jurisdiction of conscience and the judgment of promises according to spiritual criteria, there is a markedly different emphasis. The courts of love could not be indifferent to the bodies, the unique subjectivities, that were to be judged together, in the way that the canon law conception of *caritas* was indifferent to the individuality of the other person. *Caritas* was concerned with the salvation of the individual soul whereas the *amor mixtus* of the judgments of love seeks a justice appropriate to the other that exists between the lovers and not as the property of either one.

An instance of reading the relationship *between* the parties, or *entre deux*, can be taken from a further case reported in the *Tractatus*. In Judgment xvi the circumstances were these: a certain man had been arduously seeking

---

112 On the two intentionalities bonded by relationship, see Irigaray, *J'aime à toi*, at pp. 172ff. For commentary, see Pottage, 'Recreating Difference', at pp. 133–136.

the love of a woman but had not had the chance to speak with her at any length. Hoping to win the woman's love, he therefore used a confidant (*secretarium*) to mediate between them

> so that through this mediation each party might be able to discover more easily the wishes of the other, and reveal to the other with greater secrecy their own; through the confidant, too, the love between them could be more secretly conducted on a permanent basis.

The confidant took on the duty but then 'broke his faith as messenger (*sociali fide confracta*)' and began to press his own interests as a suitor. The woman quite improperly listened to his deceitful advances and finally agreed to them, 'the love was consummated and she gave way to all that he asked'. The original suitor laid a complaint before the Court of the Countess of Champagne asking for a judgment on the fraud of the confidant.

The Countess summoned sixty ladies and pronounced the following judgment:

> this deceitful lover richly deserves the woman he has found, she did not even blush when complying with this great crime. So let him enjoy the love he has gained through betrayal, if such is his wish, and let her enjoy the kind of lover she deserves. But both must remain forever seques-trated from the love of any other individual

for both have broken the code, the rules of love.[113] The size of the Court and the absolute character of the sentence, of their suspension in the purgatory of their mutual affections, both indicate the essential nature of the crime against love. What is at stake in this judgment is nothing less than the intangible space between lovers, namely the relationship itself conceived as a site of the message – of the word, the love-letter, the postcard, the salaam as well as of gifts and of tokens. It is that space of meaning, that distance necessary to communication, which the confidant destroyed by ceasing to be the interpreter or go-between and taking the place of the lover. In hermeneutic terms, the confidant, the interpreter, destroyed the text or stole the meaning of the message, and in doing so destroyed the space of love, the space in between, the space of address, of a message or a caress sent *to* the other. The confidant had taken on the role of law as thief of the message, as Janus or deceit. He had appropriated that which cannot be appropriated, stolen that which belongs to another order and thus claimed, like the lawyer, to be someone he was not and could not be.

The crime in question is properly that of sacrilege, of what in modern terms would be formulated as theft of something that belongs in the space

113 *Tractatus*, Bk 2, pp. 37–41; trans. p. 265.

of the other, and here its specific form would be that of attempting to take possession of the desire, the erotic substrate of the message, of everything that is sent.[114] At one level, it may be recollected that it was the attempt to communicate directly with the divinity, to enter its space by means of the tower of Babel, that led in the Christian tradition to the problem of communication, of an otherness that could not understand *labium proximi sui*, the language of neighbours or friends.[115] The code of love addresses itself to the other in a very similar sense to that of the myth of Babel. The desire to invade the space of the other, the desire to communicate directly, to possess the message, to take over or be inside the other, destroys the very possibility of communication as something that happens between *ego* and *alter* and happens precisely by virtue of respect of and address to the other. To be in love is to take a chance, to risk change and the dissolution of a prior identity. It is that risk of eroticism which takes the form of the communication or novelty of love and that is destroyed in the dissolution of the non-proprietary space of the message sent between the lovers. The purloined letter in this instance takes the narrative back to the realm of mere property and its various institutions or, in Irigaray's formulation, 'When the lovers, male or female, substitute for, occupy, or possess the site of those who conceived them, they founder in the unethical, in profanation. They neither construct nor inhabit their love.'[116]

## POSTFACE

It is not the history or jurisdiction of the courts of love which is 'curious and unusual' so much as the detour by means of which they have been forgotten. While I have offered a somewhat radical or wild interpretation of the judgments of love, it is an interpretation which endeavours to do justice to a literature and history of women's courts and rules of love. It is an interpretation which seeks to imagine another jurisdiction, one which is not bound by the contemporary dichotomies of public and private, self and other. It is an interpretation which willingly omits the questions of class and of property, of objectification and idealisation by means of which legal history fails either to imagine, to admit or to value the eroticism of communication and the indeterminacy of relation. The reason for that omission is simple. A history of the jurisdiction of love and of women's

---

114 For a definition and discussion of sacrilege, see Sir Henry Spelman, *The History and Fate of Sacrilege*, London, Hartley, 1632, 1698 edn, at p. 1: 'sacrilege is an invading, stealing or purloining from God, any sacred thing, either belonging to the majesty of his person, or appropriate to the celebration of his Divine Service'.
115 Ibid., at pp. 11–12.
116 Irigaray, 'The Fecundity of the Caress: A Reading of Levinas', in *idem*, *An Ethics of Sexual Difference*, London, Athlone, 1993, at p. 187.

courts is only possible if it takes as its ground or subject-matter a space that exists between and in transgression of contemporary conceptions of individual rights and their proprietary uses. What is at issue in assuming that there is something of social value and of legal significance in the domain of intimate relationships is a valuation of an ethics that recognises both the subject and its speech as necessarily embedded in desire and as belonging to a truth which is exterior to any prior proprietary right.

It would also be possible, of course, to offer a more detailed and doctrinally specific account of these courts. To do justice to their terms and substantive rules would require a rethinking of the lawyer's conception of jurisdiction and of the boundaries of law in a manner that would subvert both the language of jurisprudence and the temporal horizons of its rules. It would demand nothing short of a new form of legal hermeneutics that would take as one of its inspirations a tradition of *amour lointain* that valued literature as well as law, the erotic as well as the duration of possession, the authenticity or truth of relationships – the art of life – just as much as the roles that we have sadly come to play within institutions. Such an evanescent ground of sociality belongs in contemporary terminologies to the unconscious, to object-choice and to the therapeutic discourses of social adaptation. Those discourses, steeped as they are in the metaphors of lack, compromise and impossibility do not aspire to offer any very social understanding of the space or the desire of relationships or of the motives of those actions that touch the soul. The 'laws of Venus', however, are nonetheless laws in a descriptive sense and their effects can be seen everywhere, even if they occupy a sphere which our legal culture refuses to recognise. That we do not understand such laws is not a strong argument for continuing to ignore them. That we do not understand them is, to the contrary, the strongest of reasons for endeavouring to do them justice.

In more profane terms, it is possible to venture various concluding hypotheses. First, the courts of love and their various judgments of love were judgments made by groups of women. While it is tempting for that reason to view their judgments as simple reversals of the established order of masculine rule and its laws of male succession, I have preferred to interpret their work as that of a jurisdiction that existed, alongside numerous other geographically or topically specific jurisdictions, to the side of what became the common or 'universal' law. A close reading of the later history of the legal tradition does not support the notion of inversion but rather suggests a forgetting or repression of the feminine jurisdiction. The law of nature and of kind, to which the judgments of love contingently belong, formed part of a tradition of justice that was carried on the inside of doctrine according to the well-established civilian maxim that profane or secular law is the offspring of natural law, and as such it is a portion of the mother's entrails – *portio est viscerum mutuarum*.[117] It carries its otherness or origin inside itself, it could not but have a memory of that other line or legitimacy which pertained to the relation of mother to child. Indeed that origin was its only real certainty and hence needed the most thorough repression. In that sense the narrative of women's courts is an aspect of the history of women's law and does not reverse so much as it remembers or reinstates certain of the possibilities of law.

The second hypothesis concerns the art of life or of 'a law of the living' which this history might be taken by some to suggest. The casuistry of the judgments of love concerned the immediate and affective life of the subject. Its concerns were overwhelmingly with issues of fidelity or faith and the consequent truth or authenticity of relations within the parameters of the then existent code of love. I will use one final example. In Judgment v, the Court of the Countess of Champagne was asked to decide a case in which a man had been the lover of a certain woman for a considerable time. He had loved extravagantly and faithfully and had taken great pleasure in the consummations of that love. She, however, did not reciprocate his affections. He eventually sought to leave her, but she opposed his wishes and endeavoured to keep him in his former condition. The Court held that 'the attitude of the woman was to be judged unjust (*improba*) and illegal, for she wants to be loved yet refuses to love. It is stupid for a person to demand of another, what they themselves utterly refuse to give to others'.[118] What is at issue in such a judgment is the abuse of fidelity and the misuse of the occasions of love. It was the inauthenticity of the woman's love that was condemned as a crime against relationships and as a breach of the code of living well or living ethically.

The latter point suggests a crucial difference between the procedures of the courts of love and those of municipal law. While it would be easy to interpret such judgments in terms of an opposition between an interior and an exterior law, between affection and knowledge, that is simply a reflection of the limited horizons of contemporary jurisprudence. The judgments discussed in this chapter may appear to concern the emotive and the private, the obscure and intimate, the subjective and merely personal, but such is simply the value that we place on them. They represent in their own right something much more lasting and much less easily dismissed. They represent an attempt to think through the most pervasive, the most political and the most immediate problems of social intercourse and institutional life, namely the relation between the sexes conceived neither as a war of the sexes nor as a play of power and

---

117 For discussion of this maxim, see Sir John Fortescue, *De natura legis naturae*, London, private distribution, 1869 edn, at pp. 240ff. See also P. Goodrich, 'Gynaetopia: Feminine Genealogies of Early Common Law' (1993) 29 *Journal of Law and Society* 276.
118 *Tractatus*, Bk 2, pp. 14–16; trans., p. 255.

possession but rather as a question of reciprocal recognition and mutual right. That the desire for truth in relationships, in the interaction of the sexes, be deemed a feminine characteristic, or that values of care, relationship, fidelity and truth be regarded as matters outside of law does not reflect upon the judgments of love so much as it condemns the contemporary institutions and doctrines of law.

I will venture one final and tentative hypothesis. I have argued that the history of the judgments of love neither simply inverts the legal tradition nor masks the power or domination of law. It rather recollects an aspect and possibility of legal tradition which is not valued by contemporary doctrine and in consequence is not recognised by legal historicism.[119] In a parallel sense, it can also be argued that the same history and repression is enacted at a personal level in the repressed subjectivity of the lawyer. In biographical terms, entry into law – training as a lawyer – institutes and reproduces a comparable blindness. Legal training teaches the subject to separate the personal and the legal, it demands the repression of emotion and the privileging of the objectivity of rules over the subjectivities of truth – Aristotle's wisdom without desire. More than that, it draws the subject into a network of relations and an institutional environment which is modelled upon the legal definitions and valuations of persons, actions and things. It is an environment which, by its nature, is competitive, antagonistic and frequently damaging. Such is not to say that the institution captures the legal subject in his or her entirety. Many find escape, but that escape will generally follow the structure of the historical argument of this chapter. It is my hypothesis that lawyers will tend to find love or relationship elsewhere, either in a past which came before the law, or in a spectral domain that is outside the law and which is tenuously if not tenebrously exterior to their persona or role. It is a love which is sought elsewhere, that is attached to exteriorities, that is quite often a by-product of commodities or of the mirroring function of status. It is, in Freud's terms, either pre-Oedipal, the repetition of a primary attachment, or narcissistic, a love of self. In either form it is likely to be unconscious unless the legal persona has had the advantage of considerable therapeutic help.[120] In the language of autobiography the question that remains to be asked is: if I give so much of my time to the law, how much of the law speaks through me?

---

119 For an extended discussion of this issue in relation to the history of the mixed jury, see Marianne Constable, *The Law of the Other: The Mixed Jury and Changing Conceptions of Citizenship, Law, and Knowledge*, Chicago, Chicago University Press, 1994, especially at pp. 89–95.

120 Particularly impressive on this theme is Theweleit, *Object-Choice*, pt I.

# Chapter 3

# Eating law

## Commons, common land, common law

And it shall be a sign unto thee upon thine hand, and for a memorial between thine eyes, that the Lord's law may be in thy mouth.[1]

Undoubtedly, one can write while eating more easily than one can speak while eating, but writing goes further in transforming words into things capable of competing with food.[2]

As if at supper, at any supper, I begin with an anecdote. It dates from the mid-sixteenth century and concerns both food and law as well as what will be termed the 'homosociality'[3] of eating rites at the Inns of Court. It is reported in the work of Gerard Legh, King's herald, scholar, subsequently a member of Lincoln's Inn and author of a work of some considerable influence on genealogy and law with especial reference to armory and devices, *The Accedens of Armory* of 1562. The story begins with Legh returning from travels in the East,[4] in parts of 'the unknown world' where he had been studying 'deedes of armes'. He arrives back in England by way of the river Thames and lands some half a league from the City of London. Drawing near the City he

> suddenly heard the shot of double canons, in so great a number, and so terrible, that it darkened the whole air; wherewith, although I was in my own country, yet stood I amazed not knowing what it meant. Thus, as I abode in despair, either to return or continue my former purpose, I chanced to see coming towards me an honest citizen clothed in a long garment, keeping the highway, seeming to walk for recreation, which prognosticated rather peace than peril.[5]

1 Exodus 1.9.
2 Gilles Deleuze and Félix Guattari, *Kafka: Toward a Minor Literature*, Minneapolis, University of Minnesota Press, 1986, at p. 20.
3 See M. Borch-Jacobsen, *The Freudian Subject*, London, Macmillan, 1989, at pp. 72–80, where the concept of homosociality is elaborated as the appropriate description or 'pathology' of professional relations.
4 It is not insignificant that Dionysus, god of wine, masks and banquets (revels), comes from the East and as a stranger. On which see M. Detienne, *Dionysus*, London, Athlone, 1984. More generally, of course, the East is bringer of light: *ex oriente lux*.
5 G. Legh, *The Accedens of Armory*, London, R. Totell, 1562/1576 edn, at fol. 118 a.

Reassured by the demeanour and apparent gentility of this passer-by, Legh falls into conversation and asks for an account of the meaning of the display of arms.

The answer to his question is curious: 'it is, quoth he, a warning shot to the Constable and Marshall of the Inner Temple, to prepare to Dinner'. That so terrible a noise is deemed appropriate to the occasion is explained in terms of the nobility of the office held – 'he uttereth himself better to be that officer whose name he beareth' – and the prestige of the province which he governs, namely the most ancient and noble of the Inns of Court, the Inner Temple. There follows a passage in which the character and purpose of the Inn is given a resounding description as being

> a place . . . privileged by the most excellent Princess of the whole Island, wherein are store of Gentlemen of the whole Realm, that repair thither to learn to rule and obey by Law, to yield their fleece to their Prince and Common-weal, as also to use all other exercises of body and mind whereunto nature most aptly serveth to adorn by speaking, countenance and gesture, and use of Apparel the person of a Gentleman; whereby amity is obtained, and continued, that Gentlemen of all countries, in their young years, *nourished together* in one place, with such comely order, and daily Conference, are knit by continual acquaintance in such unity of minds and manners as lightly never after is severed . . . .[6]

Intrigued by what he has been told of this ancient Inn of lawyers, Legh subsequently visits the Inner Temple and again the narrative has the curiously other-worldly character of that Renaissance literary genre which depicts the originary: the times and rituals of repetition whose power of presence resides in a stylistic conformity to a past which was never present.[7] The originary is invariably hieroglyphic, it exists only in the trace or vestige, the ruin of a present form. It is sufficient to the logic of origin that it be repeated and through repetition lived as simulacrum. The forms of the original are thus those of reinscription of an imaginary genealogy, a lineage of structural residues in which each image plays the role of exemplar, each plastic form the figure of a sign. Thus when Legh returns

6  Ibid., at fol. 119 b (emphasis added).
7  This early historical genre exists to describe the 'originals' of all known social forms, as is most explicit in the titles of many early antiquarian works, as, for example, in Sir H. Spelman, *The Original of the Four Law Terms of the Year*, London, D. Browne, 1614; W. Dugdale, *Origines Juridiciales or Historical Memorials of the English Laws*, London, T. Newcomb, 1666; or any of the late sixteenth-century antiquarian discourses collected in Thomas Hearne (ed.), *A Collection of Curious Discourses written by Eminent Antiquaries upon Several Heads in our English Heritage*, London, J. Richardson, 1771. More generally on the 'originals' of England, see W. Camden, *Britannia sive florentissimum regnorum, Angliae, Scotiae, Hiberniae chorographica descriptio*, London: F. Collins, 1586, 1695 edn; J. Selden, *Jani Anglorum facies altera*, London: Bassett, 1610, 1683 edn. On the quality of originality see M. Merleau Ponty, *The Phenomenology of Perception*, London, Routledge, 1961.

to the Inner Temple the description he provides is as much an inscription of texts, an examination of prototypes, as it is a narrative of literal presence. The Inn is the 'most antient' of its kind, its members are the 'most noble', its justice the most provident and its tables the most replete.

The emblematic logic of the origin takes Legh first to a church, 'and passing forward [I] entered into a Church of ancient building, wherein were many monuments of noble personages armed in knightly habit'.[8] While gazing at these rare and immemorial sights, Legh is welcomed to the Inn by Palaphilos, a king of Armes, and invited to eat at his lodgings within the palace where they duly partake of 'such cheer as the time and country [does] yield'. This small repast is cut short by the noise of 'Drum and Fyfe' which transpires to be the summons of the Inn to dinner. The central event in the visit is the observation of the banquet that follows. Granted that Legh is primarily concerned with an account of signs, of the enigmas, ensigns, emblems, devices, symbols and hieroglyphs that make up the visual rhetoric of the Inn and announce the genealogy of an institution, the lengthy description of the meal which follows must be accounted for in primarily figurative terms. The order of dining – of arrival, dress, seating, service, food, speech, argument, exposition, dance, revelry and masques – is the order of a lawful world, a symbolic order in which justice, rule and law are to be understood as being expressed together[9] through culinary measures, victuals and wine.[10] To borrow from the language of armoury, the lineage and legitimacy of the community of lawyers is visually depicted in the heraldic crests, memorials and tablets of achievement that adorn the walls of the Hall. The lawyer does not merely appear, he descends from an order of symbols: that is what guarantees him as the emblem of the truth and relays his table as the Table of Justice, while it is food and drink, meat and wine, that guarantees his blood, an internal and unbroken line, an inner imperative.[11]

The meal described is that of a cloistered yet in part secular society or guild. Its order is that of a monastic routine quite possibly inherited, both directly and, more significantly, symbolically, from the early monastic

8  Legh, *Accedens*, fol. 120 a.
9  W. Fulbecke, *Direction or Preparative to the Study of Law*, London, Clarke, 1599, epistle and p. 3: 'in this heaven that is Britain . . . religion, justice and law do stand together'.
10 This is even more apparent if Legh's account is supplemented by that of the other essential sources of our knowledge of the order of service at the Inns of Court, namely Sir John Fortescue, *De Laudibus Legum Angliae*, London, Gosling, 1470, 1737 Selden ed.; Sir George Buc, *The Third Universitie of England*, London, n.p., 1615; and Dugdale, *Origines*, particularly fols. 151 a–161 b.
11 For an interesting description and illustrations of the Halls, see D. Plunket Barton, C. Benham, and F. Watt, *The Story of Our Inns of Court*, London, Foulis, n.d.. On the signification of internalisation, see A. Lingis, *Excesses: Eros and Culture*, Albany, NY, SUNY Press, 1983, ch. 5.

precursors of the profession.[12] The available records of the financial accounts of the Inner Temple and especially of who was invited and what was allowed and spent on cloth and meat[13] also suggest that Legh's description is extravagant, exemplary rather than normative: it depicts the excesses of a banquet, of heavy eating, *vanitas*,[14] precisely to indicate the priority of law over necessity, of the symbolic over the literal, of genealogy over mere reproduction – of spirit over flesh. The Tables of the law are abundant, well ordered and replete; they are also exclusive in that the first rule of the Inn is that none but the members of the Inn and certain honoured guests shall dine: 'no stranger . . . should be permitted to take any repast'.[15] The significance both of membership and of attendance will be emphasised many times for only through the communion of the Table do Law and lawyer maintain their emblematic and sacrificial place. Only through the Table, through the repetition of meat and wine, can the companions of Justice either recollect or live their priestly role.[16] In theological terms it is necessary simply to recall that it is through bread (*manna*) that God first appears in the desert, it is at a banquet that the

12 See J.H. Baker, *The Order of Serjeants at Law*, London, Selden Society, 1984, pp. 16–21, 67–70; more generally, see M. Foucault, *The Care of the Self*, New York, Random House, 1981, pp. 99–104, 140–144 at 141:

> it is a trait manifested by all Greek and Roman medicine to accord much more space to the dietetics of alimentation than to sex. For this medicine, the thing that matters is eating and drinking. A whole development – evident in Christian monasticism – will be necessary before the preoccupation with sex will begin to match preoccupation with food. But alimentary abstentions and fasts will long remain fundamental.

See further, S. Mennell, 'On the Civilizing of Appetite', and B. Turner, 'The Discourse of Diet', in M. Featherstone and B. Turner (eds), *The Body*, London, Sage, 1991.

13 See particularly Dugdale, *Origines*, at fols. 141 a–161 a.

14 *The vanitas* painting is didactic, it illustrates the material pleasures of the world for moral purposes. See, for example, the discussion in N. Bryson, *Looking at the Overlooked: Four Essays on Still Life Painting*, London, Reaktion, 1992, at pp. 115–123, interestingly observing that the *vanitas* painting is undermined by internal contradiction, namely that in denouncing indulgence it provides an indulgent image of it. More generally on the representation and visual rhetoric of food in S. Schama, *The Embarrassment of Riches*, London, Fontana Press, 1988, pp. 161f.

15 Dugdale, *Origines*, at fol. 149 b.

16 On the priestly character of the lawyer, see Fortescue, *De Laudibus*, at pp. 4–5:

> Be pleased to know then, that not the Deuteronomical, but also all Human Laws are sacred, the definition of law being thus, 'it is an holy sanction, commanding whatever is honest, and forbidding the contrary'. And that must needs be holy, which is so by definition . . . whence we, who are the Ministerial officers, who sit and preside in the Courts of Justice, are therefore not improperly, called *sacerdotes* (being one who gives or teaches Holy Things) and must 'take heed of what [they] do, for [they] judge not for men, but for the Lord, who is with you in the judgment'.

More generally see the adoption of the civilian definition in Sir John Doderidge, *The English Lawyer. Describing a Method for the Management of the Lawes of this Land*, London, I. More, 1602/1621 edn, at pp. 28–29: 'Secondly, they say that the knowledge of the Law is affirmed to be *Rerum divinarum humanarumque Scientia*, it doth contain the knowledge of all divine and humane things.'

moving finger of God writes upon the wall, it is at the last supper that Christ establishes bread and wine as the perennial symbols of his presence, and at supper at Emmaus that Christ returns after his death. It can be argued, indeed, that all the *signs* of divine presence are connected with bread and wine, with meat and fish, grain and figs.[17] It is, again and again, through food and drink, through shared nourishment, that a community is reproduced and its memory of origin, of genealogy, inscribed within, or literally incorporated: 'moreover, there was a time, not long ago and not yet over, in which "we, men" meant "we adult white male Europeans, carnivorous and capable of sacrifice"'.[18]

The Law provides no exception. We are introduced immediately to a dinner in which 'the Hall was served after the most ancient order of the Island', an order that in common law terms exceeds the 'memory of man' and so constitutes an original, an emblem of the immemorial, of that order which repeats not the mundane but the natural, not human practice but Divine Law.[19] The banquet is, of course, both communion and celebration, a mixing of solemnity and revelry, order and expense, of which Legh remarks 'I assure you I languish for want of cunning, ripely to utter that I saw so orderly handled appertaining to service.' The order of fealty and of service begins with the blast of trumpets, 'the couragious blast of deadly war', which is repeated between every course and serves, if nothing else, to remind of the guilty killing that has stocked the tables, the murder of animals which can only be expiated through communion, through the

17 For a discussion of the significance of the table in the New Testament see M. Symmons, 'A Gastronomic Interpretation of Christianity' (1990) 49 *Meanjin* 220; also G. Bataille, *Theory of Religion*, New York, Zone Books, 1989. For more general discussions see Y. Hachamovitch, 'Christ at Supper: A Semiotics of the *Bodegon*', in R. Kevelson (ed.), *Law and Semiotics IV*, New York, Plenum Books, 1991; P. Goodrich, 'The Eucharist and English Law', in *idem*, *Languages of Law; From Logics of Memory to Nomadic Masks*, 1990, London, Weidenfeld and Nicolson, ch. 3; M. Foucault, 'How we Behave' (Interview) (1983) *Vanity Fair*, p. 60.

18 J. Derrida, 'Force of Law: The Mystical Foundation of Authority' (1990) 11 *Cardozo Law Review* 921 at 951 and further at pp. 952–953:

in our culture, carnivorous sacrifice is fundamental, dominant, regulated by the highest industrial technology . . . carnivorous sacrifice is essential to the structure of subjectivity, which is also to say to the founding of the international subject and to the founding, if not of positive law (*loi*), at least of legal normativity (*droit*).

On ceremonies of incorporation, see P. Connerton, *How Societies Remember*, Cambridge, Cambridge University Press, 1990, ch. 3.

19 As specified, for example, by Sir John Davies, *A Discourse of Law and Lawyers*, London, Grosart edn, private circulation, 1615/1876 at p. 253 where the 'originals' of English law are said to be *ius non scriptum*, 'being written in the heart of men . . . which we do call *ius commune*, as coming nearest to the law of nature, which is the root and touchstone of all good lawes'. For further and striking expressions of the theological provenance in nature, see St German, *Doctor and Student*, London, Selden Society, 1528, 1974 edn, at p. 24 defining positive law as something 'derived as a thing which is necessarily and probably following of the law of reason and of the law of god, for the due end of human nature'. Similarly, Sir Henry Finch, *Law or a Discourse Thereof in Foure Bookes*, London, Society of Stationers, 1967, at fol. 75a where common law is defined as being formed in the light of natural law and reason 'and from thence come the grounds and maxims of all common law'.

constitution of fraternity which will render shameful food a holy symbol of sacrifice. That symbolisation of community, of bonding, begins with a procession into the Hall or 'commons'. This is led by the Prince, followed by 'Embassadors of sundry Princes', then by the nobility, the steward of the Inn, the Treasurer, the keeper of Pallas' seal, the Judges, Serjeants at Law, Readers, barristers, utter-barristers, mootmen and clerks, each accompanied by their alloted number of servants which would include steward, carver, cup-bearers and servers. According to records of the legislation of the Inner Temple Parliament, each rank of member is dressed according to their status and the occasion, for 'glory and beauty'.[20] On this occasion, to take but one example, the judges would wear scarlet gowns, hoods and mantles bordered with minever and pinned near the left shoulder, furred cape about the shoulders, taffeta or satin Tippets and the gold ring of inception to legal office.[21]

The order of food is the order of meats, the table of fare the law as a menu.[22] While the Prince is described alliteratively as being served with 'tender meats, sweet fruits, and dainty delicates confectioned with curious cookery, as it seemed wonder the World to observe the provision',[23] the records indicate a diet of mutton which is embellished on feast-days by game and fowl. Each rank has its allotted value of meat and for the feast-day this would be a combination from the following: there would be boar, red deer, conyes, veal, sturgeon, pike and 'calves heades' (the latter otherwise being particular to the Middle Temple) and then capon, swan, bustard, pheasant, cranes, partridges, woodcock, plover, snipe, lark, heron, bittern, mallard, hen, pigeon, curlew, godwit and teal. Accompanying the meal would be wine, again served in measures according to the status of the Table concerned, and music, then games, dance, masque and revelry, the festive rituals of community that would more ordinarily take the form of readings, mock cases, disputations, questions of law and of statutory interpretation. It is upon the latter and more usual, though no less exotic, exercises that attention should be focused. They form the deeper order of the table and of eating law.

In hermeneutic terms the obsessive listing of meats and their quantity, of wines and their quotient, and of the allotted order and ritual of service, betrays something more than simple financial accountability or record.[24]

---

20 The reference is to Names, XXVIII. II. and is mentioned by Dugdale, *Origines*, fol. 98 a.

21 Details of dress are from Dugdale, *Origines* fol. 98 a–102 a. H. Cohen, *History of the English Bar to 1450*, London, Sweet and Maxwell, 1929, provides a further account.

22 For an example of a menu, see J.H. Baker, *Serjeants at Law*, at p. 262.

23 Legh, *Accedens*, at fol. 121 a.

24 Though record and account are important aspects of the regulation, the legality of such banquets is also a frequent source of later condemnation, as, for example, in Roger North, *The Life of the Right Honourable Francis North, Baron of Guildford, Lord Keeper of the Great Seal*, London, White, 1648, pp. 149–151: 'I cannot much commend the extravagance of the feasting . . . and the profusion of the best provisions and wine was to the worst of purposes, debauchery, disorder, tumult, and waste.'

Food and the amount and price of food, service and the propriety of bodily behaviour and dress, are the intrinsic *measures* of daily life, of its routines to be sure but also of its lineage and legitimacy, its bonds and its law in the Christian West. The Table is also an altar and the meats spread upon it are forms of sacrifice which will hold those who eat together, nourished from the same source in recollection of the same fealties. It is not only a question of propriety, of symbolic order and its rules: the Table and the meal refer the objects of everyday life to a sacred world, servile use to spiritual bonds, the bodies collected around the Table to a religious body united in the subjectivity which subtends all meat.[25] It is this which lends to the 'commons' or meals of the common law their emblematic status, their power as originals. In the sense that Mass holds together the church (*Corpus Christi* and *Corpus Iuris*) and inaugurates its spiritual presence as a sacred and united body in communion with the Divinity, the order and rules of dining bind the law to its common origin and purpose in supposed antiquity and nature herself: what every meal serves to recollect is a community which holds custody of the law of God, given by him to Adam and then to Moses, 'after whom, whatsoever the prosperity has done in the holy sanction of laws, they have but as Apes, by imitation borrowed the semblable form of laws from him'.[26] In Freudian terms, the act of eating animal flesh founds the human community of Christian cultures not only through violence or the sin of killing but also through differentiation; it being only through eating the animal that the animal can be distinguished from those that eat. The ceremony or rites of common food further establish community by repressing the relation between the act of killing and the production and consumption of food.[27]

The relation between the Inn and food is an obvious one, although its significance has seldom been discussed. The received wisdom is that these Inns of 'ancient amity' or 'hostells' of the Court date back at least to the reign of Edward I and were strictly regulated and highly costly 'seminaries or nurseries' of students of law or *apprenticii nobiliores*.[28] Sir George Buc

25 G. Bataille, *The Accursed Share*, New York, Zone Books, 1988, associates eating with an intimacy occasioned by the commonality between those that eat and that which is eaten. In neo-Freudian terms the meal recollects the murder of that which is eaten and it is only the ritual of the Table which will transform that death to spiritual ends:

> Sacrifice restores to the sacred world that which servile use has degraded, rendered profane. Servile use has made a thing (an object) of that which, in a deep sense, is of the same nature as the subject, is in a relation of intimate participation with the subject.
> (ibid., pp. 56–57)

26 John Ferne, *The Blazon of Gentrie*, London, J. Winder, 1586, at pp. 40–41.
27 See S. Freud, *Totem and Taboo*, Harmondsworth, Penguin, 1939; N. Elias, *The Civilizing Process I: History of Manners*, Oxford, Blackwell, 1939, 1978 edn.
28 Dugdale, *Origines*, fol. 142 a. See also Ferne, *Blazon*, who populates the Inns with 'the sages and oracles of the lawes' (fol. A vi b) and insists that only those of noble blood can study there (pp. 92–93).

traces the term Inne to Hostelry, 'which in the Roman is *Diversoria*, guest Innes and Common houses for entertainment of all travellers for their money',[29] and Dr John Cowell provides the same etymology for *Hospitii Curiae* derived from common inns 'instituted for passengers, for the proper Latin word is *Diversorium*, because he that lodgeth there is *quasi divertens se a via*'.[30] An earlier reference from Thomas Hoccleve (1379–c. 1450) makes allusion to a dining club, 'a court of Good Company'.[31] To the description of the Inn of Court as a place for the nobility to study law we may thus add further connotations of diversion or difference, whereby the stranger or traveller is taken temporarily off their path and a certain humanity (homosociality) and community is established through food and wine. The diversion makes the difference between nature and culture, between solitude and community, body and spirit. Its particular form, that of the seminary or apprenticeship – the latter term being derived from the Latin *apprehendere*, to seize or take possession of – has a peculiarly maternal form and the institution as a nursery should be understood quite literally as a law that becomes mother to infant subjects:

> a mother that nourishes not those who want but those who follow her rule; such an allegiance already supposes an apprenticeship, the entry into the imaginary space of the institution whose subjects are infants. ... The centralised organisation works toward the production of infants.[32]

If the legal subject is an infant, it is because the infant is defined, in the eyes of the law, as a representation: the infant refers to the father, to the king. We recognise in the infant a genealogy, a son.[33] If we move to examine the further regulations of these courts or Inns, the lineage and the difference that binds Law to food in the commons becomes more apparent.

The legislation of the Inns of Court in the sixteenth century is concerned almost obsessively with details of the commons. To become a barrister or to remain a barrister requires attendance at commons. All the ceremonies of investiture or inception into the various ranks of the profession take place via the commons and so too all rituals of collective membership of

---

29 Buc, *Third Universitie*, at p. 969 b.
30 Dr John Cowell, *The Interpreter or Booke Containing the Signification of Words*, Cambridge, Legat, 1607/1637 edn, fol. Q 3 a. On the role of the Inn as a quasi-market or private substitute for the open market in sixteenth-century England, see F. Braudel, *The Wheels of Commerce*, New York, Harper and Row, 1982, pp. 42–50. He remarks at one point of this trading that 'sometimes the newcomers [i.e., merchants] would hold court in inns, which were beginning a long career as substitutes for the market' (ibid. p. 47).
31 See Cohen, *History of the English Bar*, p. 452.
32 P. Legendre, *Jouir du pouvoir: traité sur la bureaucratie patriote*, Paris, Editions de Minuit, 1976, p. 190.
33 See P. Legendre, *L'Inestimable objet de la transmission: étude sur le principe généalogique en occident*, Paris, Fayard, 1985, pp. 320–330.

the community of the Law, feasts, banquets, revels and games are held in the commons. All the exercises and disputations of training or education in Law – exercises in interpretation, readings and mooting – are incident upon meals in the commons. For the student of law the regulations are monastically strict and the legislation frequent. It should be added that at the most general level the concern with appearance, diet and conduct in the Inn is a concern with the necessary training of the body in preparation for the rigours and indeed the wasting of youth which comes with the study of Law and accompanies the rigour of an itinerant practice.[34] Its study is commonly represented as wasting and unsavoury; for Doderidge, '*multorum annorum opus*, it is the worke of many yeares, the attaining whereof will waste the verdour and vigour of youth';[35] while for Coke, 'the student thereof, having *sedentariam vitam*, is not commonly long-lived; the study [is] abstruse and difficult, the occasion sudden, the practice dangerous'.[36] Fraunce speaks of a science which is 'hard, harsh, unpleasant, unsavoury, rude and barbarous'.[37] In this generic sense all the various dialogues and tracts which treat of the proper forms of preparation for study or addiction to Law stress the need to conform to ascetic principles and to the melancholic and dark influence of Saturn; an influence which Bodin defined as that 'pretious death' which draws the soul from the body and earthly things and turns it towards spirit and law.[38]

Starting with the rules governing the entrant to the Inn, the first regulation is one requiring a minimum of noise. Those who practise law must study frequently, they must live with texts and the aura of the text is one of dust, of silence or of muted conversation. It is probably for this reason that the noble entrant is limited in the number of servants that he can bring with him to his lodgings, nor, according to a Middle Temple

34 The very real hardship of legal life and particularly of a travelling law – the common law's epic geography – can be inferred from the stress on physical virtue in the various manuals used by gentlemen lawyers. See, for example, Henry Peacham, *The Compleat Gentleman*, London, Rastell, 1615.
35 Sir John Doderidge, *The English Lawyer*, London, I. More, 1631, at p. 29.
36 Sir Edward Coke, *A Book of Entries*, London, Streeter, 1610, preface.
37 Abraham Fraunce, *The Lawiers Logike, exemplifying the praecepts of logike by the practice of common law*, London, How, 1588, preface.
38 J. Bodin, *De Republica*, London, Knoller, 1580/1606 edn, at p. 558. The relevant literature on humour and law is vast and only a few works can be singled out here. Among the earliest are Fortescue's dialogue between the Chancellor and a student, *De Laudibus*; and St Germain, *Doctor and Student*; Selden, *Jani Anglorum*, at fol. A 4 a. Specific treatises on the study of law range from Sir Thomas Elyot, *The Boke Named the Governour*, London, Dent, 1531/1907 edn; W. Fulbecke, *Direction or Preparative to the Study of Law*, London, Clarke, 1599; Doderidge, *The English Lawyer*; to the later works of Sir Roger North, *A Discourse on the Study of the Laws*, London, C. Baldwin, 1650/1824 edn; and W. Phillips, *Studii Legalis Ratio or Direction for the Study of the Laws*, London, F. Kirkman, 1667. Numerous other works, including those of Sir Edward Coke, Sir John Davies, Sir Henry Spelman, Dr John Cowell, Sir Henry Finch, John Ferne and that of forensic rhetoricians such as Leonard Cox, Thomas Wilson and George Puttenham also contain significant elements of similar advice.

regulation of 1635, can any 'foraigners, discontinuers, [strangers] or other not of the society . . . [nor] common Attorney or sollicitor'[39] be allowed to lodge with him. Deprived of all but the quiet fellowship of the order of Law, the student or mootman is required both to dress and to act with 'reverence'. They are forbidden to play certain games – 'shoffe-grotte or slyp-grote' – which suggest levity, and 'no wine or tabacco [shall be] uttered or sold in the House'.[40] They must dress on all occasions, both in and out of the College, in gowns, nor should these gowns be any 'but such as are of a sad colour'. They were forbidden beards and subject to many further rules of attire which excluded foreign fashions in clothes, coloured doublets or hoses, the wearing of ruffs, hats, cloaks, boots, spurs, swords or daggers, or long hair in any public place of the Temple Halls. The general rule was aphoristic:

> they have no order for their Apparell; but every man may go as him listeth, so that his Apparell pretend no lightness, or wantonness in the wearer: for, even as his apparell dothe show him to be, even so shall he be esteemed among them.[41]

As the outward sign of 'inward adornment' and of 'eminence over laymen', dress should eschew foreign fashions as being inappropriate to a law which was consciously seeking to expunge any remaining 'tincture of Normanism' or of Rome from the insular and antique common law.[42] That loud colours or lively dress were also forbidden probably indicates a concern to present the profession as both learned and grave: it was a sacred calling according to Fortescue and not simply royal pleasure or courtly masque as might be misguidedly supposed.[43] That dress was to be 'sad' reflected its destruction of youth, its frequently stated dark and melancholic hold upon its subjects, the rude, harsh, unsavoury and unending scope of its proper study.

Dressed to solemn advantage and compliant to rules of demeanour and decorum, the student's academic life was orientated towards fulfilling the statutory requirements of attendance and performance of tasks in the

39 Dugdale, *Origines*, fol. 192 a (1635, 11 Car cap 1).
40 Ibid., at fol. 149 b.
41 Ibid., at fols. 144 a–149 b, 192 a–193 b. According to W. Rastall, *A Collection in English, of the Statutes now in Force*, London, T. Wight, 1603 edn, sig. 12 a–14 c, there are over twenty enactments between 1509 and 1603 directly concerned with apparel and the banning of French cuts of cloth, colours and fashions in England.
42 See, for example, W. Harrison, *An Historicall Description of the Island of Britaine*, London, n.p., 1586, at fol. 20 a–b; John Hare, *St Edward's Ghost, or Anti-Normanism*, and John Warr, *The Corruption and Deficiency of the Laws of England*, respectively 1642 and 1649, reprinted in *The Harleian Miscellany*, London, R. Dutton, 1810, vol. VI.
43 On questions of status more generally, see W. Prest, *The Rise of the Barristers: A Social History of the English Bar 1590–1640*, Oxford, Oxford University Press, 1986; and for a slightly later period, D. Lemmings, *Gentlemen and Barristers: The Inns of Court and the English Bar 1680–1730*, Oxford, Clarendon Press, 1990.

commons. The received wisdom of the preparative writers and rhetorical manuals was that the essential legal art of memory (*memoria*) was an organic training, a bodily practice, and necessitated temperance both of diet and of habit. It is perhaps significant to recall that the art of memory itself was discovered at a banquet by Simonides and that it was only by chance, by virtue of the fact that he had left the banquet, that Simonides lived to invent the rhetorical art of memory.[44] The art of memory originated in the recollection of the seating plan of a banquet, but its more normal use would attach it not only to the legality of places but also to less excessive repasts. It was recommended thus 'to keep a diet, and eschew surfeits, to sleep moderately, to accompany with women rarely'.[45] Phillips, by contrast, concentrates more on rising early (*aurora musis amica*), arguing that the

> spirits of our Bodies, following the dispositions of the air, which in the morning at sun rising is subtill and thus pure and free from all gross vapours and our minds being of the same condition, are quick and nimble.... And those that change morning into evening – those antipodes of nature, that turn night into day ... do very much mistake their time. For in night the Air is thickened and corrupted with contagious Exhalations which possessing the senses, do pierce the brain and make it cloudy and heavy.[46]

Both Fulbecke and Phillips stress the need for dietetic regimentation and give copious advice on eating limited quantities of red meat:

> if a man study soon after supper, the nourishment is resolved into gross vapours which do fill the body and are very noisome obstupatives to the senses. For the meat being destitute of heat, doth wax raw and doth putrify in the stomach.

Phillips later adds that meat causes 'vapours and fumes [which] do cloud the mind and overshadow the clearness of the brain'.[47] It is the body that must be seized and trained to live the law and to obey the dictates of the planets, of the heavens. Only through control of bodily practice will law be properly remembered and so fully lived, a principle of physical regimen which Doderidge, to take one final example, spells out in terms of a memory controlled through the manipulation of bodily temperatures and

44 On Simonides, see Quintilian, *Institutio Oratoria*, XI 2. 17–26.
45 Thomas Wilson, *The Arte of Rhetorique*, London, Garland, 1553 / 1982 edn, at p. 420. William Fulbecke, *Direction or Preparative*, at p. 32: 'The next thing I require in a student is temperance ... a restraint of mind from all voluptuousness and lust, as namely, from covetousness, excess of diet, wantoness and all other unlawful delights.'
46 Phillips, *Studii Legalis Ratio*, at fol. J 9 b.
47 Fulbecke, *Direction or Preparative*, at p. 48. Phillips, *Studii Legalis Ratio*, at fol. k 1 a–b states that meat causes 'vapours and fumes [which] do cloud and overshadow the clearness of the brain, and do offend and hinder operations of the superior faculties to wit, of the senses, the imagination, the understanding and the memory'.

fluids. Again linking memory to the body and the bodily functions to dietary rules,

> Mans body being composed of elementall qualities requireth in the perfection thereof a temperature of humors, which also consisteth in the temperate disposition of heate and moisture, for that *in humido, & calido consistit vita,* and hereby it is made a more apt instrument and organ for the operation of the powers of the soule, and so consequently of Memorie.[48]

The rules of the Inns thus regulated not only the order of service and seating at Table but also the amount of meat and wine permitted at each meal on each day of the week.[49] In a sense, food would make the Law and the Table would represent the Tables of Justice. Consider further the initial and minimum requirement for qualification, namely attendance at divine service (taking of communion) at least twice a year upon pain of expulsion, seven or eight years' attendance at commons, completion of the established and ancient exercises of the commons, namely moots, petty moots and arguments, and finally the general stipulation that

> such will not be called if they fail to apply and follow their study; to keep the case, to perform their exercises, to order their habits and hair to decency and formality, and to yield due respect to Benchers and antients. . . .[50]

Even once qualified the barrister was still subject to a requirement of attendance at commons – he must keep commons for six weeks of every year and perform a moot *ex tempore* and be challenged by a puisne barrister upon a point of law – upon pain of forfeiture of chambers. The punishment for breach of any of the rules of the Inn was either by a fine or 'by putting him forth of commons; which is to say that he shall take no meate nor drynke among the fellowship' until judgment is revoked.[51] Fortescue reiterates the point, observing that

> the only way they have of punishing delinquents is by expelling them from the society, which punishment they do dread more than criminals do imprisonment and irons; for he who is expelled out of one society is never taken in by any other.[52]

The significance of the regulation of attendance and food at commons is clearly not entirely dietary nor simply a matter of servile use, of amount

48 Doderidge, *English Lawyer,* at p. 18.
49 Dugdale, *Origines,* at fols. 195 b–196 a.
50 Ibid., at fol. 192 b.
51 Ibid., at fol. 196 b.
52 Fortescue, *De Laudibus,* at p. 112.

or of whether it is bittern, curlew or godwit that constitutes the feasting. The Table and commons were the sanctuary and the communion of the fellowship of Law, its body and its blood. In a direct movement from eating to speaking, from orality to oratory,[53] it is food and the measure of food which binds the company to its forensic forms. It is food that 'opens the mouth' and leads the body to the institution: once the mouth is ceremonially opened, in ceremonies that do not differ greatly in their logic from the investiture of religious dignities through rites of *apertio oris*,[54] then the law can speak. The orality of law should not be underestimated, nor the relation between food and knowledge ignored. 'The Priest's lips', Richard Hooker proclaims, 'should preserve knowledge, and ... other men should seek the truth at his mouth, because he is the messenger of the Lord of Hosts', the Lord, according to one etymology of *hospes*, of guests and innkeepers.[55] It is through dining that the student is trained in the Law and it is through feasting that each further qualification in law is ceremonially inscribed upon the body of the Law, into its physical presence and community. Consider the ceremony of appointment of a Serjeant at Law, which is described in detail in Fortescue and in Dugdale.[56] Those selected to this office are chosen by the Lord Chief Justice 'for their general study of law and their profit to the law', having generally formerly been elected as Readers. The first information provided of the investiture ceremony is that upon the day that the Lord Chancellor grants them their state and degree they must 'keep a great dinner, (among other solemnities) like to the Feast of a King's coronation; which shall continue and last for the space of seven days'.[57] The ceremony of investiture itself lasts for three weeks and involves many further dinners, including one in which the Lord Chief Justice hides in a 'secrete chaumber'[58] or cupboard before hearing arguments on points of law and then retiring to dine. Alongside innumerable regulations as regards the appropriate dress for the various and lengthy stages of investiture should be noted also the wearing and giving of gold rings. At the ceremony before the Lord Keeper of the Great Seale at Westminster a gold ring is to be given 'in token of their duties and thanks to their majesty'. Further rings of specified weight are given to other officials and members of the Inn, for 'the same betokeneth their bountiful-

---

53 On which see L. Marin, *La Parole mangée et autres essais theologico-politiques*, Paris, Meridiens Klinckseik, 1986, ch. 1.

54 In the investiture of cardinals the Pope would lay his hand on the mouth of the new cardinal while reciting the words *nos aperimus tibi os* (we open your mouth). See P. Legendre, *Le Désir politique de Dieu: étude sur les montages de l'état et du droit*, Paris, Fayard, 1989, pp. 156–157.

55 R. Hooker, *Of the Lawes of Ecclesiastical Politie*, London, Scott, 1593, 1667 edn, at pp. 48–49.

56 For a detailed description of a Reader's feast, see Roger North, *Life of Francis North*; also, A. Wigfall Green, *The Inns of Court and Early English Drama*, New York, Bloom, 1928, ch. 3.

57 Dugdale, *Origines*, fol. 112 a–b. See also Fortescue, *De Laudibus*, pp. 112–121.

58 Dugdale, *Origines*, fol. 115 a.

nesse; they be round, they have no end; it sheweth their integrity. The Prophett sayeth *ambula corem me et sis integer*.[59] After the giving of the ring – a symbol of knowledge and of union (*conjugere*) akin to marriage to Law, a symbol of a closed community and exclusive love – they proceed to change costume and to dine.[60] To dine and to dine again, for at each sitting, at each bench-table case, at each reading or argument, moot or bolt, the law is spoken at the same time as food is eaten, the feast is a feasting within the order of sumptuary law.

Why attach such rituals of argument and of mental exercise to the act of dining if not to situate the Law within a hierarchy of reproduction which food both measures and enables?[61] It creates, first, a pattern of community or, following Freud, homosociality of professional relation in which the slightest deviation from the code of honour of the male group is taken as a slight or humiliation, in which the order of food represents and mediates homosocial tensions, rivalry and competition. The commons establish an order of community and emblematise the proper hierarchy of honour or worth through and across rites of eating that both join and differentiate a profession of men of law.[62] Why open the mouth of the Law with food if not to indicate a certain paternity linked to carnivorous sacrifice and to the internalisation, through food, of the principle of a community held together, if not through the recollection of a pre-existent or primordial guilt at an earlier act of lawlessness, of killing, then at least through a common bond established through the denial or destruction of the flesh. That which binds men to a common role and order of productivity, to the intimate and exclusive community of law, is precisely figured in ceremonies that deny the body, the feminine reality and certainty of reproduction, in constituting a perfect and so abstract law extrinsic both to contingency and to contact. Sacrifice, melancholy and food are joined by a common theme, that of symbolising a transition from body to spirit, from real to symbolic, from feminine certainty to masculine systematicity, the bond of homosociality which is constituted historically by the denial of the body and its theological correlates of pollution, uncleanness and lust.[63]

---

59 (Walk around me and I am not touched.) Ibid., at fol. 122 b.
60 For the investiture of Readers, many similar ceremonies are held in the Inn, including their acting as ushers in the Hall – they usher in the meat and then the music.
61 It is of interest here to note that by legislation of 1346 (20 E. III. cap 1): 'our Justices shall not . . . as long as they shall be in [that] office take Fee nor Robe of any men but Ourself . . . except meat and drink'.
62 Borch-Jacobsen, *The Freudian Subject*, pp. 74–76, discussing Freud's conception of homosexuality as allowing for the translation of the egoistic into the erotic, of sociality into sexuality. The professional man experiences a sublimated conflict (over prestige, profession, job and status) in his professional life, a conflict whose unconscious cause lies in erotic homosexual competitiveness, a 'rivalrous resemblance' or confraternal paranoia.
63 For an analysis of this terminology of pollution and uncleanness, see P. Goodrich, 'Antirrhesis: Polemical Structures of Common Law Thought', in A. Sarat (ed.), *Rhetoric and Law*, Ann Arbor, Michigan University Press, 1993.

To eat is also, however, to consume the Law both in the analytical sense of acknowledging and through repetition living the Law as the union and genealogy symbolised through shared food, while in a more popular – though admittedly somewhat different – sense it linked food to law in the minds of contemporary sixteenth-century England. Common nourishment was linked to a perception of a common addiction: the academy of lawyers threatened the commonwealth with a class of citizen possessed by law, a profession that imbibed nothing but law, whose only thoughts were those of an irrational myriad of arcance particulars, of an ill-organised and little understood oral tradition which they would impose – as 'arithmeticall judgement, by rigour of law onely' – without reason or mercy upon the populace. In William Fulbecke's *Parallele or Conference*, the metaphor of food is used to castigate the lawyer as one too full of law, too stuffed with meats and measures so that they are

> so full of law-points, that when they sweat, it is nothing but law; when they breath it is is nothing but law; when they sneeze it is perfect law, when they dream it is profound law. The book of Littleton's *Tenures* is their breakfast, their dinner, their boier [tea], their supper, and their rere-banquet.[64]

As one nineteenth-century commentator (somewhat inaccurately) observes, 'the whole care of education seems to devolve on the cook, the only necessary part of the ancient regulations being that the student shall eat his commons for a certain number of terms'.[65] Sir Roger North is more concise in advising the student of law to pursue the subject without interruption: he must 'not only read and talk, but eat, drink and sleep law . . . *nulla die sine linea*'.[66]

## EXCURSUS: NOMOS, MEASUREMENT AND COMMONS

The derivation of common law from the commons of the Inns of Court, from the homosocial time and place and terms of eating at the *Hospitii Curiae*, gains a slight though significant support from the pervasive historical confusion as to the meaning of common law or *ius commune*. The derivation of the term is best understood by reference to genealogy, that is to say that the common law has many ancestors and that the role of commons in its formation could only ever be understood as one graft upon a complex series of lineages. In terms of the way in which the authors of

---

64 W. Fulbecke, *A Parallele or Conference of the Civil Law, the Canon Law, and the Common Law of the Realme of England*, London, T. Wright, 1602, fol. B 2 a–b.

65 Anon., *The Law Student's Guide; containing an Historical Treatise on each of the Inns of Court with their Rules and Customs*, London, Butterworth, 1827, at p. 11.

66 (No day without its legal texts.) North, *Discourse on the Study of the Laws*, at p. 7.

the early histories pose the problem of originals it was never likely, of course, that there would be a single answer to the question of the origin of that which is by definition before 'Time of Memory', immemorial or 'time out of mind'. Its sources, in that acceptation, will never exceed the traces of an origin which was never present although our authors, oracles and sages of the common law have never tired of ascribing roots which range from the eccentric to the hagiographical.

Certain of the ascribed sources have a fairly obvious mythological function within the doctrinal tradition and its contemporary polemics and require only the briefest of allusions. Druidical, Greek, Israelite, Trojan and Cornish origins are presented without any very manifest attempt at historical or other justification and I will discuss briefly two such examples. Sir Henry Spelman is probably the most remarkable in his attribution of the unwritten character of English (namely Saxon) law to Lycurgus of Sparta:

> We find among the Saxons, the example and reason why our common law was an unwritten law. They were originally a Grecian colony coming out of Lacedaemon and the territory of Sparta; where Lycurgus . . . among other of his decrees . . . ordained this for one, that their laws should not be written, because he would have every man to fix them in his memory; and for that purpose made them short and summary, after the manner of maxims.[67]

The implication of this particular genealogy is probably that of providing an historical image which links the source of law to an inner writing or, in Derrida's terms,[68] an arche-writing, which structures and binds the soul according to a divine law to which we have internal access through faith or external (positive) access through the Crown as *vicarius Christi*. To reduce such laws to writing was thought, at least by Lycurgus, to threaten the inner bonding of soul to Law, by replacing a lived and habitual obedience with the artifice of writing.

Sir Henry Spelman also refers dismissively to early British sources which he deems 'little to the purpose: they judged all controversies by their

67 Sir Henry Spelman, 'Of the Original of the Four Law Terms of the Year', 1614, in *idem*, *English Works*, London, D. Browne, 1723, at p. 102. Sir Edward Coke, *Reports*, London, J. Rivington, 1777 edn, in the preface to vol. III, at fol. B 1 a, mentions terms in the Greek tongue; while W. Hakewill, 'The Antiquity of the Laws of this Island', 1604, in Hearne (ed.), *Curious Discourses*, at p. 1, refers to an agreement between the old laws of Greece (of laws humane the most ancient) and those this Island.

68 J. Derrida, *Of Grammatology*, Baltimore, Johns Hopkins University Press, 1976, at p. 66. See also, in this respect, Doderidge, *English Lawyer*, pp. 161–164, for the notion of 'the conversation of men' as a source of law accompanied by what is possibly a comparable justificatory logic, discussed in Goodrich, *Languages of Law*, at pp. 116–122. M. Hale, *The History of the Common Law of England*, Chicago, Chicago University Press, 1656?/1971 edn, at p. 16 refers to 'Learned Men's Arguments and Opinions'.

priests the Druids, and to that end met but once a year'.[69] Sir John Fortescue,[70] William Lambard,[71] John Selden,[72] William Harrison[73] and William Dugdale[74] all also make reference to the Druids, with varying degrees of scepticism. Again, the logic of this ascription of origin refers the law both to extraordinary antiquity and to the influence of the divine, although here that divine intervention is played out across the immediate rites of sacrifice. The most severe punishment known to Druidic law is said to have been exclusion from the ceremony of sacrifice (*sacrificiis interdicunt*), the significance of this excommunication being first that the subject would be shunned by his fellows for fear of contagion and second that exclusion cut the excommunicant off from recourse to the gods.[75] The rite of sacrifice, the offering of flesh and blood to the divinity has interesting connotations of the later use of the Table, of food and of exclusion from the fellowship of the commons: the religious significance of the sacrifice and the psychological root of the rites of consumption do not lie in consumption as ingestion or as use but in the act of violence or immolation whose virtue is that of

> detatching from the *real* order, from the poverty of *things*, and of restoring to the *divine* order. The animal or plant that man uses (as if they only had value *for him* and none for themselves) is restored to the truth of the intimate world; he receives a sacred communication from it, which restores him in turn to interior freedom.[76]

The essence of such immolation is to consume profitlessly, to destroy so as to consecrate and in the act of destruction to reinstate the intimate order of commonality through and across the wasted thing. The consumption of food at Table is to be understood as a rite of the *sacra*, of the thing or object placed upon the altar which acts as the screen between a mundane world of separation and a sacral world of unified being. It may be added thus that the writ of outlawry as described in Bracton lies as a significant

---

69 Spelman, *Four Law Terms*, at p. 103.
70 Fortescue, *De Laudibus*, at pp. 29–33.
71 William Lambard, *Archeion or Discourse upon the High Courts of Justice in England*, London, H. Seile, 1591/1635 edn, at pp. 5–7.
72 Selden, *Jani Anglorum*, at pp. 16–18.
73 Harrison, *An Historicall Description*, at fol. 20 a–b.
74 Dugdale, *Origines*, at fols. 3 b–4 a, 96 a–97 a.
75 The description of the sacrifice is derived from Caesar and states that the punishment makes those 'interdicted' into 'number of the most impious and wicked, all people shunning them, and refusing their conversation, lest they should receive damage by the infection (*contagione*).' Dugdale, *Origines*, fols. 96 b–97 a.
76 Bataille, *The Accursed Share*, at pp. 57–58 (emphasis in original). Consumption in this sense is only completed through being performed in the face of the other, its utility being its power to destroy rather than its product. See also, in a different context, the description of the slaughter of pigs among the Hagen of Papua New Guinea, well discussed in M. Strathern, 'Discovering Social Control' (1985) 12 *Journal of Law and Society* 111.

middle point between sacrifice and eating: the outlaw forfeits his county and his realm,

> he is made an exile, and the English, call such a person an outlaw, and of ancient time he was accustomed to be called a friendless man, and so it seems that he forfeits his friends, and hence if anyone knowingly *fed* such a person after his outlawry and expulsion, and received and held communication with him in any way . . . he might be punished with the same punishment.[77]

It is again through the control of food, the common measure and meal, that the law goes within and possesses an interiority: communion has as its inverse a contagion, a speech that comes back from outside the law and comes back in the form of infection.

The better accepted originals differ from the above claims to divine source and immemorial antiquity only in the attempt to link common law to specific localities and it is in the use of the term common to mark and measure the place of the law that the stronger arguments of genealogy initially reside. Aside from occasional and erratic references to Samothes, Neptune, Arthur and Brutus as the first Kings and authors of English law, the derivation of common law is referred to a human geography which links the law to the inner life of the inhabitants of the various parts of the realm and to their local institutions. Sir John Davies gives the most extensive account in reiterating and elaborating Fortescue's claim that the common law is indissolubly woven to the needs and comforts of the inhabitants of the Island:

> Neither the law of the Romans, which are cried up beyond all others for their antiquity, nor yet the laws of the Venetians, however famous in this respect, their Island not being inhabited so early as Britain, neither was Rome at that time built. Nor in short, are the laws of any other kingdom in the world so venerable for their antiquity.[78]

Davies adds lengthy lucubrations on the theme of a common law

> which is written only in the hearts of men, [and] is better than all the written lawes in the world. So the customary law of England which we doe likewise call *Ius Commune*, as coming nearest to the law of nature, which is the root and touchstone of all good lawes . . . and written only in the memory of man . . . doth far excel our written lawes.[79]

The excellence of this insular inheritance is deemed to be its coextensive-ness with the populations of the Island and Dugdale lends support to such

---

77 H. Bracton, *De Legibus Angliae*, London, Longman, 1879 edn, at 2 cap XIII. i (emphasis added).
78 Fortescue, *De Laudibus*, at pp. 32–33. Futher statements to the same effect can be found in Coke, *Reports*, pt 3, at sig. A 7 a–B 5 b, and pt 8, at sig. L 3 a–L 4 a.
79 Davies, *A Discourse*, at p. 253.

a theory by tracing the common law to the laws of Mercia (*Merchenlega*), of Saxon England (*Saxon lega*) and of the Danes (*Danelega*) which Edward the Confessor – 'not unworthily to be accounted our English Justinian'[80] – did reduce into one body and called them the Common Law.[81] This Anglican *ius commune* was a pre-Norman law tied to the original blood and stock of the Island and it was this native law or *lex terrae* which was supposedly restored time and again after the Conquest (*pro bono pacis*) and most notably in that 'great manumission' of the English law, Magna Carta.

When later attributions are made to a common law which is the law of the Crown and of the realm or *regalis* it should be recollected that the jurisdiction of the antique common law is thought to incorporate and annex the later accretions of written or statutory law into its own vestigial forms and ancient geographies.[82] The itinerant royal judges, termed *itinerantes* or *quasi-errantes* by Lambard,[83] after all, simply go out to find the local law while those who stay in London, termed *residentes* or *sedentes*, hear appeals from the local jurisdictions and enrol judgments and fines recorded *nisi prius*. This time, finding the original of the courts in the story of Moses,[84] the principle of division is both numerical and agricultural. In theory the local courts are simply numerical groupings – by county, hundreds, tens (*tithings*) – yet in practice the Saxons are said to have made law through village and neighbourhood (*Jura per pagos et vicos reddere*), a Justice tied to Town and Territory. The question then arises of the principle of division itself in that the groupings are only in one aspect numerical and if one adds the other local courts, the Court Baron, the Court Leet and the Shireeves Court, the specific measure of such groupings is clearly agricultural and administrative as well as cabbalistic. The measure of law here recollects the Greek root of *nomos* in division or sharing: the correlate or supplement of numerical or, in Deleuze's terms, nomadic accounting is distributive, a 'sedentary structure of representation' according to strict boundaries and limits.[85]

The classical system of measurement, and the mark of both town and

80 Lambard, *Archeion*, at p. 55.
81 Dugdale, *Origines*, at fol. 5 a–b. The Venerable Bede, *Ecclesiastical History of the English People*, London, Penguin, 731/1955 edn, pp. 111–112 gives a rather different view of the same issue. The source of Dugdale's account is probably John Stowe, *The Annales or General Chronicle of England*, London, T. Adams, 1614.
82 See particularly Coke, *Reports*, Pt 3 at fol. C 3 a: even where statute abrogates, diverts or alters common law 'from his due course, yet in revolution of time, the same . . . have been with great applause, for avoiding many inconveniences, restored again'. Davies, *A Discourse*, at p. 253, reiterates the same point, while Hale, *History of the Common Law*, pp. 3–5 develops a theory of the incorporation of statutes over time into the unwritten law.
83 Lambard, *Archeion*, at p. 30.
84 Ibid., at pp. 13–14; also Dugdale, *Origines*, at fols. 26 b–32 a. The biblical reference is to Names, 18. 21–27.
85 G. Deleuze, *Différence et répétition*, Paris, Presses Universitaires de France, 1969, at p. 54. See also, G. Rose, *Dialectic of Nihilism*, Oxford, Basil Blackwell, 1984, pp. 104–105.

city, is the plough. The common law divisions base themselves upon a civilian definition of dimensions, the underlying principle of which can be found initially in the *Digest*, where 'the term *urbs* is derived from *urbo*: *urbo* is to mark out by plough (*urbare est aratro definire*). And Varus says that *urbus* is the name for the curved part of the plough which is customarily used in the foundation of an *urb*'.[86] So too the specific measures of land and tenure are marked by the plough: Doderidge, in a brief treatise *Of the Dimensions of the Laws of England*, thus defines an acre as being the equivalent of the Latin *Jugerum*, so called 'quod uno Bovum jugo per diem exarari potest' (because one ox could plough it in a day).[87] Similarly *carucata terrae*,

> [which] may contain a house, a mill, a loft, and divers parcels of land of divers kinds . . . and it seemeth in quantity to be so much as a plough land, *viz.* a tenement, whereupon a man may keep a plough for husbandry with all necessaries and incidents thereto.

The word *carucata* is indeed said to mean a plough or wainload and Doderidge cites the august Judge Henry Prisot as authority for the view that a carow 'should be so much land as a plough shall plough in one year'.[88]

The measurement of Law is the measurement of the productivity of arable land and so it is the plough which dictates the boundaries of a village, a town or a city and its jurisdiction. That precious and closely guarded sense of dimension ties a people to its food and to the quantification of the production of food, for behind every common table is a common land and common food. Rastall's *Exposition* thus defines common as

> the right that a man hath to put his beasts to pasture, or to use and occupie the grounde, that is not his owne . . . and alwaies [note] that common is by prescription and of common right, and it is appendaunt to errable land only, and not to any other land or house.[89]

Cowell's *Interpreter* likewise defines common in terms of measurement and dependence:

> commen (*communia*) commeth from the French (*commun id est quod ad*

---

86 *Digest* 50.239.6 (*de verborum significatione*). For a quite remarkable phenomenological jurisprudence of the plough as an instrument of law and of faith, as 'the instrument to which all instruments of law are only ever forms of homage', see Y. Hachamovitch, 'The Ideal Object of Transmission: An Essay on the faith which attaches to instruments' (1991) 2 *Law and Critique* 73.

87 Sir John Doderidge, *Of the Dimensions of the Laws of England*, in T. Hearne (ed.), *Curious Discourses*, at p. 41. The same definition is given in A. Alciatus, *De Verborum Significatione*, Lugduni, Gryphius, 1530, lib 1.

88 Doderidge, *Dimensions*, at p. 42.

89 J. Rastell, *The Exposicions of the Terms of the Laws of England*, London, T. Wright, 1566/1602 edn, (amended), at fol. 43 b.

*omnes pertinet* [common is that which attaches to all]) and signifieth in our common law, that soile or water, whereof the use is common to this or that towne or lordship; as common pasture.[90]

In the logic of originals, which logic Locke[91] among others confirms, all land was common in this sense and where later use or conquest removed the common pasture and water from its collective tenancies, it changed the political relation between individual, group and land but it did not change the measure or form by which the land was accounted as a unit. The Law as *lex terrae*, in other words, subsisted as both measure and rule, as a calculation of labour and produce, it was in Lambard's phrase an 'Arithmeticall Government'[92] which regulated and accounted equivalences between common land and common table, and perhaps later between a town or city and 'the necessaries' of its reproduction.[93] If we recollect Legh's narrative, it begins with his arrival near the City of London and it is in a particular sense the Law of that City which he then describes. According to the law of armory each town or city has its lineage and its ensign, its model of identity being both familial and heroic. John Ferne in the *Blazon of Gentry* thus speaks ardently of the unifying 'urban' character of common law: 'for the law is said, the bond of the city, the foundation of liberty, a flowing spring of equity, the mind, the soul, and the definite sentence of the city'.[94] It might be added that it is not simply bond and soul, but flesh and blood, the Table of the Law being the repetitive rite of the consumption of meat completed through the testimony or witness of the other, through the evidence of being seen to eat in common.

The village, the town and the city all mark the common earth, the tellurian substrate of human community. In the most mundane of terms, the Law and the plough are equally instruments which regulate what the eminent Russian geographer Woeikof has termed the 'moveable bodies', the earthly surfaces over which humans have control.[95] The crust of the earth is marked and marked again by the mechanical action of surface agencies

90 Cowell, *Interpreter*, at fol. Q 3 a.
91 John Locke, *Two Treatises on Goverment*, ed. P. Laslett, Cambridge, Cambridge University Press, 1970.
92 Lambard, *Archeion*, at p. 72.
93 On the general conception of law as regula, see P. Stein, *Regulae Iuris*, Edinburgh, Edinburgh University Press, 1966; see also, D. Kelley, *The Human Measure*, Cambridge, Mass., Harvard University Press, 1990.
94 Ferne, *Blazon*, at p. 41.
95 A. Woeikof, 'De l'influence de l'homme sur la terre' (1901) X *Annales de géographie* 98. His work is well developed in terms of the marks of possession that constitute the semiotics of property by Y. Hachamovitch, 'From a Tooth to a Flesh: A Semiotics of Moveable Bodies', in R. Kevelson (ed.), *Law and Semiotics III*, New York, Plenum Press, 1990. For further discussion of surfaces as a semiotic field, see A. Lingis, *Libido: The French Existentialist Theories*, Bloomington, Indiana University Press, 1985, ch. 4.

such as running water, frost, winds, the roots of plants, the transference of particles by animals and the constant tread of their feet [under which] lies a residue, the result of decomposition, constantly being renewed and prepared for use, capable of being modified and of taking on different forms.[96]

It is the movement of the surface, the extension of the plough or the territorial movements and pastures of herds that initially become subject to law's *regula*, the calculation or accounting of repeated forms of movement that constitute the first negotiable signs of possession and the nascence of the market. Fig or grape, grain or mutton, it is impossible to think of the emergence of the village or the city without an account of a proprietorial relation between community and those evanescent yet repeated surfaces, those movable bodies and the marks by which they are known and bound to Law. These are the measures of *Domesday Book*, of judgment, of fealty[97] and of subsequent hierarchies of faith:

the land does bring a certain kind of servitude to the possessor. For no man holds land simply free in England, but he or she that holds the crown of England: all others hold their land in fee, that is upon a faith or trust . . . in fee or feoda, which is as much to say as in *fide* or *fiducia*; that is in trust or confidence;[98]

a confidence marked or estimated by reference to worth, to produce, to reproductive capacity.

In place of a conclusion it may be noted finally that our dear and sullied common law does not escape the genealogical principle of institutional reproduction, namely that only through the sacrificial rites of food, through communal ceremonies of consumption, can the human group create and affirm a space of Law. The measures that first mark the flesh of an animal or the quotient of grain as property are the intrinsic signs of the *lex terrae*. By the same token food eaten in the gaze of the other, at the familial Table or at the legal commons, is the intrinsic sign of that civility which marks the space of civil law. It is thus through the commons that lawyers gain admission to Law and it is equally through commons that the ancient erudition of the lawyer was kept alive as a principal source of Law, as *communis opinio* or the opinion of the commons, which aphoristic,

96 Vidal de la Blache, *Principles of Human Geography*, London, Constable, 1926, at pp. 21–22.
97 Selden, *Jani Anglorum*, pp. 56–58, remarks that

in the primitive state of the kingdom after the conquest the kings had payments made them out of their lands, not in sums of gold or silver, but only in victuals or provisions . . . and those that were deputed to this service (the purveyors) knew what quantity arose from each several lands.

98 Sir Thomas Smith, *De Republica Anglorum*, London, Middleton, 1565 / 1584 edn, at pp. 111–112.

topical and essentially pragmatic oral tradition lived on in the Inns.[99] Perhaps it still does, for according to a document lately fallen into my hands the ancient, consolidated and continuing rules of the Inns appear to state the following: 'The student must be at least twenty one years of age, must have passed the Bar Examination and must have kept eight terms, that is to say dined in the hall of his Inn three times a term for eight terms.'[100] The history of that rite of dining is rehearsed here simply to observe that no rite is innocent, no symbol without its attachment to an ethics and practice. It can legitimately be observed that any move beyond the homosociality of the common law would require, at the level of scholarship, an account of the repressed homosocial basis of law's sociality, and at the level of practice, a move to more humanistic rituals. In substantive terms, the lists and codes that governed dining can be argued to have had a considerable hermeneutic significance insofar as the *communis opinio* of the commons, the common sense of propriety and reasonableness that governed the institution, were also, both directly and indirectly, sources of law.

99 A point well stressed by J.H. Baker (ed.), *The Reports of John Spelman*, London, Selden Society, 1978, vol. II, 'it was a learning kept alive primarily by the oral traditions of the Inns of Court and Chancery' (p. 161), where, it might be added, the law was both eaten and spoken. For a more recent version of the same argument, see W.J. Loftie, *The Inns of Court and Chancery*, Southampton, Ashford Press, 1985 edn, where he remarks of dining at the Inns that here one finds that 'there are rules for eating and drinking very anciently established, as intricate and as much guided by precedent as an ecclesiastical suit, or a bill in the old Court of Chancery', and concludes with a most excellent example of common law logic: 'The first of the immutable precedents is seniority, but the second, that the wine goes round with the sun, prevails over it' (ibid., 31).

100 *A Career at the Bar*, London, printed for the Inns of Court, 1985.

# Chapter 4

# Specula laws
## Image, aesthetic and common law

The sixteenth-century legal humanist Alciatus defines the concept of an image in a classical aphorism: *Quid est pictura? Veritas falsa.*[1] The significance of this concept of image is embedded in a complex tradition of doctrinal writing upon the question of signs, representations and personality. At its strongest, the legal definition of the person (*ius personarum*) is determined by the theory of images as the form of human appearance, of human presence. The legal person is a mask (*persona*) and that mask is governed in its representation – so also in its rights and capacities – by the law of the image (*ius imaginum*) and the drama of masks. It is, first, a law of the *imago*, of lineage, of the succession of the paternal form through each generation, symbolised in the household by the pride of place given to the painted death-mask – the effigy – of the ancestral father. It was also, in more mundane terms, a question of likeness, of imitation, through which the image gave a face to things and so semblance to inchoate matter. In these terms, the legal subject itself is in one respect to be understood or recognised as a visual fiction drawn upon the natural person, and is defined by dogmatic tradition as *simulacra fugacia . . . repercussae imaginis umbra*, and later, to use Alciatus again, as *mens incarnata, fantasma temporis, speculator vitae.*[2]

The power of the visual, of the image, crosses the boundaries of natural and legal personality. In its strongest definition, law itself proceeds through the representation of likeness or resemblance, its classical definition, adopted by Bracton, being that of *procedere ad similia*, and in its early judgments is collected across Europe in the 'Mirror of the Justices' (*Speculum Justitiariorum*), in reflections or specula of the law, fixations of

1  A. Alciatus, *De Notitia Dignitatem*, Paris, Cramoisy, 1651, edn, at p. 190. (What is an image? A false truth). The definition is attributed to Epictetus.
2  The first citation is from Ovid, *Metamorphosis*, III v. 415 (likeness in flight . . . shadow of a reflected image). That from Alciatus is from *De Notitia*, at p. 192 (incarnate mind, visibility (image) of time, observer of life). For an excellent commentary on this point, using Ovid, see P. Legendre, *L'Inestimable objet de la transmission: étude sur le principe généalogique en Occident*, Paris, Fayard, 1985, pp. 54–56.

the image inscribed in the text.[3] The memory of Law – as custom and tradition, as precedent and antiquity – is held and 'sealed' in images, imprinted though visual depiction or textual figures that bind, work and persist precisely through the power of the image, through a vision, for example, of 'neighbourhood', 'reasonableness', 'national security' or simple authority.[4] The legal art is in many respects to be taken quite literally as a plastic art; it stands against an imagistic background of architecture, statuary, dress, heraldry, painting and insignia – gold rings, rods, coifs, seals, rolls, banquets and dramatics – which provide popular consciousness with a Justice which can be seen and so remembered.[5] The form of such 'painted law' is borrowed directly from the traditions of the western church and particularly from the doctrinally central role of iconography as well as of miracles, sacraments and further signs of the presence of the Other, of God, within the temporal world. The visible sign represents an invisible presence, it manifests a deep structure or law which otherwise escapes the senses and could not hold (fascinate) the imagination or soul of its subjects to the order of natural forms. It is that sense of attachment which will be the object of this chapter. Without an appreciation of its visual and aesthetic forms, its plastic presence and the doctrines which designate such presence, it is impossible to comprehend either the method of Law – its hermeneutic – or the procedures by which Law as judgment and measure (*ius est ars boni et aequi*) inscribes itself upon

3  As, for example, in Sir Edward Coke, *Reports*, London, Rivington, 1777 edn, at IX, fol. A 3 a.

4  See Thomas Wilson, *The Arte of Rhetorique*, London, Garland, 1553/1982 edn. The art of memory requires learning to have places (rooms) and to 'digest images' in them accordingly (ibid., p. 423). He adds later the general scholastic precept that 'those things we keep best in our minds which we know by sight and have marked with our eyes – the sight printeth things in a man's memory, as a seal doth print a man's name in wax' (ibid., p. 430). For an account of the Renaissance development of conceptions of image and imaginary, see D. Summers, *The Judgment of Sense: Renaissance Naturalism and the Rise of Aesthetics*, Cambridge, Cambridge University Press, 1987:

> The principle of the memorability of the inner visual was extended beyond the art of memory proper to become one of the most basic principles of rhetoric itself, that the first appeal of speech was to the inner eye of the beholder, and that conviction was achieved, or could be achieved, when the matter being argued stood as if real before the inner eye of the listener.
>
> (ibid., pp. 39–40)

5  For general elaboration of this point, see David Freedberg, *The Power of Images: Studies in the History and Theory of Response*, Chicago, Chicago University Press, 1989. On the philosophical history of images see M. Le Doeuff, *The Philosophical Imaginary*, Stanford, Stanford University Press, 1989: 'now that the notion of thinking in images has come to acquire a degree of cultural respectability it is no longer feasible to go on ignoring the importance of imagery in philosophy' (ibid., p. 2). See also the excellent G. Didi-Huberman, *Devant l'image*, Paris, Minuit, 1990, for a powerful account of a psychoanalytic reading of the image, its conditions of possibility and its unconscious labour. See further G. Deleuze, *Logic of Sense*, London, Athlone, 1990.

everyday life. Without a head for the symbolic, the classical basis and history of the dogmatic tradition simply escapes us.

There is a second preliminary point to be made concerning methodology. The definition of image taken from the jurist Alciatus is aphoristic and implies a number of further points relating to the Roman law definition of both truth and image. On the surface Alciatus appears to be reviving the glossatorial correlation of truth and image, which variously spans the law of death, the *imago* being that which survives, the death-mask of the father in the atrium of the household,[6] to the principle of *accessio* whereby words inscribed or images painted on the property – the parchment or tablet – of another became, in the revised interpretation of the glossators, the property of the owner of the tablet: *pro lectione pictura est*, the picture takes the place of knowing how to read. The image, in this account, was to be tied by accession to a truth – an author, reference or physical property – that exceeded it, that formed its attachment to the world and guaranteed it an identity within the order of images or *systema simulationis*. Thus the appropriate hermeneutic of the image was one which would perceive truth both in fiction (*fictio figura veritatis*) and in likeness or simulation. That truth was in conceptual terms the Law, while in material terms it was the text, from which principle the glossators adduced the hermeneutic rule that in reading it was not the letter but rather the truth that was to be observed, *non solis litteris adhaerere*.[7] The significant feature of this early statement of exegetical principle is not simply that it textualises the image, reducing the figure to an index of identity within the Law as a system of truth. A careful reading can also evidence a reverse causality whereby the further consequence of the correlation of *pictura* and *scriptura*, image and text, resides in making the text itself an image, a symbol, a painted word. My point is that in the development of the tradition, the text circulates as an image and the power of its effect is largely resident in that aesthetic quality rather than in its supposed rational content, for few ever read the law, none ever read all of

6  The literature discussing the *imago* is extensive. See particularly, L. Dupont, 'The Emperor God's Other Body', in M. Feher (ed.), *Zone: Fragments for a History of the Human Body*, New York, Zone Books, 1989, pt 3, p. 397; also, T.G. Watkin, 'Tabula Picta: Images and Icons' (1984) 50 *Studia et Documenta Historiae et Iuris*, p. 383. In classical Roman law the image was an exception to the principle of *accessio*, it was an icon and as such was to be understood as a reality in itself, as both sign and referent rather than as substitution for an absent presence: 'the *imago* is not an image consisting of a signifying medium and a signified form. Both *ossa* and *imago* were parts of the emperor's body, and in the ceremonies they functioned in similar ways as figures for the whole body' (Dupont, 'Emperor God's Other Body', at p. 403). The image was a real presence. The glossatorial revolution in interpretation deprived the image of its reality. See also P. Legendre, *Le Désir politique de Dieu: étude sur les montages de l'état et du droit*, Paris, Fayard, 1988, pp. 228–240.

7  (One should not adhere only to the letters of the law.) *Novels* 146. Coke, *Reports*, III E 7 b, states the principle as *in lectione non verba sed veritas est amanda*, in reading it is not the words but the truth that is to be loved.

it.[8] The forensic rhetoricians in particular reverse the commonsensical ascription of literary properties to the plastic arts and read the text through its visual images and icons, its tropes and figures.[9] It is through its imagery, its visual tropes and figures, that the text attaches itself and binds its reader, for only through such forms of visual depiction could a literary tradition bind an audience which, even where literate, is seldom literate in the language and forms of law.[10] A reading of the legal text which ignores the power of its imagery or the aesthetic of its reception is a reading which is in many senses beside the point in that it ignores precisely that dimension of the text and its context which performs the labour of signification and so gives the text its effect.

## EXEMPLUM

I will begin with an example from a case decided in 1318 in the Court of the King's Bench, from the beginning of the common law, and conclude with one from the end of the tradition, a Court of Appeal decision of 1990. In both instances the purpose of analysis is to illustrate the substantive conditions of possibility of an aesthetic of law. It is also, by implication, an argument against certain other protocols of reading which would

8  Thus, for example, F. Hotman, *Anti-Tribonian ou discours d'un grand et renomme iurisconsulte de nostre temps sur l'estude des loix*, Paris, Perrier, 1567, at pp. 110–111, commenting upon the glossatorial tradition, remarks that

> in the following 300 years [since the publication of the *Corpus Iuris*] such a vast literature grows up in the books that Baldus, at forty seven years of age, comments that he is still an apprentice; even the Judges admit to being dazzled by the authorities and to judging more by chance than by reference to assured and certain law.

For the English tradition and its reception of the text, see M.T. Clanchy, *From Memory to Written Record*, London, Arnold, 1979; and also P. Goodrich, 'Literacy and the Languages of the Early Common Law' (1987) 14 *Journal of Law and Society* 422.

9  Quintilian, *Institutio Oratoria*, trans. H. Butler, London, Loeb Classical Library, 1921–1922, in particular, emphasises the importance of visual figures grouped under the label of *energeia* or *illustratio*. The later tradition concurs with that emphasis as, for example, we find in Susenbroto, *Epitome troporum et grammaticorum rhetorum*, n.p., 1563, at fol. G 6 b (Icon, Imago): 'est cum vel rerum vel personarum imago exprimitur. Vel est formae cum forma ex quadam similitudine collatio. Vel est oratio demonstrans corporum aut naturarum similitudinem'. In more juristic contexts see: Thomas Farnaby, *Index rhetoricus. scholis et institutioni tenerioiris aetatis accomadatus*, London, Robert Allot, 1633, especially pp. 9–14, 59ff. (on *imagines* and *allegoriae*); H. Peacham, *The Garden of Eloquence*, London, Jackson, 1593, at fol. X i a (icon); G. Puttenham, *The Arte of English Poesie. Contrived into Three Books: the first part of poets and poesie, the second of proportion, the third of ornament*, London, Field, 1589, at p. 201 (icon); R. Sherry, *A Treatise on Schemes and Tropes, very profytable for the better understanding of good authors, gathered out of the best Grammarians and Orators*, London, Day, 1550, at fol. F vi b (Icon and *Imago*).

10 The visual or heliotropic character of the tradition is well discussed in J. Derrida, *Margins of Philosophy*, Brighton, Harvester, 1982. A rather more complex discussion can be found in G. Deleuze, *Différence et répétition*, Paris, Presses Universitaires de France, 1968. For a discussion of the relation of knowledge to image in the theological tradition, see M. Aston, *England's Iconoclasts*, Oxford, Oxford University Press, 1988.

restrict the interpretation of the legal text to an analysis and reconstruction of its legal content severed from those images and symbols whereby that content is transmitted. Such readings follow a doctrinal definition of legal language and text as 'unspoken' memorials or monuments of law's *regula*, its rule.[11] It will be suggested that such a monumental hermeneutic or anti-aesthetic should be interpreted quite literally, it gives a reading of those elements of a law which died, a reading of the legal sepulchre, of tombs and monuments which inscribe not the living but the dead. There is, however, also a symbolism to the monument and it may be observed initially that the monument is, in classical law, differentiated from other forms of memorial in that no part of the corpse nor the head can be buried under it: 'but if the body itself be not there, and it was erected for a dead bodies' sake, it is a monument'.[12] The further feature of the monument is prescribed and adopted from 'Roman lawes' which 'forbid the garnishing of monuments with buildings, and hermas, that is ymages'.[13] In other words, there neither should nor could be any image – neither trophy nor mask – for a grave which does not contain any body: the monument dissimulates and so too do certain forms of legal hermeneutic.[14]

The first case, *William de Thorp* v *Mackerel and another*,[15] is one of many from the Year Books of the fourteenth century concerned with the offence of contempt of the crown and its court. William Thorp, 'the king's sworn clerk', was walking from the Inns of Court to the Court at Westminster in the company of sundry other 'men of law'. While proceeding along Fleet Street William was attacked 'with force and arms and beat, wounded and ill-treated'. While he was on the ground Mackerel 'pissed on him' (*urinam super ipsum*) and trampled him underfoot. The writ later issued by the plaintiff in the case (a writ of *venire facias*) stated that the defendant was in contempt of the king and his court (*in contemptum domini regis et curiae*) and further that this contempt was committed in the presence of the court (*in presencia curie*). The judgement in the case accepted the writ as

---

11 Coke, *Reports*, III at fol. L ii a, defines a record as 'a monument or act judicial before a judge ... it hath this sovereign privilege, that it is proved by no other but by itself – *monumenta (quae nos Recorda vocamus) sunt vetustatis et veritatis vestigia* – a record is perpetual evidence'.

12 Anon., 'Of the Variety and Antiquity of Tombes and Monuments of Persons deceased in Englande', 1601, in T. Hearne (ed.), *A Collection of Curious Discourses written by Eminent Antiquaries upon Several Heads of our English Antiquities*, London, Richardson, 1771, at p. 225.

13 Ibid., at p. 224.

14 Though it may be noted that the legal tradition had early realised the importance of such dissimulation in the maxim *qui nescit dissimulare nescit regnare*, cited by the lawyer Puttenham, *The Arte of English Poesie*, London, Field, 1589, at p. 155 (he who knows how to dissimulate knows how to rule). The most significant legal figures of speech are thus grouped under the heading of allegory, the figure of false semblance ('we speak of one thing and mean another').

15 (1318) in 74 *Selden Society*, p. 79.

stated and agreed that the contempt, while being committed some mile and a half from the Court at Westminster, was committed in its presence. It was, in short, a contempt or scandalising of the court which was to be treated at common law according to the geographical fiction that what occurred some one and a half miles from court occurred in court, in the presence or image (the face) of the law. William de Thorp was awarded damages of 100 shillings and, according to records later published by William Dugdale, he subsequently became Lord Chief Justice.[16] Utilising this admirably succinct example I wish to make three points concerning the broadly aesthetic dimensions of legal presence and simultaneously to draw certain further conclusions with regard to the openings offered by a semiotic reading of such legal material.

## Canonic geography

The first and most obvious point concerns the specific character of legal presence, the place of the Court and of the Law. The decision in the case is instituted upon the presupposition of a non-physical geography in which the place and presence of the Court extends from Westminster to Fleet Street. The legal presence or aura of law is no longer attached to a specific building but is rather an intensive and internally governed property of those who speak for or work within the Law. In that sense we may begin by considering the notion of presence itself. It is *prae-sens*, that which is before the senses to be sure, but also that which is in advance of sense, for the Latin adverb *prae* connotes 'going in advance', 'extremity', as 'above', 'beyond', 'higher than', all of which meanings imply an indexicality to presence insofar as that which appears *before* the senses is never more than a sign of other qualities or of the non-present. Fittingly, *prae* also has two further meanings: 'comparison with' or 'compared with' and 'for', 'because of', 'by reason of', 'on account of' in which latter connotations the implication of indexical reference is even stronger, that which is before the senses, the image or sign or thing which we see is there

---

16 Thus proving that not all that is pissed upon is flushed away. See W. Dugdale, *Origines Juridiciales*, London, Newcomb, 1666/1671 edn, at fol. 99 a. On the question of why the decision was made in the manner described, some further light can be extracted from the earlier case of *Henry of Naburn* v *Walter le Flemyng, Richard of Duffield and others* (1316) 74 *Selden Society* 72, where it was held that the defendants, who arrested the plaintiffs as they returned from Parliament to York, were in contempt of the King and in prejudice of his crown (*in regis contemptum et corone regie preiudicium*). In a sense well analysed in E. Kantorowicz, *The King's Two Bodies*, Princeton, Princeton University Press, 1957, any interference with the passage of the King's subjects was an offence against the crown, that is, against the mystical body of the crown (*corpus mysticum*) and is to be interpreted as a breach (*vi et armis*) of his personal peace and will.

for a cause and by way of likeness or semblance to some hidden quality, reason or causality.[17] Presence is in this acceptation always imminent.

In geographical terms, the cartography that would map such presence is initially to be understood as an intensive geography whose object would be not simply the physical or plastic manifestations of law but rather a mental geography, a mapping of inner spaces and qualities which accord or conform quite closely with the canonist rule that the institution, the church, does not inhabit a territory – *ecclesia non habet territorium*.[18] The *lex terrae* or law of the realm takes its hold upon the space of circulation and action, its effects are measured not through any immediate corporeal threat but through a metaphysics of presence or better of self-presence of the law in all those sites where its officers and representatives, its dignities and honours are to be found. The etymology of territory as legal juris-diction can remind us usefully that both text and territory as legal concepts have their roots in a terror (*terreo*) mapped upon the order of the soul and only secondarily upon the body, upon the image as that which represents the mere visibility or written memory of law.[19] Thus when William de Thorp is attacked it is not, or is only coincidentally, a natural person who is so injured but rather a subject of law who already carries with him both the place and the dignity (the presence) of the Court. The principle is one of a classical hierarchy of imitation or *imitatio imperii*: just as the Court is the suite or following of the King and by legislation of 1300[20] 'was not to be divorced from the person of the King' but always to be deemed as travelling with him, so also with time and the expansion of the legal system, each itinerant judge and officer of the court was likewise to be an

---

17 For an analysis of presence along these lines, see L. Marin, *La Parole mangée et autres essais theologico-politiques*, Paris, Meridiens Klinckseick, 1986, pp. 210–215. See also E. Benveniste, *Le Vocabulaire des institutions Indo-Européenes*, Paris, Minuit, 1969.

18 For commentary on this principle, see P. Legendre, *Ecrits juridiques du moyen age occidental*, London, Variorum, 1988, ch. XI, at p. 530. In later usage we may note that ecclesia or church is precisely that spiritual congregation inaugurated through the collective mass, through the eucharistic displacement of the physical world whereby the communicants are transported to the realm of the spirit. See, for discussion of this point, P. Goodrich, *Languages of Law: From Logics of Memory to Nomadic Masks*, London, Weidenfeld and Nicolson, 1990, ch. 3.

19 The importance of this hierarchy of the places and forms of inscription of law gains one of its most striking expressions in Sir Henry Spelman, *Of the Original of the Four Law Terms of the Year*, London, D. Browne, 1614/1723 edn, p. 102. It is interesting to note further that the continual struggle within the history of the western church over the status and legitimacy of images revolves around their role as vestiges or marks of God's presence: for the reformers, the image, like writing, served to obstruct memory, to engender forgetfulness of that to which the image referred. See, for example, W. Perkins, *A Warning Against Idolatrie of the last times*, Cambridge, J. Legat, 1601: 'the right way to conceive god, is not to conceive any form; but to conceive in mind his properties and proper effects. So soon as the mind frames unto itself any form of God an idol is set up in the mind.' (pp. 107–108). For a legal version of this view, see J. Selden, *Table Talk*, London, E. Smith, 1589, at p. 23.

20 *Statutes of the Realm*, i, p. 139 (*Articuli Super Cartas*, c. 5).

extension of the Crown and its law and to travel (*iter*) *as if* it were in the suite of the King's Court.[21] Thus according to Lambard 'it must be true, that the King and his councell are not to be tyed to any one place, seeing that the place itself neither addeth, nor derogateth to, or from their authoritie; and their be many causes of remove and change, from place to place' whereby the 'Royall presence' is detached first from Westminster and then from the person of the King.[22]

A geography of mental space clearly cannot be reduced to its physical presences, even if the latter are deemed simply indexes or ruins of the former. A structural principle is operative which attributes causes strictly to the hidden or unconscious order, to the imagination of the senses (*formae imaginariae*) and in doctrinal terms to the spirit. In a preliminary sense, that order of terror or mental territory, of text and truth, is a positive unconscious within which are stored the originary and repeated themes of institutional life. They constitute an historical a priori, the patterns and forms of an intinerant law, those memories of the tradition which by virtue of their structural quality are no longer represented but simply lived without the need for representation.[23] A canonic geography is a geography of those structures, those forms of terror or manipulation that bind invisibly and from within, for they are the measure of that most complex of theological and legal constructions, namely presence.

## Iconic lives

The second point, then, is to ask what populates a mental geography? What phantasms occupy the space where life is not yet? What is inherited through and across and beneath the structures of everyday life so as to reconstitute, again and again, the same judge? the same judgment? the same universe of persecutions? the same confessional zone? The form of presence implied by such spectral geographies also implies a particular legal conception of person and personality. If legal presence is to be understood as exceeding any specific architectural site and any merely

21 For a relatively recent version of this power and presence of the Court see *Balogh v St Albans Crown Court* (1975) QB 73, per Lord Denning.
22 William Lambard, *Archeion or Discourse upon the High Courts of Justice in England*, London, Seile, 1591/1635 edn, at p. 148.
23 The key reference here is Deleuze, *Différence et répétition*, as at p. 29:

> The mask is the true subject of repetition. Such is the case because the nature of repetition differs from that of representation, because the repeated cannot be represented, but must alway be signified, while masking at the same time that which it signifies . . . I do not repeat because I repress. I repress because I repeat, I forget because I repeat. I repress because, at first, I cannot live certain things or certain experiences except in the mode of repetition.

For an excellent analysis of the relation between image and repeated act, see A. Lingis, *Deathbound Subjectivity*, Bloomington, Indiana University Press, 1989, pp. 158f.

physical presence, that is because its function is ideally performed through an insidious terror, through a textuality of definition and naming, through a transcendent presence in image and measure collated initially through repetition and the various forms of homage. The law should here be understood as mystic body, as the King's peace and as the King's measure of all institutional forms of service and tenure: the territory or realm which the Crown governed was to be understood quite specifically as being in each and every part or member an element of His body and a part of His paternity or *patria*.[24] The text of the law becomes the territory of the realm, in the apposite civilian definition it institutes life (*vitam instituere*)[25] in both its parochial and normative forms: to enter the realm of law it is necessary to be a legal subject and that is by definition a question of being both already a subject of law and of wearing the mask, the sign, of legal institution: it is only as a legal sign that one can enter the discourse of law.

The geography of canon and norm, of law as the foundation of presence and person, is best understood as a regulation, an accounting, of the habitus of the institution. In instituting life, the law founds subjectivity as a place, as sign or mark, from which the subject speaks. In analytical terms its object is the unconscious, for only through Law does the subject gain a name and know its place, the space from which it came. To the superficial point that law institutes and repeats in the form of memory (precedent) can be added the more foundational significance that should be attributed to tradition as lineage and as genealogy. In demarcating the place of the individual the law accounts a movement from originals to specific forms of subjectivity. The underlying or unconscious structure of legal place and presence is genealogical: it is through relating image or appearance to their instituted forms, to their legal originals, that law takes hold of social being through the institution of a history and a name, paternity and family. What law offers is an account of that structure through which the individual has a place and speech within the social:

> what does it mean to *institute subjectivity*? Whenever possible, I have evoked the concept of prior fabrication (*pré-fabrication*) . . . so as to convey the thought of a process of reproduction, a process which western legal thought can only think of in terms of logical being, in the sense of the political animal. That is to say, following Aristotle's

24 See *Willion v Berkley,* Plowden Reports, 3 Eliz, 177 a. It is the *corpus morale et politicum* of the people. For further discussion, see Kantorowicz, *The King's Two Bodies,* at pp. 320–345.
25 *Digest* 1. 3. 2 (Marcian). Pierre Legendre, *Transmission,* pp. 139–141, 349–351. In Legendre's admirable analysis, this fragment is to be understood in an immediate and direct way: the law, as the discourse of foundations, of all things divine and human (*lex est omnium divinarum et humanarum rerum regina*), quite literally institutes subjectivity: 'one should not forget that institutions, in their juridical and most violent sense (that of *vitam instituere*), touch the most fundamental aspect of human reproduction: differentiation by means of speech (*la parole*)'.

interesting explication, the speaking animal, whose uniqueness from other species lies precisely in that access to speech. From an anthropological viewpoint, there is neither western law nor occidental legality save from this perspective.[26]

Returning to the case of William de Thorp it is necessary to ask what it was that was infracted – what body of law or image of place and presence – fell with him, fell as him? Only if the humble clerk to the court is perceived as being the bearer of a genealogy and legitimacy, only if the legal subject is in this exemplary case taken to be itself a place or *locus* of a particular kind of speech, a speech which emanates 'in the name of' the law which it serves, can the offence be detailed in the way in which it was, namely as being in the face of both Crown and Court. The point has a more general significance. The Court is that place in which the law is spoken, its speech is foundational and it is also universal: in classical terms it is inaugural insofar as it summons the omens and the gods, the fates and the presence of the divine source of all law. It is a discourse of permanence, a discourse which will bear repetition precisely through its endurance. In that sense the law of the court which attaches to the person of the clerk is an inescapable law, one which is at all times addressed to all subjects. It is both past and future: 'the subject only exists as subject by virtue of the place where it is instituted'.[27] It is that place which continued and in whose face the contempt was committed.

A more general point concerning personality also follows in the logic of this early legal doctrine drawn from Rome. The image – the face – governs reference, it orders by law that the person be perceived in a particular way, as belonging to a lineage and an institution, as 'coming from' and so having a place already mapped by the civil law. The person as mask or *persona* must not only be perceived according to an identity constructed by law but must also be heard to speak in the name of that law of place. The image speaks of origin and so designates place. In the classical tradition this formulation finds its place in the theory of effigy and emblems, the emblem is the sign or insignia of lineage and its etymology indicates its function, the emblem, from the Greek *emballo*, 'throws within'; it gets under the skin and holds the subject up as the index of law. In that sense perception is always perception of a legal construction, of a sign within the iconic order of law, of a law which is seen to be done to the exclusion of all other laws and to the exclusion of other gods. It may be noted also that in this respect the tradition can itself be traced to earlier Judaic forms within which writing and image, law and icon, are in-

---

26 Legendre, *Transmission*, at p. 354. The analysis offered by Legendre owes much to the philosophical reworking of Freud by Lacan and specifically to the notion of an unconscious which is structured as a language. See J. Lacan, *Ecrits*, London, Tavistock, 1977.
27 Legendre, *Transmission*, at p. 357.

dissolubly linked: in the book of *Names* (i.e. *Exodus*) the law is given in the Ten Commandments, inscribed upon tablets of stone, precisely to counter the image of other gods assembled by the tribes of Israel in the form of the idolatrous golden calf. The inscription and image of law is made possible by virtue of the destruction of the idol, the law is written again once the false images have been destroyed.[28] What then populates a mental geography? What is taken a hold of by the icon? In legal terms it is a non-physical control: the law controls attributes of respect and behaviour that are in essence symbolic or in a strict sense iconic. The icon is indicative and refers to another order, always in excess of what can be seen. We need, in short, to understand legal presence as being intrinsically iconic – as referring to an invisible order, more so, we need to understand that this invisible order itself has a history, a history which can be called the positive unconscious of law.

## Common law

In theological dogmatics the icon in its plastic form is also a mark of place: it signifies the space of the liturgy, the space – however sudden or contingent in architectural terms – within which the church (as *ecclesia*) may gather. The icon thus demarcates a place of transmission from the mundane to the sacred, the space of the eucharist, of the possibility of sacrament and miracle whereby one world will pass over to the next. What is portrayed in religious art as the site of annunciation, of the appearance of the spirit to its human subjects, is in legal terms a matter of maintaining an image and presence of the court. More than that it is a question of throwing the legal image into the life of the subject for only through that visual presence can the law move beyond the text and so spill into the nervature of everyday life. That life must in important respects become the book. The book or books of the law are in that sense no more than symbols of that other scripture through which the soul is prepared for its final reckoning, its day of judgment.

The notion of an absolute or originary textuality is more familiar to the continental tradition than it is immediately recognisable within the common law. In one sense the common law differentiates itself from civilian tradition precisely through its historical refusal to accept the symbolic and political power of the code. The common law was tradition and that tradition was oral and aural, an oratorical memory perpetuated through the common opinion of the bar, through customary practice, through the conversations, the disputations and the repetitions of an

28 For an excellent analysis of this relation of writing to idolatry, see A. Jacobson, 'The Idolatry of Rules: Writing Law According to Moses, With Reference to Other Jurisprudences' (1990) 11 *Cardozo Law Review* 1079. The biblical reference is to Names, 32.

itinerant judicial tradition. In such a tradition oral reason rather than precedent was the law. Yet if such was the case it simply made those available monuments of legal record – both writings and persons or judges – more striking and more significant than might otherwise have been the case. At one level the oral character of the tradition was a fiction, recollection was always aided and abetted by symbols – by daggers, by runes, by ceremonies of seisin, by lists, charters and the like – while the very notion of an unwritten tradition was only ever a partial one. As Hale not inaccurately describes it:

> when I call those Parts of our Laws *Leges non Scriptae,* I do not mean as if all those Laws were only Oral, or communicated from the former Ages to the later, merely by Word. For all those laws have their several Monuments in Writing, whereby they are transferr'd from one Age to another, and without which they would lose all kind of Certainty . . . [they] are for the most part extant in Records of Pleas, Proceedings and Judgments, in Books of Reports, and Judicial Decisions, in Tractates of Learned Men's Arguments and Opinions, preserved from ancient times, and still extant in Writing.[29]

Where the law enters life, in the symbolic form of Book or Tractate, Record or Report of the unwritten tradition and constitution, where it mingles in this form with the generic order of unwritten custom pursued 'time out of mind', might it not be most plausible to see these texts as *mnemonic* signs, as triggers of habit and repetition? To study the text in this context is to examine the relation between written and plastic mnemonic forms and their oral surrounding: the purpose of image or text is here to remind the judge or the subject of those rites or behaviours, those ceremonies or acts, which constitute their community and the form of their institution. Repetition, it should be recollected, itself has an etymological basis in rehearsal and rehearing,[30] it is that which is said and said again, that which the community of common lawyers carries with it as an auditory memory, as 'auricular' testimony, as the tropes and figures of collective reminiscence of the legal form. The mnemonic refers the viewer or listener to that order of unwritten law which is carried as authority alongside the text, the plea roll or record as the common opinion of law, as unwritten tradition or interpretation.[31]

29 M. Hale, *The History of the Common Laws of England*, Chicago, Chicago University Press, 1656/1971 edn, at p. 16. For detailed discussion of this relation between text and orality in early common law, see M.T. Clanchy, *From Memory to Written Record*, London, Arnold, 1979; also P. Goodrich, 'Literacy and the Languages of the Early Common Law' (1987) 14 *Journal of Law and Society* 422.
30 On the implications of this etymology see G. Rose, *Dialectic of Nihilism: Post-Structuralism and Law*, Oxford, Blackwell, 1984, pp. 102–108.
31 For a more detailed account of the mnemonic role of precedent within the oratorical tradition, see P. Goodrich, 'We Orators' (1990) 53 *Modern Law Review* 410.

The relation between the image of the textual and the unwritten discourse which surrounds it ensures that no text of law can ever be understood as the simple or 'closed' representation of its content, its signified. The tradition is one of memory and even where memory simply recollects (invents) prior practice as authority, it does so through an act of recollection or *actus memorandi* whose function, even according to the legal textbook writer, is explicitly that of 'representing the image of things forepassed in the same manner as if they were now actually and really present'. Such a process of repeating presence or of summoning the original inevitably also entails acts of inference and association, of imagination and representation. The second aspect of memory is thus depicted in terms of an *actus reminiscendi*, defined as 'a kinde of discourse of Memory [whose] operation [is] to inferre, collect and discourse upon' the topics discovered through the *actus memorandi*. The process should ideally lead to the drawing of 'conclusions from a thing conceived to another thing concealed, and to extract out of things knowne the knowledge of things unknowne'.[32] Where the classical tradition referred to such memory as *traditio* or *interpretatio*, the unwritten authority that would accompany the custody of the various codes or written laws, the common law would harbour its common memories in the *communis opinio* of the Inns of Court, in half-remembered conversations and half-heard recollections of proceedings and pleas in Court.[33]

To understand the law as both text and speech it is necessary to develop a hermeneutic which pays attention both to the image, to the aesthetic and plastic remains of practice, and to the oral and literary forms of the tradition. At a substantive level the development of common law was as much a product of Equity as it was of custom or writ and the jurisdiction of Equity was quite simply that of mercy, of the recollection of motives which the doctrinal tradition itself described as 'Geometricall judgement', that is as spatial measure, as 'lesbian artifice', 'harmonicall justice' or simple cunning that would mitigate those decisions of the lawyers that erred from *Regia via*: for

> there be no ordinarie Medicine of Lawes for infinite Maladies, that be caused by evill humours, yet I doubt not . . . it would be fruitfull or beneficiall to the Common Good . . . to checke the isolencies and outrages (if any such shall happen) of the judges, justices and other men that be great by their places.[34]

The reference to greatness of place, of course, refers us once more to the

---

32 Sir John Doderidge, *The English Lawyer*, London, I. More, 1631 edn, at pp. 15–16.
33 See J.H. Baker (ed.), *The Reports of John Spelman*, London, Selden Society, 1978, vol. II at pp. 151–161.
34 Lambard, *Archeion*, at pp. 70–73.

itinerant presence of the court, to the genealogical law whereby the person of the judge is itself a place, an accounted mark upon a lineage and legitimacy. More than that, however, even where it is not Equity but rather law – 'Arithmeticall Government (as they call it)'[35] – which is at issue, it must needs still be recollected – discovered, deployed and developed – through a rhetorical grasp of its forms. The curricula manuals thus list those tropes, figures and images, those illustrations and allegories, through which it is most likely to persuade. The mnemonic and often visual quality of such legal figures is stressed time and again by the rhetoricians, while the liturgical place of legal speech also gains a passing recognition. To the generic attribution of maximal effect to visual figures, to *hypotyposis*, *prosopopeia*, *prosographia*, *aposiopesis*, *metalepsis* and other metaphoric and expressive figures, should be added broader rhetorical classifications of legal argument as best served by 'auricular', elliptic, gnomic and imagistic formulations. In each case the figure is in some measure dark or occlusive, it is its very opacity which serves to trigger a memory of place or of logical association, inference or analogy, which will complete the statement or argument.[36]

## EXCURSUS

To read the legal text and its oral and plastic context as an imaginary structure of belonging, as an imagery of filiation and descent, is to read it against itself. It offers an attempt – a protocol – for deconstructing the boundaries of the text and for reviving the problematic of that revolution in legal method which founded the western tradition upon a hermeneutic of the spirit as the source of text and law.[37] To read the tradition against itself is in that sense to endeavour to revive the problematic of the legal body and of an aesthetic of law, to revive the underside of the tradition which had always recognised in the lawyer a poet and mythmaker, an author of fictions and oracular teller of truths that took the form of fictions. It may be observed initially that this other tradition of legal dogmatics coincides quite closely with the antique meaning and practice of dogma, from the Greek *dokein* – to think – which referred to the unconscious unravelling of thought, to reverie and the recounting of visions and dreams. Dogmatics was here associated directly with the institutional

---

35 Ibid., at p. 72.
36 For various arguments to this effect, see Sherry, *A Treatise on Schemes and Tropes*, especially fols. D vii b–F vi b (pistis or 'proves'); Puttenham, *Arte of English Poesie*, at pp. 148–167. Thomas Farnaby, *Index rhetoricus*, at pp. 40–58.
37 That inaugural revolution of legal method is the principal object of the historical work of Pierre Legendre, and is best approached through *L'Empire de la vérité*, Paris, Fayard, 1983, and *Le Désir politique de Dieu*. See also, H.J. Berman, *Law and Revolution. The Formation of the Western Legal Tradition*, Cambridge, Mass., Harvard University Press, 1983, especially pp. 99ff.

unconscious and with a discourse of law which had its roots in those sacrificial, miraculous and sacramental practices that are the literal connotation of all inaugural, liturgical and oracular forms of speech.[38]

The discourse of law as a 'poetical sermon', as the institutional dream that would magically fascinate and magnetise the legal subject to the fixations of sovereignty was a commonplace of medieval glossatorial analysis. To be bound – fixated – to law was to be held in the mirror of the text, to be alive in the book, and the symbolism of legal rite and textual practice, of ceremony and of scripture, had its most fundamental place in creating the medieval love of law. What is significant in that practice is not so much the recollection of a love of power, expressed through all the diverse forms of *hominium* and *feu*, of fidelity and honour, so much as the very existence of that imaginary space which underpinned and accompanied the casuistic reasoning of the text. For even the text had its aura and symbolism of sanctity, it was not dissociable either from the magic of inscription or from the sacral aura of record, of the chapel, the *thesauria regis* or treasure chest and hiding place (*sacramentorum latibula*) in which the text would lie.[39] The connection which should be made, however, goes beyond that between law and soothsaying, between text and fascination. It is that which dates back at least to Sophocles, and gains its first juridical formulation in Plato, in Book 12 of the *Laws* which most explicitly links the discourse of law to that of the Fates, to the *Moira*, a collocation which is later taken up in Roman law, in terms of the discourse of destiny, that of the *Fata*.[40]

Plato describes three Fates, born with each individual, *Lachesis* or the distributor of lots, *Clotho* or the spinner, the teller of tales, and *Atropos* or the fulfiller of destiny, the inflexible one, the rule of irreversible law inscribed upon the soul. Together the Fates state a destiny, tell the narrative of the life lived according to its horizons and then bind the soul to that destiny – it can have no other fate than that 'foreign will' or *fatum* always already inscribed in the soul. In the substantive terms of the Roman tradition, the Fates are the discourse of law as spoken before a life begins, they announce in advance the inescapable, the tragic course of a life to

38 I have spelled out this aspect of common law discourse in a preliminary manner in *Languages of Law*, at pp. 140–141. On the legal concepts of *fascinum* and the associated theories of magnetism, discussed in the *De Arte Magnetica*, see Legendre, *L'Empire de la vérité*, pp. 110–113.

39 Hotman, *Anti-Tribonian*, at pp. 120–121, describes the procedure for consultation of the manuscript of the *Corpus Iuris* in terms of the 'original being guarded like a sacred and precious relic, only being very rarely shown accompanied by candles and torches', in a barred and otherwise unlit room. For descriptions of the common law library, see Coke, *Reports*, III at fol. L iii a; Sir John Davies, *A Discourse on Law and Lawyers*, private circulation, 1615, at pp. 262–267.

40 As far as I am aware, the only extended contemporary discussion of this theme is to be found in Pierre Legendre, *Le Crime de caporal Lortie: traite sur le père*, Paris, Fayard, 1989, especially pp. 27–33. For interesting comments on the Greek tradition, see E. Levinas, *Totality and Infinity*, Pittsburg, Duquesne University Press, 1969, pp. 226ff.

come. The tragic quality of destiny is precisely its prior statement, it cannot be avoided nor can it be escaped: in its most generic form it is simply the sentence of death pronounced at birth. In a more particular sense, however, the Fates are linked to the specific form and horizons of the future life. Fate is the law which speaks the individual life in advance, the law as authority and reason mapped genealogically in the form of the family, both *patria potestas* and the fatherland of the text, *Roma communis nostra patria est*.[41] Those two paternities prescribe both life and death and again the *Digest* is quite explicit as to their structural status: *veluti erga Deum religio: ut parentibus et patriae pareamus*.[42]

The family, of course, is destiny in Roman law and its conception of familial fate includes the social as family. In the more modern discourse of psychoanalysis that classical genealogy reappears as the model for explaining unconscious structures: the Law is the law of the Father and the destiny of the subject is played out in relation to the Father in whose name it speaks. Paternity guarantees both legitimacy and succession or more simply the future. In more specifically legal terms the Fates as the oracles of law may be understood in a more generic sense as the structures that determine place and speech within the institution: the law speaks in advance both the reason that will determine the course of institutional action and at the same time, through the proprietorial forms of bequest, through covenant, contract, testament and will, through all those forms of legal deed and obligation, corporate personality and fiction of office, that exceed the temporality of an individual life it binds in advance, as destiny or fate, the place and institution of future lives. In a sense that is not far removed from the classical forms, it is that foreign will or fate already inscribed upon the soul at birth, that external structure that dwells within, that presence of the Other or of law that accompanies the person, the image, of its representatives. It was with that nomadic space or place of law that *Thorp* v *Mackerel* was concerned and I will end by briefly considering a contemporary case that strives in the same manner to preserve that sense of presence.

In *X Ltd and Another* v *Morgan Grampian (Publishers) Ltd and others*[43] the issue before the Court was initially that of the disclosure of documents obtained by a journalist from the plaintiff company. The specific question before the Court of Appeal was that of whether or not the appeal should be heard at all in the light of the stated intention of the journalist concerned not to pass the documents over to the Court even if judgment went to the plaintiff. In refusing to deposit the documents in the Court pending the

---

41 *Digest* 50.1.33 (Rome is our common fatherland).

42 *Digest* 1.1.2 (in the same manner as we are bound by obligation to God: so we must obey both our parents and our fatherland).

43 (1990) 1 All ER 616. The appeal is from the decision of Hoffmann J. in *Re Goodwin* (1990) 1 All ER 608.

outcome of the appeal the journalist sought to protect his source and to abide by the moral obligation of his promise not to betray that source. He was equally prepared to face whatever sanction the Court deemed fit to impose for failure to comply with its hastily invented order for deposition of the documents.[44] The issue was interpreted by the Court of Appeal as one of contempt. Arguing among other things that the relation between lawyer and client alone is the equivalent of that between priest and penitent and therefore that it alone could allow the superimposition of a moral bond upon legal obligation,[45] the Master of the Rolls stated that the legal subject is to all intents and purposes a 'servant' to the law. That servitude is the logical consequence not only of the subject's destiny at law, his Fate as spoken in advance by the very form of an imperative juridical reasoning, but is also the necessary corollary of the fact that law alone can speak the conditions of future acts. By virtue of his defiance of that monopoly upon the discourse of the future, by virtue also of his failure to recognise the extended place of the Court – its presence outside of its physical space – the journalist was held (though only momentarily) to be in contempt. The principle to be upheld was that whereby the Court represents the 'final arbiter', the law as 'given through the mouth of Parliament', to which it was added that '*honour* surely equates with the acceptance of, and obedience to, the rule of law'.[46] The invocation of honour suggests an immemorial law which is still tied to inaugural functions and liturgical spaces. The journalist's refusal was no simple or mere contempt of a secular law. He was rather to be understood as threatening the image of justice itself, and he was held to be in contempt to such an extent that the Court refused to hear his argument on appeal. Counsel for the journalist were therefore not allowed to speak on appeal and the Court thereby exercised an inherent power not to hear a cause. His fault was not that of defiance of the course of law but rather his defiance of the discourse of truth for which the penalty was silence. Yet that silence is eloquent. Within that silence resides an entire iconography of the territory of law for it is in that silence that law may properly be said to speak and in speaking to erase all claims to any other destiny, any other fate or reason but its own. In that silence the subject of law is erased from its book or, in biblical terms, it is blotted out from the text of law's creation.

---

44 *Re Goodwin*, at p. 611: (Hoffmann J).

> I suggested that, following the procedure commonly used against unidentified sellers of counterfeit merchandise, I might make an order against the respondent as representative of the class of persons who had received the confidential information without the plaintiff's authority . . . this was admittedly a doubtful expedient. . . .

45 *X Ltd v Morgan Grampian*, at p. 622 h: (Lord Donaldson MR) 'if any secular relationship is analogous to that between priest and penitent, it is that between lawyer and client. That is sanctioned both expressly and impliedly by Parliament'.

46 Ibid., at p. 622 e–f (emphasis added).

# Chapter 5

# Of law and forgetting
## Literature, ethics and legal judgment

Here we are all, by day; by night we're hurled
By dreams, each one, into a several world

(Robert Herrick, 1653)

The relation of literature to law is a question of genre. In the most immediate or contemporary of senses, the status of the legal genre is predicated upon a paradox. Law is a literature which denies its literary qualities. It is a play of words which asserts an absolute seriousness; it is a genre of rhetoric which represses its moments of invention or of fiction; it is a language which hides its indeterminacy in the justificatory discourse of judgment; it is procedure based upon analogy, metaphor and repetition and yet it lays claim to being a cold or disembodied prose, a science without either poetry or desire; it is a narrative which assumes the epic proportions of truth; it is, in short, a speech or writing which forgets the violence of the word and the terror or jurisdiction of the text. Law, conceived as a genre of literature and as a practice of poetics, can thus only be understood through the very act of forgetting, through the denial, the negation or the repression by means of which it institutes its identity, its life, its fictive forms.

In claiming to escape from the contingencies of genre, in forgetting its sources, its languages, its judges and legislators, law aspires to assume the modern character and quality of the discourse of fate. That law can claim to be a science outside of science, that it can assert itself as a genre that through a mixture of self-evidence and predestination or simple precedent is both more and less than a literary genre can only be understood critically in terms of a negation which both represses and incorporates that character or evidence of the literary which law most fears and most wishes to dissemble. The procedure of reading or criticism which would allow the recovery of the trauma of legal genre is necessarily constrained or confined to analysing that space within law which asserts or legitimates its legality, a space of self-evidence and so of forgetting. That the genre of law is in essence and practice unconscious, that its literature is reproduced in the form of an exorbitant demand for repetition, means that in a manner very close to that of psychoanalytic reconstructions, the literary critic engaged with law must read the literature of law through the evidence of its absence, through its repetitions and through the failures which indicate the return of that which is repressed in law.

A literary reading of law must offer an analysis in the strongest of senses. It must listen to what the subject does not wish to address, it must attend to the slight indications, the symptoms or lapses, which hide that which law seeks to forget, namely, the ethic and desire of legality as genre and as text. To address this non-question, this unconscious or undisclosed space of speech and of writing is also to bring literary analysis into conflict with law in that it seeks in law that which law does not wish either to give or to give up. In the most radical of senses, literature demands the end of law in the precise sense that in rendering the legal text to consciousness, in reconstructing the contingency of language and the fiction of a genre without genre, it questions the difference that demarcates law as a singular enterprise. A literary analysis, in short, promises eventually to collapse both the modernity and the unitary identity of law, it promises to tear down the absolute pretension of law, to destroy the idols of the legal form, to deconstruct or cast aside that character, identity or fate which claims for law a superiority or truth which neither logic nor science can ever fully impose. Literature, as a genre in relation with law, threatens the end of law through the very fact of that relationship between the literary canon and the norms, the canons, of law. It is equally possible to read in the dual etymology of canon as injunction or law and canon as legitimate genre the trauma and the repetition in which the closure of the legal canon testifies to the contingency of law.

For those who still believe in the unity and universality of law, and trust in its momentary closures, the autopoietic or self-referential quality of the legal idol or ideal rests upon a peculiarly positive form of forgetting. Specifically, the jurisprudential claim to a unity of judgment and to the *universalia* or normativities of law forgets both the history and the historical genre of law, its practice and its place within the *longue durée* of fealty and the violence of institutional attachment. The first argument to be addressed will thus be that of the form and practice of legal forgetting and it will be approached ironically via a series of arguments put forward by the literary and legal critic Stanley Fish. His claim that legal judgment as an activity depends upon forgetting the disciplinary and critical sources and contexts of judgment will be analysed in terms of a return to a peculiarly legal form of *anamnesis*. To claim that judgment rests upon forgetting, or put more strongly upon a necessary amnesia, is simply to substitute one order of causes for another. The conscious elaboration or public statement of the reasons for judging is here displaced by an inchoate conception or phantasm of other causes and unconscious reasons. The theory of judgment as amnesia or loss of memory institutes habit as law and intuition as the strongest form of judgment. In doing so it reinstitutes the phantasm of an immemorial or unknowable knowledge as the only proper source of law. Amnesia, in short, is predicated upon *anamnesis*, forgetting upon a memory beyond knowledge, law upon the displaced causes named destiny or fate, providence or despair.

It will also be argued that the irony that accompanies the notion of legal judgment as a practice of forgetting is a double one. First, it negates the explicit training in and historical practice of law as a discipline of memory. The *ars memoria* was supposed to inscribe the rules of legal practice and precedent in the permanent forms of the legal archive, in codes, statutes, Year Books and rule books; in the legal *memorandum* or the other forms of mnemosyne; in the *thesaurus*, treasure chest or royal and corporeal recollection.[1] Law's forgetting, in other words, has to be understood as taking place within the confines of institutional memory, just as tradition or unwritten law is recollected through interpretations of law's texts. In that the mode of legal recollection is textual and its judgment is institutional, the argument will then proceed to address a second irony. The notion of law as a practice of forgetting can be used to elaborate a theory of legal memory. The practice of legal judgment within a positivised conception of law depends upon a series of institutional repressions or positive acts of forgetting. A theory of law as literature can act as a powerful form of critical jurisprudence in recollecting the plural history of legal genres and the extended narrative of jurisprudential attempts to understand what may legitimately be termed the unconscious of law, in terms of genres of penitence and poetics. Finally, it will be argued that, both historically and philosophically, literature or more properly rhetoric as criticism is the discipline most appropriate to the analysis of the linguistic practice of judgment and law. The tradition of legality represents a peculiar fiction of institutional truth, it is to be located as a symbolic practice within the rhetorical genre of allegory and its success – its survival – has always depended upon an essentially literary conception of meaning best captured in the antique maxim *fictio figura veritatis*, namely, that fiction is the figure of truth in the theatre of justice and law (*theatrum legalis et iustitiae*).

## THE MOST MASCULINE OF APPROACHES TO THE MOST FEMININE OF OBJECTS

In a series of articles, the literary critic and lawyer Stanley Fish has repeated the argument that the difference of law and the distinctiveness of legal practice are to be attributed to a species of forgetting. This

---

1   The classical maxim is *omnia iura habet in scrinio pectoris sui,* the emperor carries all the laws in the archive of his breast.

forgetting is depicted in terms of the priority of practice over analysis and simultaneously in terms of the necessity of distinguishing separable and separate contexts of genre, specifically those of literary criticism or, rather improbably, philosophy and law. The first argument is stated in the context of an article on the misuse of theory in legal studies and is elaborated in the generic terms of an argument that to judge, as a transitive and unique activity, requires that the judge forget the contingency and the irrationality of social life and act rather as if the object of judgment, the rules to be applied to the circumstances of the case, were determinate and available to simple manipulation and application. 'Forgetfulness, in the sense of not keeping everything in mind at once, is a condition of action, and the difference between activities – between doing judging and doing literary criticism or doing sociology – is a difference between different species of forgetfulness.'[2] In the peroration to that argument, Fish memorably states that philosophical argument will not get rid of legal concepts: 'law is not philosophy, and it will not fade away because a few guys in Cambridge and Palo Alto are now able to deconstruct it'.[3]

Implicit in the latter argument is a distinction which Fish is fond of wheeling out when it serves his rhetorical purposes. It is that between the classroooom, the College or University and their disciplines of literature, philosophy and criticism, and the harsh world of practice and activity, the Protestant realm of act and purpose. It is a distinction as old and as tenuous as that between *vita activa* and the Roman Catholic escape into contemplation and has, for Fish, the same moral undertones: the two are not simply and inexplicably deemed to be separate, as if teaching or discipline belonged somewhere topologically outside the real world of activity, but also hierarchically related, as if it were somehow better and more normal to act unthinkingly, to forget, to repress. At all events, this particular trinity of arguments is so fond or so persuasive to Fish that he has frequently repeated them, both in the sense of using similar arguments in different essays but also in the republication of articles in different journals, collections or books. Fish, it would seem, does not wish his argument on forgetting to be forgotten and so repeats it. It may therefore be permissible to advert briefly to the later, and in Freudian terms charged, repetitions in which the argument as to the place of forgetting itself becomes a

---

2 Stanley Fish, 'Dennis Martinez and the Uses of Theory', in S. Fish, *Doing What Comes Naturally: Change, Rhetoric, and the Practice of Theory in Literary and Legal Studies*, Oxford, Oxford University Press, 1989, at p. 397, commenting on P. Goodrich, *Reading the Law: A Critical Introduction to Legal Method and Techniques*, Oxford, Blackwell, 1986, p. 209:

> In short, lawyers have always been indecently zealous to reduce behaviour to rules and, in constructing the abstract world of the doctrine and science of law, have tended to be forgetful both of the irrationality and chance embedded in social life as well as of the instability and change intrinsic to human purpose and personality.

3 Fish, 'Dennis Martinez', at p. 397.

figure, a symptom of memory or a condensation of a certain desire for continuity.

In an article entitled 'Play of Surfaces' discussing the hermeneutics of law, Fish makes the argument for the autonomy of law in more direct and stronger terms:

> autonomy should be understood not as a state of hermetic closure but as a state continually achieved and reachieved as the law takes unto itself and makes its own . . . the materials that history and chance put in its way . . . autonomy and the status quo are conceivable and achievable only within movement; identity is asserted not in opposition to difference but in a perpetual recognition and overcoming of it.[4]

In this analysis the self-referential or autonomous and hence forgetful quality of legal practice is a more active or indeed bellicose form of denial:

> A politically earned authority is *always already* in a relation to the Other it is accused of scorning, and the problem (as some see it) of opening the law's self-referential procedures to the pressures of the 'real world' is no problem at all because that very self-referentiality (autonomy, unity, integrity, etc.) has been constructed (and reconstructed) in response to those pressures.[5]

The hermeneutic argument has both a greater attraction and a lesser plausibility. While it is attractive in that it recognises the intrinsically political and embattled character of legal activity, its greed and its unpopularity, it is equally implausible in that it simply asserts the need to recognise the autonomy that is produced through this conflict between the disciplines. While Fish does not here resort directly to the metaphor of forgetting or of dissimulating the dependence of legal normativity upon the repression of its genre and its language, it is difficult to imagine any other claim. If genre is the structural form of institutional memory and the canon is its accepted textual expression, the autonomy of law can only be interpreted as a symptom of the repression of genre, as a sign of the forgetting of what Derrida terms 'the law of genre', namely the historical inevitablity of its adulteration or mixing:

> [Genre] is precisely a principle of contamination, a law of impurity, a parasitical economy. In the code of set theories, if I may use it at least figuratively, I would speak of a sort of participation without belonging

---

4   S. Fish, 'Play of Surfaces: Theory and the Law', in G. Leyh (ed.), *Legal Hermeneutics: History, Theory, and Practice,* Los Angeles and Berkeley, California University Press, 1992, at p. 312, commenting on P. Goodrich, 'Ars Bablativa: Ramism, Rhetoric and the Genealogy of English Jurisprudence', in Leyh (ed.), *Legal Hermeneutics,* pp. 44–45. 'Play of Surfaces' is also published in S. Fish, *There is no such Thing as Free Speech,* New York, Oxford University Press, 1993.
5   Ibid., at p. 313 (emphasis in original).

– a taking part in without being part of, without having membership in a set. The trait that marks membership inevitably divides, the boundary of the set comes to form, by invagination, an internal pocket larger than the whole; and the consequences of this division and of this overflowing remain as singular as they are limitless.[6]

What is surprising is that in a discussion of hermeneutics, conducted by a literary critic, the mediation of all law through textuality, through a literary practice, through a genre which invariably escapes its own classifications, should be so easily forgotten in favour of the fiction that law's practices, its texts and their subjects, should be and are best conceived in terms of autonomy. Again, the claims of the *vita activa* implicitly triumph over the conscious elaboration of the plurality and the institutional dispersion of law's intrinsically symbolic practices.

It might be noted also at this point that the very conception of *vita activa*, of Protestant commitment to the world, is itself a notion based upon a life lived in and according to the text, namely, that prior to action the subject was enjoined by ecclesiastical law to live in and according to the text, pursuant to the maxim *sola scriptura* or the text alone. There was no other guide nor contour to life than the text or, in one striking assertion elaborating the Protestant doctrine of the priority of the word as the 'word of the father' it is stated not only 'that *man* is a *word* that clasps together bodily and spiritual, visible and invisible, mortal and divine substances' but equally that, 'Man is Gods Text; and all the creatures are but so many commentaries upon him; Heaven resembles his soul, Earth his heart'.[7] Where the unity or autonomy of religious truth has suffered the fate of a secular world, the 'word of the father' or the autonomy and unity of meaning as practice according to the word returns as rhetoric in the writing of Fish. What Fish desires is the blindness of practice, the specific *eros* and peculiar oblivion of immersion or belief in a Text, that is to say, a textual system without subject or desire. What is referred to is no more than a return to faith in textuality, to a Judaic reformism, and its preordained structure of affections and subjections, a return to what might be termed, according to one's doctrine, either the imbecility of jurists or the dream of law.[8]

The last example reiterates the first, and is interesting not least for that reason. Again following a trinitarian structure, Fish begins by announcing

6   Jacques Derrida, 'The Law of Genre', in D. Attridge (ed.), *Acts of Literature*, New York, Routledge, 1993 at pp. 227–228.
7   M. Griffith, *Bethel or, a Forme for Families: In which all sorts, of both sexes, are so squared and framed by the Word of God, as they may best serve in their severall places, for usefull pieces in God's Building*, London, Jacob Bloome, 1633, at p. 145 (emphasis in original).
8   This theme is lengthily and strikingly elaborated in Pierre Legendre, *L'Empire de la vérité* Paris, Fayard, 1984, as also in Legendre, *Jouir du pouvoir*, Paris, Minuit, 1976, and most recently in Legendre, *Les Enfants du texte*, Paris, Fayard, 1993.

the political necessity of legal autonomy: 'Were law to deploy its categories and concepts in the company of an analysis of their roots in extralegal discourses, it would not be exercising, but dismantling its authority; in short it would no longer be law.'[9] It is presumably because of the implicit trauma of such a recognition or rewriting of law that Fish instantly moves to preclude, to occlude, the possibility which his own analysis has brought to the surface:

> the practice of law requires . . . forgetting, requires legal discourse to 'appropriate the meaning of other discourses . . . while specifically denying that it is doing so'. And if you reply that a practice so insulated from confrontation with the contingency of its foundation is unworthy of respect, I would reply, in turn, that every practice is so insulated and depends for its emergence as a practice – as an activity distinct from other activities – on a certain ignorance of its debts and complicities.[10]

Yet such could only be true if we were prepared to distinguish rigidly practice from theory, activity from thought, consciousness from the unconsciousness which Fish is so eager to achieve and so unable to handle. Like Hermes, Fish steals from law so as to find a message, a content for his analysis, but he neither writes as a lawyer nor engages in any practice that would differentiate him from the criticism or the mere theory he is so keen to exclude. The third moment of analysis thus follows rapidly:

> It is more than a little ironic that Goodrich finally scorns the material setting of the law's exercise and seeks to set it, instead, in the leisurely precincts (no less material but differently so) of a philosophy seminar. The law, however, is not philosophy; it is law, although, like everything else it can become the object of philosophical analysis, in which case it becomes something different from what it is in its own terms.[11]

The law, in Fish's depiction, is and must be a genre separate from literature and distinct from all types of theory. It would be interesting to pursue the logic of that difference and the immediate form of law's formal existence. As an initial observation it would be worth examining the implications of the seemingly incidental peroration, the third element in Fish's trinity, his version of the Holy Ghost, the setting, context or precinct which disallows the discourse of the University, the practice of theory or the materiality of the seminar. While it is possible in historical terms to argue that University, seminary and Inn or Court can all be viewed as

9   S. Fish, 'The Law Wishes to have a Formal Existence', in A. Sarat and T. Kearns (eds), *The Fate of Law*, Ann Arbor, Michigan University Press, 1991, at p. 203. Reprinted in annotated form in A. Norrie (ed.), *Closure and Critique. New Directions in Contemporary Legal Theory*, Edinburgh, Edinburgh University Press, 1993; also in Fish, *Free Speech*, ch. 11.

10  Ibid., at p. 204, citing P. Goodrich, *Legal Discourse: Studies in Linguistics, Rhetoric and Legal Analysis*, New York, St Martin's Press, 1987 at pp. 5–6.

11  Fish, 'The Law Wishes to have a Formal Existence', at p. 205.

genres, as being both governed by and practices of law, Fish's *vita activa* or real world of practice is presented as being forever external to such merely rhetorical conceptions of knowledge as power or to such a mundane political concern with institutional being. The stronger irony is that such exclusion of the other world of thought and institutions is contrary to Fish's own practice or more properly his preaching. In one respect it can simply be noted that a practice predicated upon forgetting is a practice which must depend entirely upon a prior inculcation, upon habit, ethos or breeding as the mechanisms that have trained the spirit or fashioned intuition. In a less abstract sense it can also be observed in the technical rhetorical terms that Fish holds so dear and yet so infrequently uses, his own practice is best characterised as a species of the *ars praedicandi*, the persuasion of the pulpit and of pedagogy which again, and not without irony, are discursive practices which lay claim to the most substantial of stakes and not least to a priority, both theoretical and material, over real life. His desire to have an effect through his discourses, through this preaching and his teaching, through his many texts and other performances, is predicated upon a collapsing of the very distinctions which his argument endeavours to establish. While it could be argued that he is not engaged in any material way in the practice of law, his concern being essentially to persuade others to act, to reform, to rethink and to recognise the truth of his discourse, the very faith which leads him to write equally pushes him to deny, if only implicitly, the distinction or separation between ideality and materiality, between thought and the real, between idea and matter that he wields to such effect within his own rhetoric. What, it might be asked, are we to make of his own repetitions, his own and apparent desire to be loved without question: where the law may well wish to have a formal existence, Fish wishes to have a material pleasure, and material effects.

At one level, that of the rhetorical, it can simply be observed in the most classical and obvious of terms that rhetoric itself is nothing more nor less than the study and practice of discursive effects, it trains the speaker in language that will make a difference, that will lead to action, and it cannot be doubted that, for good or ill, Fish has had his effects. More than that, Fish undoubtedly comprehends enough of rhetoric to understand that the discipline acts as a form of training, that it inculcates the ethos, habit and memory to which the professional subject or the amnesiac judge will return through the forgetting of judgment. In this respect Fish seeks the greatest following through the most occluded power. At another level, that of psychoanalysis, we are returned to the question with which this chapter is concerned, namely that of origins and forgetting. In this instance, what is forgotten is not simply the instability or impossibility of the distinction between discourse and the real, together with the desirability of examining the hierarchy of their opposition, but also the significance of the very enunciation through which the opposition is constituted. What is the real and what is the material if not, in Lacanian terms, the phantasm of certainty and the desire for that certitude which in psychoanalytic terms is joined not to matter but to *mater* or mother, to the 'Thing' in its strongest and most hallucinatory form either as part object, as something beyond the subject, or as the obscure object of desire.[12] The search for a power that will govern through the opacity of language or through the darkness of the body, through style or through writing is in the end a confession of a peculiarly masculine distance or estrangement from a femininity which appears historically as fluidity and as forgetting.[13] Fish evidently pursues in the most masculine of fashions the most maternal of objects, the phantasm of an origin, certitude, Freud's metaphor of the breast. In more appropriate terms, it can be said that Fish's forgetting is predicated upon a fear of femininity or of the fluidity with which femininity is associated: 'the question of ethics is to be articulated from the point of view of the location of man in relation to the real'.[14] Always assuming that the relation between man and the real is the relation between man and woman, and generically between masculinity and femininity, the fear which Fish evinces is a fear of ethics, a fear of relation and of materiality expressed in the desire to define the real as outside of the seminar, philosophy or the University, in short, a real defined as being external to the self and its practices, a real which is other to and so defined by a masculine practice. For Fish the feminine is the other, either unconscious or exiled it can be named only upon the condition that it is silent.

Fish is, of course, and no doubt much to his distress, no more than a symptom, his forgetting but a species of a more generalised desire to deny the ethics of writing or the undecidable effects of the text. In particular, it is to the question of what is forgotten when a man, such as Fish, embarks upon a practice or engages in an activity, albeit the activity of defining the activity of others, that I will return. In contradistinction to the analysis of the motive, the positive force or power of forgetting, the specific question

12 On which, see Jacques Lacan, *The Ethics of Psychoanalysis*, New York, Norton, 1992, at pp. 43–71.
13 On the body and the feminine unconscious see Luce Irigaray, *An Ethics of Sexual Difference*, London, Athlone Press, 1993; and most recently Irigaray, *J'aime à toi*, Paris: Grasset, 1992. For a spectrum of critical discussion, see Rosi Braidotti, *Patterns of Dissonance*, Cambridge, Polity Press, 1991; Drucilla Cornell, *Beyond Accommodation*, New York, Routledge, 1990; Somer Brodribb, *Nothing Mat(t)ers*, Melbourne, Spinifex, 1992; Judith Butler, *Bodies that Matter*, New York, Routledge, 1994. For a final comment:

The feminine – the other, the itinerant, law – must be affirmed not as the unconscious of the masculine but as having its own unconscious, the feminine must be affirmed not as being the phallus but as having the phallus. Only then is it possible to think through difference, through the body, through the unconscious.

(Peter Rush, correspondence, 25.11.93)

14 Lacan, *Ethics*, at p. 11.

with which I am concerned is that of what the law is 'in its own terms' or according to the fictive precepts of its distinct and unitary practice. Alternatively, what is law in the specific and autonomous language of its own genre and what must it forget so as to institute and to preserve its own identity as the genre of law? It is necessary, of course, to begin with the act of forgetting and to observe again not only that to forget is a positive activity, 'that all thought by its very nature occurs according to un-conscious means',[15] but also that repression, the unconscious positivity of forgetting, does not exclude but rather incorporates or lays out an internal space of repression, a repression that constantly returns to consciousness through its very positivity, its failure. To finish with Fish, forgetting as the style of judgment does not simply imply a form of hubris, the assumption of an effortless superiority, but it is also expressive of a frightening anti-intellectualism, of a fear of the symbolic which takes its most usual political form as nihilism or an unbearable lightness of thought.[16]

## AMNESIA AND ANAMNESIS

Forgetting, just as much as memory, is the manner in which biography and historiography are alike instituted. Because I am concerned with the question of genre and specifically with that of the genre of law, the genealogy of this specific forgetting can be traced, though necessarily in partial and inconclusive terms, through the institutional history of the discourse of law. The argument will be that just as critical historiography reads forgetting as a positive act, so a critical jurisprudence must confront the positivity of law's amnesia or loss of memory and endeavour thereby to read the unconscious body of law. At the level of legal historiography, the argument will be that if genre, the canon of texts and the laws of style, of writing and reference, of source and citation, are the structural form of institutional memory then forgetting of genre must be correlated initially to the phantasm of an origin. Forgetting institutes an invisible and so absolute cause, a non-empirical source, an image or symbol of certitude,

---

15 Ibid., at p. 32.
16 Pierre Legendre, *L'Inestimable objet de la transmission: étude sur le principe généalogique en occident*, Paris, Fayard, 1985, at p. 357: 'it is imperative to fear intellectual lightness or irresponsibility as a weapon of absolute destruction'. It might be appropriate at this point also to cite Jacques Derrida, 'Force of Law: The "Mystical Foundation of Authority"' (1990) 11 *Cardozo Law Review* 919, at 931–932:

> [critical legal scholarship] responds, it seems to me, to the most radical programs of a deconstruction that would like, in order to be consistent with itself, not to remain enclosed in purely speculative, theoretical, academic discourses but rather, and with no disrespect to Stanley Fish, to aspire to something more consequential, to change things and to intervene in an efficient and responsible, though always, of course, very mediated way, not only in the profession, but in what one calls the public sphere, the polity and more generally the world.

of a creative and so feminine form, which memory cannot directly supply and yet which science needs as the most basic justification of its enterprise. In Platonic terms forgetting is the means both of displacement and of recovery; it offers elliptically both desire and knowledge, phantasm and truth in the unity of image and memory, or more technically the conjunction of *eros* and *anamnesis*.[17] The displacement and repression that make knowledge appear absolute in the theatre of law can also be given a literal reading as the history of loss and of failure, the history of what was given up or suppressed in the inauguration of a science of law. *Anamnesis* itself hides a form of *amnesia*, it masks the history of the suppression, loss and death of all those subjects and texts which resisted or challenged the certainty of law or who proposed the undecidability, fluidity or contingency of law's judgments. This 'positive unconscious' of doctrine or legal science is the narrative of the repression of other laws, of the negation of the proximities, relationships and other bodily qualities that science must incorporate yet simultaneously exclude in the name of the distance or objectivity of law. The second feature of the analysis will thus be to shift attention directly to those forgotten texts or institutionally unremembered subjects who most directly and so obscurely spoke to the question of the genre of law. Such a history of law's rhetoric inevitably forms a critical contribution to the analysis of the language of power, an analysis which is ever likely to oppose the closure of the legal genre and specifically its silence as to the form of its most material of practices, the enunciation of law, its texts and other judgments. The history of law's genre is thus best conceived as a history of resistance, an oppositional narrative which can only be patiently recovered from the memory, the trauma, enclosed within the forgetting of law.

The initial and fond question of all jurisprudence is that of sources and of origins, that of the myths that found law itself in forgetting. At this jurisprudential level, namely that of the representation of the system of law, the forgetting or more technically repression which founds law does not relate immediately either to its practice or to the activity of lawyers but rather and ironically to the theory of law and the phantasm of its unity in a single cause or source. For Freud the foundation of law lay in the

---

17 Anamnesis is defined by Plato as recollection rather than memory, a distinction between active and passive but also between memory as reminder and recollection as recovery. See Plato, *Meno*, at 81D:

Thus the soul, since it is immortal and has been born many times, and has seen all things both here and in the other world, has learned everything that is . . . . All nature is akin, and the soul has learned everything, so that when a man has recalled a single piece of knowledge – *learned* it, in ordinary language – there is no reason why he should not find out all the rest . . . for seeking and learning are in fact nothing but recollection.

For an excellent discussion, see Richard Sorabji, *Aristotle on Memory*, London, Duckworth, 1992.

mythological trauma of the killing of the father and in the subsequent guilt, the internalised prohibition, experienced by the sons who had committed this act of murder. In literary terms, the narrative simply relays the impossibility of directly confronting the source of law or the origin of legitimacy, it is immemorial, beyond memory or, in short, repressed.[18] Such repression has, for Freud, the general form of repetition although it is of the utmost significance to observe that such repetition repeats a phantasmatic past rather than real events: 'repetition is in its essence symbolic; symbols or simulacra are the letter of repetition itself'.[19]

In a more generalised expression the same point is made at length by Derrida in his reading of Kafka's 'Before the Law': 'To be invested with its categorical authority, the law must be without history, without genesis, without any possible derivation ... this silence and this discontinuity constitute the phenomenon of law'.[20] It is based, in short, upon repression, upon becoming fate, upon being law:

> This is what we call destiny. Destiny ... implies non-localisable con-
> nections between successive presents, it implies actions at a distance,
> systems of replay, resonances and echoes, objective chances, signs,
> signals and roles which transcend spatial locations and temporal succes-
> sions.[21]

At the same time, however, this repetition or organic forgetting, to which Fish was in part referring in arguing that law would lose its quality of legality if it abandoned its autonomy, is simply a reference to the conceptualisation of law and to one of its most prominent forms of self-representation. It is still possible, in other words, to confront legality with its practices and with the materiality – the textuality – of its history. While these may replicate or repeat the narrative of forgetting so as to dissimulate both their authorship and their genre, such a rhetorical strategy is only effective when it succeeds: for those who wish to suspend belief in the myth of law or in turn to abandon the desire to belong to its system and identify with its truth the forgetting at the base of law simply incites an analysis or history of its present and its practices. It does not offer either

---

18 On which point, see S. Freud, *Totem and Taboo: Resemblances between the Psychic Lives of Savages and Neurotics*, Harmondsworth, Penguin, 1942. For a remarkable commentary on that text, see Alphonso Lingis, *Excesses: Eros and Culture*, New York, SUNY Press, 1983, at ch. 5.

19 Gilles Deleuze, *Difference and Repetition*, London, Athlone, 1993, at p. 17, commenting on the organic basis of the theory of repetition compulsion set out in Sigmund Freud, *Beyond the Pleasure Principle*, London, Hogarth Press, 1961, especially at pp. 30–34, 50–54. See also, for an interesting discussion, Sarah Kofman, *The Childhood of Art*, New York, Columbia University Press, 1988, at ch. 3.

20 J. Derrida, 'Préjugés: devant la loi', in J. Derrida, J. Luc-Nancy and J.-F. Lyotard (eds), *La Faculté de juger*, Paris, Editions de Minuit, 1985. A longer version of a comparable argument can be found in Derrida, 'Force of Law', at pp. 935–943.

21 Deleuze, *Difference and Repetition*, at p. 81. (Translation modified.)

panacea or cure: 'we are not therefore healed by simple anamnesis, any more than we are made ill by amnesia. Here, as elsewhere, becoming conscious counts for little'.[22] Nor, it might be added, is such a disbelief nihilistic but merely critical in the sense of questioning the validity or the value of a specific assumption of legality and the particular form of the myth of law in the modern age.

What is forgotten in the repetitive act of founding law is not so much the origin or genesis of law, nor even the relation of law to external causes, but rather the specific and particular practices of law, the materiality of its institutions, the history of its injustices, a history occluded in the mask of legal repetition, hidden within the phantasms of precedent, incorporated in the imaginary of a system or body of law. The normative question of pure morality or of foundation of law, of the law of law, is no more than a symptom of the desire to belong to and to believe in law and in consequence to accept its practices. What is forgotten, or indeed quite positively pre-empted in this institutionalisation of repression is not the source or genesis of law but rather it is the practice of law, its presence and its violence, which is displaced into the abstract formulation of the necessity and normativity of its practice.[23] It is this latter fiction or narrative of propriety in judging that Fish manipulates in the unnecessary terms of the constant movement of law towards its own closure. While the argument for closure and correlatively for the autonomy of law may have a certain plausibility as a description of the dream of legal rationality it neither does justice to the extant history of legal practice nor does it reflect the complexity and the differences within the theory of law and its conceptions of judgment and interpretation.

To return to the question of genre, to the question of what it is possible to say in the space of law and as law, requires a return to and sense of the full dissonance and discontinuity of the tradition. The question of genre is a question of institutional memory and of the criteria that govern the circulation and interpretation of texts. In these terms of the archive and of inscription the tradition of law was a question of philology and trans-mission or in contemporary terms of hermeneutic custody, while the profession and practice of law was a branch of rhetoric. In terms of judgment and the practice of law with which I am here concerned, the profession of law was placed quite evidently and self-consciously within, at the very least, a dual definition of genre. In terms of ecclesiastical and latterly royal law or equity, the figure that represented the genre was that

22 Ibid., at p. 19.
23 It does no harm to stress the political character of this observation. Legal doctrine has a tendency to present itself as external to the constraints of the particular situations in which its systemic elements – its rules – are applied. Such generality or abstraction is only purchased, however, at the cost of abandoning judgment to the mere circulation of texts.

of *paranologia* or confession.[24] The legal genre was established in the space of the human relation to the divine, law was announced in the place of inauguration[25] as a means of invocation of the spiritual, it was communication in the strongest and most classical of senses, that of transmission from the secular to the order of nature and of conscience. The church was the institution which established and interpreted, through its texts, its traditions and its rites, the signs and the speech of the judgment of God. In that the institutions and rites of law were always invoked, administered by and imposed upon the temporal agents or subjects of divine will, their address to and relation with law was to be understood in terms of confession and of penitence.[26] To be judged at law was to submit not simply to providence[27] but also to participate in procedures of trial and appeal which demanded an absolute exposure or transparency of the soul.[28] In an existential formulation, it might be said that the subject coming before the law had no choice but to appear in the mode of subjection or of self-abrogation. The law was to be approached through a confession which would both empty the soul and also display a filial fear of the parent law, a fear of the father and of judgment, a fear which would abrogate the subject and render it in its turn or in its trial a cypher of the judgment of the absolute.

The genre of such spiritual law was either a species of pagan divination, of seeking a 'hidden truth'[29] through ordeal or combat, or in its Christian form submission to *praeceptum iuris divini*, namely, an appearance before a court of conscience which would examine and judge both outward behaviour and inner observance.[30] The spiritual court judged the subject both *in foro interiori* and *in foro exteriori*, its charge being that of nursing

---

24 For an early example of this definition within the English tradition, see George Puttenham, *The Arte of English Poesie. Contrived into three books: the first part of poets and poesie, the second of proportion, the third of ornament*, London, R. Field, 1589, at p. 190.

25 On the concept of law as inaugural speech, see Legendre, *L'Empire de la vérité*, at pp. 147–151.

26 See, for example, Sir John Davies, 'Of the Antiquity of Lawful Combats in England' (1610), in Thomas Hearne (ed.), *A Collection of Curious Discourses written by Eminent Antiquaries upon several Heads of our English Antiquities*, London, Richardson, 1771.

27 Boethius, *The Consolation of Philosophy*, London, Stock, 1897 edn.

28 Davies, 'Of the Antiquity of Lawful Combats', reports that the 'chief justice . . . searched [the parties] if they had any charm or herbe about them' to confirm that neither had 'advantage of the other, by weapon, charm or enchantment' or means to interfere with the 'strength, the spirits, and the powers of nature [which] do decide the controversy'. (at pp. 181–184).

29 A lengthy description is provided in William Dugdale, *Origines Juridiciales or Historical Memorials of the English Laws, Courts of Justice and Forms of Tryal*, Savoy, Newcomb, 1666, sig. 65ʳ–88ʳ.

30 For the form of such trial, see, for example, R. Cosin, *An Apologie for Sundrie Proceedings by Jurisdiction Ecclesiastical*, London, n.p., 1591, at pp. 112–121. For further discussion, see P. Goodrich, *Oedipus Lex: Psychoanalysis, History, Law*, Los Angeles and Berkeley, California University Press, 1995.

and curing the soul.[31] It is precisely in this sense, and in both its pagan and its Christian forms, that law was subject to justice and governed by conscience. It was intrinsically a discourse of ethics conducted within and judged through the signs and the texts that gave evidence of another law or greater fealty. In more contemporary terms, the history of spiritual law and of its incorporation within the secular jurisdiction gives evidence of an aspect of the legal genre which is forgotten at the exorbitant cost of instituting a discourse which no longer recollects either its purpose or its transformative power as a law that writes itself upon the soul. While, in a relatively banal sense, the language of legal justification and of precedent is self-evidently replete with narratives of the good community and of the myriad proprieties of behaviour, such features of ethical governance and justice, such rhetorics of penitence and improvement, are deemed jurisprudentially to be incidental or simply rhetorical. They are repressed, in short, because they are repeated, they are repeated because they are unconscious, they are repeated because the positive jurisdiction of law has forgotten its genealogy and role as 'nursing father', its jurisdiction of internal governance, its regime of 'ghostly powers' which was classically spelled out in terms of *specula pastoralis* or of spiritual watch-tower.[32]

The penitential character of the legal tradition stems ultimately from the patristic texts of the early church, for which, in a famous passage from Gratian, 'culture consists of the reading of omens [or interpreting of signs] and the examination of the course of the stars'.[33] The dual significance or mystical character of law was transmitted to the medieval West through the reception of Roman and canon law in the twelfth-century revolution in interpretation.[34] The Renaissance and the English reception of Roman law, together with the Reformation and the arrogation of the spiritual jurisdiction to the secular law in the Act of Supremacy, ensured that the nascent tradition of common law took on the character of an unwritten tradition, and a hierarchy of sources, texts and meanings of law which was based upon the priority of their invisible or spiritual source. The tradition and institutions of common law inherited and practised a law which was

---

31 For the distinction between internal and exterior court, see Edward Stillingfleet, *Ecclesiastical Cases Relating to the Duties and Rights of the Parochial Clergy and Resolved according to Principles of Conscience and Law*, London, Mortlock, 1698, at pp. 24–25.

32 See Roger Coke, *Elements of Power and Subjection or the Causes of all Humane, Christian and Legal Society*, London, T. Newcomb, 1660, pp. 98–99, on the law as 'nursing parent' with the duty of watching over the spiritual realm.

33 Gratian, C 26 Q 2 c 9 (Origen). For discussion, see Pierre Legendre, *L'Amour du censeur*, Paris, Seuil, 1974, at pp. 145ff and at 263; see also Legendre, 'Aux Sources de la Culture Occidentale: L'Ancien Droit de la Penitence', in *idem, Ecrits juridiques du moyen age occidental*, London, Variorum, 1988.

34 For an extended analysis of this concept, see Legendre, *Les Enfants du texte*, at pp. 237–276.

unified by virtue of the hierarchy of its sources and which was interpreted and applied through a conception of jurisdiction which incorporated, though most frequently in the form of negation, an interior space of the spirit and force of law which was essentially sacral in its formulations of justice. It is in this penitential sense and genre that the law acts upon the soul. It is in this sense that it claims access to a system of rules which precedes and exceeds its momentary applications. It is in this sense that law relies upon unwritten meanings, upon both tradition and text and proclaims through these very institutions the innocence or the forgetting that lie at the source of its practices. It is for this reason and by virtue of this history and genre that the law can only be addressed in the penitential terms of innocence and guilt, and for this reason that the subject must appear before the law in the guise of appeal or confession. In its longest of durations, law institutes belief in power and in that aspect it is concerned with the mystical casuistry or the soul, with the manipulation and control of desire and the socialisation of its libidinal exchanges.

For all its obviousness and for all its common sense, Fish's conception of judgment as predicated upon forgetting is lodged in a unified notion of judgment – as if all legal judging were of a comparable character – and so rests both upon the existent hierarchy or *hieros* of spiritual sources and equally upon the absolution or penitence of a judge whose innocence depends upon the identity of internal and external sources of law. To judge by not thinking, to decide actively through forgetting is simply to offer a modern form of the Platonic theory of *anamnesis* within which knowledge pre-exists subjectivity and is best recollected through the unconscious memory of the body. To forget is to think otherwise and in secular or modern terms it is to invoke a poetics that exceeds writing, a knowledge of law which lies beyond law, in the order of language and the laws of the soul. The contradiction, therefore, between the practice and the theory of judging is not simply evidence of an inadequate jurisprudence or of a failed historical sensibility but also of a dissimulation. The conception of judgment as forgetting is in part a statement of faith, of faith in law and in lawyers, it is a mystical belief in the absolute and unchallengeable character of power. That faith, however, is always a faith in and of law in the sense that it is the text – scripture or statute, canon or rule – that institutes the particular and peculiar unconsciousness of judgment. The most active form of judgment, namely, forgetting, is at the same time the most textually based, the quiescence of the *schola* or classroom being here replaced not by any radical practical activity but by the memory of another seminar, that of the Judicial College, of Chambers, Law Offices, Inns of Court or the hidden libraries of law.

Forgetting transpires to be dissimulation. Ironically, the second classi-fication of legal genre is, historically, that of dissimulation, of pretending not to have what one has. According to the barrister and scholar of rhetoric,

Puttenham, the legal genre is to be defined also in terms of allegory, or of 'the Courtly figure of *allegoria*'.[35] Citing a classical maxim, *qui nescit dissimulare nescit regnare*, he who knows how to dissimulate knows how to rule, Puttenham classifies the figures and tropes of secular law as belonging primarily to the art of deception. In this depiction, the pervasive legal use of analogy and metaphor is interpreted not so much or so directly in terms of reason, as in terms of allegory. In the context of law the extended use of metaphor is defined as allegory, as the saying of one thing while meaning another, a rhetorical or figurative form which prolongs indefinitely the legal task of dissimulation. What is interesting is not so much the juxtaposition of this definition of legal genre in relation to other, equally possible, rhetorical elaborations – in the more normal or familiar terms of accusation,[36] memory,[37] conflict, antirrhetic,[38] or probable logic[39] – as the fact that Puttenham, a lawyer writing within a literary genre, chooses to define law in terms of poetics.

The first speech with the power of life and death, the original genre of communal belonging and of governance was that of poetics. The first legislator was the bard, the first law a poem. Sir Philip Sidney's *Apologie for Poesie* labours the same point at length in arguing that from the laws of Solon to contemporary use, law appeared best when it came in the mask or *persona* of the poet.[40] Not only did poetry most accurately reflect the birth of community, the originary contract in language itself, but equally poetry was the first legislation insofar as it was the role of the poet or Roman *Vates* to foresee the future, to divine, to augur, to give expression to destiny and so to foretell.[41] Being the language of nature, poetry was the speech closest to divinity. Being the direct expression of natural law it was not simply creative force, *poiesis*, but equally the *prosopopoeia* or linguistic face of God. While it is true that there is a sense in which it is possible to define poetics as a species of forgetting, in that the poet, being carried ecstatically by language, may forget both fact and nature or ignore

35 Puttenham, *Arte of English Poesie*, at p. 155: 'The Courtly figure of *Allegoria*, which is the figure of false semblance (we speak of one thing and mean another) – common and indeed essential to public life – *qui nescit dissimulare nescit regnare.*'

36 Thomas Farnaby, *Index Rhetoricus. Scholis et institutioni tenerioris aetatis accomodatus*, London, Allot, 1633, at p. 9.

37 Thomas Wilson, *The Arte of Rhetorique*, London, Garland, 1553, 1982; see also John Doderidge, *The English Lawyer*, London, I. More, 1631.

38 Anthony Munday, *The Defence of Contraries*, London, Winder, 1593. On the concept of antirrhesis, see P. Goodrich, 'Antirrhesis: On the Polemical Structures of Common Law Thought', in A. Sarat and T. Kearns (eds), *The Rhetoric of Law*, Ann Arbor, Michigan University Press, 1994.

39 Abraham Fraunce, *The Lawiers Logike, exemplifying the praecepts of logike by the common law*, London, Howe, 1588. For discussion of this and related texts, see P. Goodrich, *Languages of Law; From Logics of Memory to Nomadic Masks*, London, Weidenfeld and Nicolson, 1990.

40 Sidney, *An Apologie for Poesie*, London, Olney, 1595, at pp. 2–3.

41 Ibid., at p. 5.

the mundane levity of prose, the fictions of poetry are traditionally defined as being as close as is humanly possible to law or to the rendition of the spiritual causes of things. In this sense the poetic is to be understood as the truth of speech and as the force of law. While the dissimulation of poetics was always open to abuse, its proper form reflected both the uncertainty and the distance that separates the visible order of things from the ethical causes of community and law.

Within the post-reception tradition of civil law the explicit recognition of the poetic genre of law was always embattled or at the least somewhat less than explicitly avowed. That lawyers spoke in the form of allegory, that metaphor and antithesis would lead from an apparent object of legal discourse, from facts or conflicts, to other orders of normative and disciplinary truth could hardly be denied. An express awareness or advocacy of the poetics of law was, however, the exception rather than the rule. There were, nonetheless, those that conceived directly of the discipline in the tradition of the history or myth of poetics. The most remarkable and eloquent of such proponents of legal poetics was the twelfth-century jurist Placentinus, the author, among other works, of the *Sermo de legibus*.[42] Written in the form of an address to commencing law students, the address attempted to spell out the conditions and specifically the interior spaces and fealties of law. Taking the form of an attack on or of resistance to the glossatorial tradition, and its panoply of rules, definitions and elaborations of the grammatical details of antique and fragmentary Roman texts, the *Sermo* addressed the indeterminacy of legal meaning through the analysis and use of images, figures and the other forms of poetic use. The address was in this sense concerned quite directly with the relation of law to conscience and correlatively spelled out the place of the discipline within the practice of ethics. It was the figure of a woman, Justice in the form of the Goddess *Jurisprudentia*, who was to act as the emblem of Placentinus' opposition of the art of law to the withered and antique science of legality (*stulta scientia*) and which grounded his ensuing critique of the glossatorial discipline and its narrow or constrained written forms, the *literae* or dead letters of law.

The *Sermo de legibus* took the exceptional form of a satirical poem and its key stanzas oppose age or the *ager vetus* of Justinian's science to the spirit and creativity of youth. In literary terms, the critique of the *Sermo de legibus* is polemical and dramatistic and at one point explicitly counterposes the figure of a youthful woman, our mistress ignorance – *domina Ignorantia* – and legal science, an old, deformed, ugly and disfigured woman.[43] The *prosopopoiea* of *domina Ignorantia* is not, however, to be

---

42 Herman Kantorowicz, 'The Poetical Sermon of a Mediaeval Jurist. Placentinus and his "*Sermo de legibus*"' (1938) 2 *Journal of the Warburg and Courtauld Institute*, p. 22.
43 *Sermo de legibus*, in Kantorowicz, 'The Poetical Sermon', at lines 80–87.

understood as mere forgetting or the stupidity of a pure activity; she opposes one knowledge to another and comes in the form of critique. Ignorance is the adversary of custom (*contra morem*) and of the dessicated text of convention. The metaphor of ignorance is related not to forgetting as such but rather to vitality and a bodily hedonism with which the critic opposes the life-destroying characteristics of legal science, its idolatry of texts and its pedagogy of privation and sophistry. The interminable and myopic concerns of legalism, the literalism of glossatorial practice and the ascetism and abstraction of its belief in a domain of pure rules is challenged in the form of an irreverent and pre-stoical cynicism. The public life of this poetics is concerned with the play of words and with a law predicated upon virtue and desire; its art being that of a wisdom that lives indeterminately, that thinks each law through on each occasion of its promulgation.

*Domina Ignorantia* impugns the appearance of learning and the pretence of science and ends by inveighing against a science which kills both its subjects, its students, and also its object, the law: 'while you use your body in this way/you are destroying yourself/you are murderer'.[44] To this denunciation of a self-nihilating activity is added a lengthy and reasoned critique of a science which offered affectation rather than authenticity, tears and not pleasure, jealousy and not desire:

> O you stultified science,
> What can your diligence bring forth
> When your study is itself but punishment?
> You are pallid and impoverished
> Your life cheap and nihilating. . . .
> You teach nothing![45]

In short, it was a science which proffered punishment and not teaching, flight from the world and not attachment, death in the midst of life.[46] The concern of *Ignorantia* with the body, with the materiality – the delirium – of the text and with the purposes or virtues of law offers a stark contrast to the boredom and the rigidity of contemporary practice. To forget the unworldliness of law was to remember its violence and its immediacy. To forget the abstraction and the casuistry of glossatorial grammar and concordance was to recollect the plenitude and the poetry of textuality. To forget the nihilism or emptiness of a specific tradition was to return to the plurality of arts and languages through which law could be rewritten or renewed. It is thus not the particular character of Placentinus' satirical and essentially peripatetic jurisprudence that is of concern but rather the

---

44 Placentinus, *Sermo de legibus*, at lines 104–106.
45 Ibid., lines 93–96 and 116: 'O tu stulta scientia, / Quid prodest diligentia/Quam tu ponis in studio?/ Tu es macra et pallida, /Morieris vili vita/ . . . Noli inculcare!'
46 Ibid., at lines 99–100: 'Tu morieris in vivendo/Atque vivis moriendo.'

opposition of poetics to a specific and extreme reception of antique law. What also needs to be emphasised is that Placentinus shared his critique, if not its peculiar expression, with a lengthy tradition of resistance to the pretensions and the closures of legal science.

What Placentinus recognised and endeavoured to teach or transmit was a sense of the necessarily rhetorical and so emotive performance or practice of law. It was because law was indeterminate that it needed ethics, it was because judgment entailed not simply discrimination but also creativity or *poiesis* that the student must study the virtues and develop the internal faculty of justice or *synderesis*, it was because law sought an effect not simply upon the surface – the body – but also upon the soul that both judge and lawyer were always orators and rhetoric was the first legal art. It is this duality of legal genre and jurisdiction, this plurality of laws, against which the later tradition most frequently reacted and in the face of which forgetting might seem the appropriate description of the identity and difference of law. Such forgetting, however, is itself a surface phenomenon. It is in a dual sense a misrecognition. It is not simply a desire not to understand but is equally an impoverishment of the idea of law in that it refuses to contemplate either the historicity of legal character as judgment or the plurality of forms and languages of institutional practice.

## HERMES OR LEGAL COMMUNICATION

The discourse of law is a discourse of political love: it is both a grammar, a philological enterprise, and a symbolic attachment, a love of texts and an addiction or capture of the subject by the institution.[47] The stake of law, its classically defined purpose is essentially to hold the body of the subject to the dictates of the soul. In this sense it has as its object the training or art of creating effects within the soul or *foro interiori* of its subjects. Equally to this end the discourse of law can never be precise, it can never close off the uncertainty, invisibility or fluidity of the emotions which attach the subject to the icon or the aura of legal presence. To the degree that language and image, rhetoric and aesthetics are conjointly the forms of access to the soul, in that words and signs, letters and figures direct the attention from visible to invisible, the concentration of the legal genre upon the language and specifically the textuality of law is neither a surprising nor a dis-functional feature of the tradition. In another sense, one which comes close

---

47 This theme is lengthily surveyed and elaborated in the work – the *Leçons* – of Pierre Legendre. See, particularly, P. Legendre, *Le Désir politique de Dieu: étude sur les montages de l'état et du droit*, Paris, Fayard, 1988; and also Legendre, *L'Amour du censeur*, at pp. 143ff. A collection of translations from the work of Legendre is forthcoming: P. Goodrich and A. Pottage (eds), *Law and Desire: Readings in the Jurisprudence of Pierre Legendre* (London: Macmillan, 1996). For an introduction to his work, see Anton Schütz, 'Sons of Writ, Sons of Wrath: Pierre Legendre's Critique of Rational Law-Giving' (1994) 16 *Cardozo Law Review* 979.

to that of contemporary psychoanalysis, it can be added that the discourse
of law entails an enfolding of separate languages and jurisdictions, those
of conscious and unconscious, of word and image, of *simulacrum* and
*symbolum*.

The contribution of the reception to the study of law was precisely that
of elaborating a theory of genre and of its texts. Where Placentinus used
the poetic prehistory of law to construct a satirical critique of the methods
and certainties of the dogmatic tradition, later jurisprudence utilised the
conceptions both of the penitential and poetic genres to elaborate the terms
of a legal hermeneutic, of a 'labile *ratio*' or spirit of law (*anima legis*).[48] The
philological impetus of the reception was not always as blinkered or as
bound to the words or sentential figures of the text as is sometimes
suggested. Certainly by the Renaissance the rhetorical formulation of legal
argument and meaning extended far beyond the *ipsissima verba* or bare
letters of the text. The predominant form of reception was indeed contained in treatises that spelled out both the rhetorical goals and also the
linguistic forms of legal judgment and argumentation. The main form of
practical treatise on law was the compilation of the places of legal
invention and of commonplace or topic, in textbooks or formbooks that
were published under the title *De Verborum Significatione*, or in English the
*Interpreter* or *Exposition of the Words of the Law*.[49] These works explicitly
sought in legal philology and the work of linguistic memory an expansive
truth, a 'universality'[50] which preceded and watched over all other
inquiries and which endowed all other disciplines with their eloquence
and their force.[51]

The purpose of the lists of terms, tropes and figures of law was never
simply lexical but was rather artistic and specifically either rhetorical or
hermeneutic. Without endeavouring to spell out the conventions or the
details of this early legal literature it may simply be noted that the method
of definition and classification was set up to provide the means of
discovery not simply of the appropriate forms of legal argument but also
the manner of interpretation of both text and tradition, both letter and
spirit of the law. Thus Rastell conceives of his *Expositions* as an aid to virtue

---

48 For discussion of the concept of 'labile *ratio*', see particularly Ian Maclean, *Interpretation
and Meaning in the Renaissance. The Case of Law*, Cambridge, Cambridge University Press,
1993, at pp. 142–158.

49 Most famously Andrea Alciato, *De Verborum Significatione libri Quator*, Lugduni, Gryphius,
1535. In England, see J. Rastell, *The Expocisions of the Terms of the Laws of England*, London,
Totell, 1566; J. Cowell, *The Interpreter: Or, Booke Containing the Signification of Words: wherein
is set forth the true meaning of all, or the most part of such words and termes, as are mentioned
in the Lawe writers, or statutes. . . .*, London, Roycroft, 1607.

50 John Selden, *The Historie of Tithes* (BL 517.b.4, 1618), at p. xix.

51 A theme extensively and instructively pursued in Guillaume Budé, *De Philologia*, Paris,
Vascosan, 1536. For a general commentary, see Donald Kelley, *Historical Foundations of
Legal Scholarship*, New York, Columbia University Press, 1970.

and cites Aristotle to the effect that 'ignorantis terminis ignorantur est ars',[52] while Cowell introduces his *Interpreter* as intended 'toward the beautifying of this ancient palace', namely the art of law.[53] Even more explicitly Alciato devotes a considerable portion of the first book of his much published *De Verborum Significatione* to the definition of the figures of speech and the listing of definitions of rhetorical terms.[54] Language was the great 'Ladie of Learning', common law was no more than her attendant, and the great sages of law were her 'Chiefest Darlings'.[55] Time and again the love of texts and the coincident addiction to philology, to the *arcana* of language, reappear as the essential passion or thinly veiled desire of law. The figures of diction and the techniques of philological reconstruction were essential to the art of legal speech and to the practice of interpretation with which it was also indissolubly bound. Again using an early example, Thomas Phayr in the introduction to his *New Boke of Presidentes* enjoins the student of law to learn the language and the figures of law so as to be able to interpret and write law in a 'pleadably recorded fashion'.[56]

The language of law was always far more than mere appearance; its surface was but a screen for hidden causes and true meanings which could only appear to those with the knowledge and hermeneutic skill that could look beyond the letter to the spirit and substance of law, with the ear for a sense that existed *subauditio* or *subintellectio*.[57] The law, for Sir Edward Coke and the early modern doctrinal tradition, was built from

> *Vocabula Artis*, from the Vocables of Art, so apt and significant to expresse the true sense of the laws, and [which] are so woven into the laws themselves, as it is in a manner impossible to change them, neither ought legall termes to be changed. . . [they] cannot defend themselves *in Bello Grammaticali*, in the Grammatical War, and yet are more significant, compendious, and effectual to express the true sense of the matter, than if they were expressed in pure Latine.[58]

The peculiar feature of this common law was not the arcane character of its language but rather the strength of its expression and the scope of its

---

52 Rastell, *The Expocisions*, at fol. A ii b (he that is ignorant of the terms of any art is ignorant of the art).

53 Cowell, *The Interpreter*, at sig. 3[r].

54 Alciato, *De Verborum Significatione*, pp. 88–94.

55 Selden, *Historie of Tithes*, at p. xix.

56 Thomas Phayr, *A New Boke of Presidentes, in manner of a Register* . . . ., London, Whytchurche, 1544, at sig. iii[v].

57 See the divisions presented by Stephanus de Fredericis, *De iuris interpretatione*, in *Tractatus iuris universis*, Venice, 1574, at Book 1, 208–225; Jerome Sapcote, *Ad primas leges Digestorum de verborum et rerum significaione*, Venice, 1579, 56.

58 Sir Edward Coke, *The First Part of the Institutes of the Laws of England. Or, a Commentary upon Littleton, not the name of a lawyer only, but of the law itself*, London, More, 1629 at fol. C b a.

faith in and love for the law, a sentiment expressed at length in a notable passage from the *Reports*:

> If the language or style do not please thee, let the excellency and the importance of the matter delight and satisfy thee, thereby thou shalt wholly addict thyself to the admirable sweetness of knowledge and understanding: *In lectione non verba sed veritas est amanda*. . . . Certainly the fair outsides of enamelled words and sentences, do sometimes so bedazzle the eye of the reader's mind with their glittering show, as they cause them not to see or not to pierce into the inside of the matter; and he that busily hunts after affected word, and follows the strong scent of great swelling phrases, is many times at a dead loss of the matter itself, and so *projicit ampullas et sesqipedalia verba*. . . .[59]

Each letter of the text, for Coke, was significant and known to the law, a view he shared with a tradition that ran from Fortescue to Fulbecke and from them to the heritage of common law. For Fulbecke, to take but one further example, the words of the law were *sileni Alcibiades* 'whose outward feature was deformed and ugly, but within they were full of jewels and precious stones'. As for the speech of law, 'it is an external act, which is ordained for the declaration of inward meaning, and therefore words are said to be the limits of our meaning'.[60]

Again borrowing an established metaphor, philology was a 'tower of judgment' from whose heights could be discerned numerous hidden things and through whose techniques knowledge could be disencrypted from its textual forms of custody. The text which contains this combination of treasure and danger, wisdom and deceit, does not belong to any model of mundane or secular textuality but rather to an inaugural conception of text and of genre. It takes little historicist presence of mind or acumen to observe that the impossible unity of artistic meaning and dead letter (*litera mortua*) was in the strongest of senses located within the genre of the word made flesh as both father and son in the same form. The Anglican law borrowed directly from the Anglican text, the visible word was the sign of an invisible presence, the secular meaning of a spiritual truth. John Jewell, in the course of a polemical defence of the Church of England, gives what is perhaps the most explicit account of the nature of the word in arguing that

> the *word* of God has different meanings according to its various properties and effects: where it multiplies it is *seed*, where it cuts the heart it is *sword* and divides flesh from spirit; where it binds together it

---

59 Sir Edward Coke, *Reports*, London, Rivington, 1777 edn, part III at fol. C 7 b.
60 William Fulbecke, *Direction or Preparative to the Study of Law; wherein is shewed what things ought to be observed and used of them that are addicted to the study of law*, London, Clarke, 1599, at pp. 55–56, 91.

is called *net*, where it washes us clean it is called *water*; where it enflames, it is called *fire*; where it feeds – *bread*; where it opens and gives entry – the *key*. . . .[61]

Within such a tradition of the word and of *sola scriptura*, the language and texts of law borrowed their significance and their rhetorical force from an explicitly figurative usage. They were but 'outward tokens' to be read and understood as tropes or *ad tropicam intelligentiam sermo referatur*.[62] In Coke's terms, they were necessarily true by virtue of their art, their usage and their age.

The late Renaissance concern to assert and institute the artistic or poetic quality of the legal text belongs to the oldest of juristic traditions in which the permanence of the letter of the law is matched by the fluidity of its meaning. It was, after all, the sacral quality of the Twelve Tables, the fact that it was beyond the power of the lawyer (*juris consultus*) to change even so much as a letter of the earliest Roman code, which first gave rise to the need and practice of fictions that would elaborate new legal meanings without touching so much as a syllable of the law. Indeed each letter and syllable of the law was known and significant to the lawyer, each error of a letter being likely to be treated as misprision and so to invalidate an obligation or a writ.[63] The maxim *fictio figura veritatis* referred, in other words, to the initiate knowledge or hidden truth that existed within yet beyond the proximity and the opacity of the literal text. Philology, in short, and with it hermeneutics resurrected the poetic and dissimulative character of legal writing and interpretation and so returned law to its place within the diverse arts and disciplines of the drama of public life and of institutional enunciation. What it argued was no more and no less than that this speech of law was inherently symbolic, that it was tied in imagination and in practice to an unseen yet knowable body and meaning. The law regulated the subject through a 'ghostly power' and tied the meanings of servile use to the true bonds of law, to the *corpus mysticum* or inner truth of secular speech. Whatever the specific content of that mystical dimension to the secular realm, it is the relation of text and memory, image and body, to the soul of the subject and to the imaginary forms of its attachment to law that deserves a certain recollection, recovery or *anamnesis*.

The fictions of law rest upon their own diverse histories and play out the dramatic game of social meaning within the metaphors of jurisdiction and the imaginary realms of community or polity. Their identities are

61 John Jewell, *A Defence of the Apologie of the Churche of England*, London, Fleet Street, 1567, at p. 144 (emphasis in original).
62 Ibid., at p. 205 (the word refers to a figurative meaning).
63 See, for examples of misprision, Sir Henry Finch, *Law or a Discourse Therof in four books*, London, Society of Stationers, 1627, pp. at 226–232; see also Coke, *Reports*, at pt. II.

derived from the art of Hermes and like his messages or communications between divinity and humanity, they are plural and borrowed. In place of Hermes, Selden speaks of Janus as the face of common law, but does so to similar effect.[64] The emblem and so too the genre of law, whether Hermes or Janus, is always a species of mercurial and so deceptive transmission of meaning in the face of history and death. The two faces of Janus look upon the two dispositions of legal thought, the past and the future, the divine and the human, the masculine and the feminine, while like Hermes the law steals its meanings from sources that exist in the spectral realms beyond the engagements of secular exchange. Legal hermeneutics thus listens to what cannot be heard and looks upon what cannot be seen. To perform such feats of meaning requires an apprehension of the text as a sign and of speech as an adequation to causes that exist beyond the immediate consciousness of legal *regulae* or norms of law.

Both Hermes and Janus are also thieves. They take from one order and dispense their gain in another: one face looks upon the people and one upon the gods (*haec facies Populum spectat; at illa Larem*).[65] They hide the mode of that transmission and therein lies another theft, a mixing of genres undisclosed to the audience. Hermes seeks to hide his sources and possibly to forget. Such dissimulation is doubtless proper to the legal genre but it is not appropriate to the analysis of that genre nor to its critical potential. Jurisprudence, in other words, is doomed to elaborating and criticising the fictions of law, its *poiesis*, the forms of its theft, its modes of transmission. Therein lies not simply the poetry, the *poiesis* and also the creativity of law and of legal writing, but also the inevitable and dangerous proximity of law to its others in the sense that it is not possible to distance or disassociate the role of Hermes or the figure of Janus from the practice of law. That jurisprudence should disrupt the legal love of order is its most singular and significant role. As an analysis of the literary value of law, of law's genre, it speaks to the life in law and summons the ethics of its practice. In more mundane terms literature as law recollects not simply the tradition of legal critique but also the internality of legal rule. It recalls that the business of law is the fashioning of the soul.

It may be appropriate to end by reference to a further work of satire. In a curiously postmodern sounding treatise, *De incertudine et vanitate omnium scientiarum et artium*, first published in 1530, Hienrich Cornelius Agrippa addresses the two arguments rehearsed in this essay. The first is the tyranny of law, which theme is addressed in terms of a knowledge

64 John Selden, *Jani Anglorum facies altera*, London, Bassett, 1610, preface: 'Dum tuus ambiguam *Janus*, facieque biformi / Respicit antiqua, et posteriora videt: / Archivos Themidis canos, monumentaque legum / Vendicat a veteri semi-sopita situ / Hinc duplex te *Jane* manet veterane corona, / Gratia canitie, posteritate decus.'

65 Selden, *Jani Anglorum*, frontispiece (one face looks to the public sphere, the other to the soul).

which presumes to bear sway over all other arts and exercises tyranny: . . . preferring itself to all other disciplines as it were the first begotten of the Gods, [it] doth despise them as vile and vain, although it be altogether made of nothing else but frail and very weak inventions and purposes of men, which things be of all others the weakest. . . .[66]

The genre of law cannot avoid a mixture of sources and styles, a dependence upon other loves and upon the wisdom and the desire of other disciplines. Amnesia as to the diverse disciplinary sources, contexts and motives of legal practice or judgment can no more establish an autonomy of law than a text can maintain its boundaries within the exigencies of law's literary practice, canon or precedent. The genre of law, as a practice of memory is caught between origin and custom, the immemorial, the forgotten and the repeated. Forgetting takes its place within memory but it does so according to a curious legal dialectic in which the recollection of the past is subject to an essential forgetting, one in which the source of law is always conceived as empirically lost and so open to the phantasmatic prospect of adaptation or bridging between its lost instance and its present interpretation.

The claim to the unity of judgment or to the closure of law at best represents a fiction and at worst a symptom of a confused forgetting or deeply unhappy repression. Agrippa reminds us also and finally that 'all sciences and arts are subject to death and forgetting'.[67] My argument has been that such forgetting is no more than displacement and as such it is a resource for the analysis and critique of law. Forgetting allows the return of memory and the reconstitution of its desires. Recollection refigures jurisprudence as a law mixed with justice, while memory allows for a history of resistance to the fiction of the autonomy of law, an objection to the addiction to law and to its capture of subjectivity by the absolute order of a beautiful but hidden norm. Forgetting serves to mask the genre and the ethos of judgment, and in this it is not only unethical but in its turn it forgets that what is forgotten will return as *anamnesis* or a knowledge of the soul. In its most extreme form, forgetting is death, and yet death is not inarticulate nor without its traces and remains. Death passes on, it is the exemplary subject of memory and of mourning, the first form of reminiscence, of one thing leading to another. Death is the phantasm that creates the register and the necessity of institutional memory. Law is born of death, of recent death as also of the relics of classical lives. And of death it can only be said that it is not yet.

66 Translated as Henrie Cornelius Agrippa, *Of the Vanitie and Uncertaintie of Artes and Sciences*, London, Bynneman, 1575, at sig. 160[r].
67 Ibid., at sig. 181[r].

# Chapter 6

# Transmission and law
## Or, a sorrow beyond words

*Haeres est nomen iuris, filius est nomen naturae.*[1]

There are certain incidental narratives that on occasion alleviate the boredom of law. One such marginal anecdote is included in an influential discussion of the law of marriage in Juan Luis Vives' *De Institutione foeminae Christianae*, first published in England in 1523. In the course of depicting the 'charter of the laws of wedlock' in terms of 'unity and affinity' rather than 'love of beauty' or 'bodily pleasure', Vives offers a curious reminiscence:

> when I was in Paris, I talked with Guillaume Budé, at his own house and his wife came by . . . . he said 'this is my wife which so diligently follows my pleasure, that she entreats my books no worse than her own children, because she sees my love of study so well'. . . .[2]

The story is offered by Vives as an illustration of the desirable form of concord or harmony within the 'bond of that most holy fellowship', marriage. The great Renaissance lawyer and humanist scholar, Budé, had an attentive and observant wife who not only followed but also predicted or divined his pleasures. She would equally appear to have subordinated her own desires to the needs of legal scholarship, the life of the emotions and of the family to Budé's stronger passion or other lover, the 'Great Ladie of Learning', Philology.[3]

1 (An heir is the legal name, a son the natural name.) Francis Bacon, *Maximes of the Law*, in *Elements of the Common Lawes of England*, London, J. More, 1630, at p. 52.
2 Jan Luis Vives, *De Institutione foeminae Christianae*, translated as *A Very Fruteful and Pleasant Boke Called the Instruction of a Christen Woman*, London, H. Wykes, 1523, at fol. Z i a (translation modified). A stronger translation of the same passage would be: 'my wife is so sweet, so diligent, so nice and so good with my books that she is almost as desirable as no wife at all'.
3 On Budé's guilt-ridden relationship to his much younger wife, see Donald Kelley, *Historical Foundations of Legal Scholarship*, New York, Columbia University Press, 1970, at p. 61. For another strikingly laudatory depiction of philology, see John Selden, *Historie of Tithes*, London, private circulaton, 1618, at pp. xix–xxi describing 'true Philologie' as the 'first philosophie (or universality)' and as the basis of all legal and historical knowledge.

It will be my argument in what follows that the story of Budé's wife and of her submission to the will of her husband is neither as unexceptional nor as marginal as it might at first appear. It is a vignette which relates the life of one of the founders of the modern legal tradition to three of the greatest emblems of legal transmission or inheritance. The first is genealogical and relates to the legal institution of an order of differentiation and of succession. The context of the anecdote, that of the family, is paradigmatic of the stake of all law: the family establishes the means of social reproduction and the first order of prohibition, obedience and norm exist in *patria potestas*, the power of the father and of the husband, and correlatively in the various duties of the wife and children of the marriage. The story indicates a wife who obeys her husband and predicts his wishes through an understanding which transcends simple observance, through a love which allows an internal and anticipatory obedience, a spiritual subjection made whole through both habituation and belief. The initial significance of the story thus relates to the legal place of the wife and to what in psychoanalytic terms would be analysed as the institution of subjectivity, the role or adaptation of husband and wife to a hierarchy or order of pre-established communicative exchange. One serves in the sphere of *res publica*, the other in the *gynaeceum*; one communicates within the order of texts, the other within private space and through the contingency of the body.

The lesson of genealogy, though it is certainly not incontrovertible, is that the first order of transmission and of law is historically and conceptually the family.[4] The familial demarcations of subjective place, however, are always marked in advance of the subject and so the anecdote offers a further significant emblem of transmission, namely that of the text and specifically of love of the text. The virtue of Budé's wife is that she recognises his love of texts and is aware, however dimly, of the priority which they have over the immediate family or merely apparent progeny of the marriage. The humanist's belief in the text institutes an order of relations within which *ratio scripta*, written reason, or *corpus iuris*, the textual body of law, pre-exist and so also predetermine the places and possibilities of subjective life. The text of the law is not only a sacred object of veneration, but more broadly philology, the study of texts, is viewed as the source of all knowledge, the law that determines all future laws. Budé's love of his wife is thus secondary to a greater love, a passion which burns almost too fiercely and to which 'sweet loving companionship' he readily confesses: 'I must admit that I have also a second spouse (*altera coniux*)

---

4  Thus, for example, *Digest* 1.1.2 (Pomponius) 'Veluti erga deum religio: ut parentibus et patriae pareamus,' (Just as we are bound by obligation to God: so we obey both our parents and our fatherland). For an extended elaboration of this theme, see A. Papageorgiou-Legendre, *Filiation. Fondement généalogique de la psychanalyse*, Paris, Fayard, 1990.

whom I often call *Philologia*.'[5] To which he adds elsewhere, that to this 'princess and source of all thought', to the 'singular *Philologia*, I devoted all the ardour of my soul and all the energy of my nature'.[6]

The various personal marginalia in *De Philologia* suggest that Budé's love of law and learning, his passion for texts and for the revival and restoration of antiquity, was not an untroubled affair or an unalloyed pleasure. His second love, his small infidelity, was at times too demanding, a source of unspecified ills, a Pandora. In the language of those that followed him, Budé's passion for texts, his infidelity, was often described as an addiction, an obsession that was wasteful of youth, unfaithful to femininity and harmful to both feeling and life. It was also potentially a self-destructive pleasure, an indiscretion of age, a sepulchral lust born of the indifference of the body. Yet however disturbing or troubled, the priority of the text over the body and of philology over femininity is indicative of a further and crucial aspect of Vives' narrative. The story of Budé's wife was concerned to illustrate a harmonious conjunction, a concordant family. It evidenced a home as it should be, everything in its place, the relationship established and the order and hierarchy of communication already given. In this respect the significance of Budé's reported remark is that it indicates a wife who recognises that love which Guillaume elliptically names *studium* or *literarum studium*, a spouse who yields to the priority of the text, who comes with care into the presence or domain of textuality and effaces herself before the wisdom and the written form of law. One might say that it is an everyday story of a woman married to a lawyer, a sad reminder of gender and sacrifice, of law and of its abrogation of feelings. In this respect, and without further pretext, it could be added that the virtue or foresight of the wife is obviously likely to be interpreted as a suppression of her feelings, that any positive communication or transmission of law established through philology, the custody and interpretation of texts, will be accompanied by the repression of emotion or, in the example given, the silence of the wife. The tradition has its underside and it will be argued that this 'other scene' of legal communication, the silent message or absent voice, is logically as significant as the explicit *literae* or letters of law. The sorrow of the wife is just as much a feature of institutional meaning as love of law.

The third emblematic feature of the story is thus in a sense monumental. The transmission of law is a question of textuality, of a literary tradition and of its interpretation through its textual and auditory forms. The transmission of law, its passage over the *longue durée* or indefinite time of institutional structures is a matter of the communication or passing on of the dignities, places, roles and other sites of subjectivity, of the *personae* or

5  Guillaume Budé, *De Philologia*, Paris, Vascosan, 1536, at sig. 26ᵛ.
6  Ibid., at sig. Vᵛ.

identities of historical being. What the story relays in this respect is not only a matter of the custody and love of texts, but also of the power and the cost of interpretation. It relays these features of tradition in both positive and negative or repressed forms. Vives offered a picture of successful communication, a model of law as the order and agreement of spouses, a pure surface reflecting an inner devotion, a silent communication achieved through effacement, an order of texts that would play on the narrative of the living. The digression, or incidental narrative, of Budé's love of two spouses can thus serve as an emblem of the duality of transmission or communication within the dogmatic tradition. The positivity of the text is predicated upon the negation of those that support or serve the archive and its interpreters. The communicative power of a textuality recovered and disseminated by legal humanism is accompanied by a certain non-communication, by the abandonment of the contemporary, the loss of life and the postponement of feeling in the demands of philology and the dead letters of tradition. The literal meaning of the tradition was bought at the cost of displacement and of borrowing, its textuality depended upon denial and upon metaphor, silence and theft. To resort again to the image of two spouses, the humanist lawyer represented, both in his person and in his passion, the two faces of all institutional transmission, a duality encapsulated in the delirium and in the pain of an addiction to law, an ambivalence expressed in a love that was also an infidelity, in a passion that was also cadaverous, a proximity that spoke the distance of law.

## THE CASE OF THE PURLOINED HANDKERCHIEFS

The significance of the historical conjunction of philology and law, of the coincidence of textual reception and the formation of the western legal tradition, has become, if only indirectly, an increasingly vocal theme within contemporary and critical legal studies.[7] In place of Budé's great love, philology, modern jurisprudence has elaborated a plethora of lesser passions or minor deliriums in the form of rhetorical and hermeneutic conceptions of law. The most recent additions to the market-place include 'semiotics and legal theory',[8] 'law as an autopoietic system',[9] 'literary

---

7   Such attention is, however, largely indirect and most usually ignorant of the philological history of the legal tradition. The most notable exceptions, in addition to Kelley, *Foundations of Legal Scholarship*, and his more recent, *The Human Measure*, Cambridge, Mass., Harvard University Press, 1990; are Ian Maclean, *Interpretation and Meaning in the Renaissance: The Case of Law*, Cambridge, Cambridge University Press, 1993; Pierre Legendre, *Les Enfants du texte*, Paris, Fayard, 1993.

8   For example, Bernard Jackson, *Semiotics and Legal Theory*, London, Routledge, 1985; Peter Goodrich, *Languages of Law; From Logics of Memory to Nomadic Masks*, London, Weidenfeld and Nicolson, 1990; and most recently Dennis Klinck, *The Word of the Law*, Ottawa, Carleton University Press, 1992.

9   As, for example, Gunther Teubner, *Law as an Autopoietic System*, Oxford, Blackwell, 1993.

jurisprudence',[10] an 'aesthetics of law'[11] and a 'psychoanalytic jurisprudence'.[12] The phantasm of communication, it might well be said,
continues to disturb the law, while the art of interpretation similarly
disrupts and exceeds the capabilities of modern jurisprudence.[13] Were it
not so overused and dull a concept, it might be appropriate to speak of a
crisis in legal communication, manifested most obviously in the return to
the question of the meaning of tradition and equally expressed in the re-
emergence of the theme of transmission in ever more diverse legal contexts.

The concern with communication, and over longer time spans with
cultural and legal transmission, is predicated upon an obscure sense of the
failure of communication or the loss of meaning within the texts of law.
There is a deep sense in which the linguistic critique of law expresses not
only failure but mourning, a distress located vaguely in the extremity or
distance that separates legal science or the positivised profession of law
from the appreciation or life of its symbols, the poetics of its texts, the
imaginary of its reason. It is not simply that in the breakdown of its
identity, law faces the incursion of its others, the return of its repressed.
The sense of loss or of things not going well relates more directly to the
collapse of the symbolic and the coincident absence of any historical sense
or ethical purpose to institutional being. The overwhelming force of legal
communication, the mere fact of judgment, is matched only by the
increasing weightlessness of its reasoning and the estrangement of its
concepts. The concern with transmission may in consequence be understood as a concern with the intellectual health of the institution and its
subjects: perhaps they do not love enough, perhaps they are too faithful,
too haunted by a past which they neither understand nor know.

It is in this sense that the various contemporary attempts to rewrite or
renew jurisprudence refer to a history of law's other genres and its
dependence upon other disciplines. Whether such critique is conducted
in the name of deconstruction, literary criticism, linguistics or psychoanalysis there is a certain commonality to its theme. It returns, whether in
the spirit of play or taste, truth or cure, to the question of interpretation or
commentary in its strongest of senses, that of sounding the conscience of

10 Richard Weisberg, *Poethics*, New York, Columbia University Press, 1992, at p. 35ff. It would
   be wrong in this context to exclude Stanley Fish, *Doing What Comes Naturally: Change,
   Rhetoric, and the Practice of Theory in Literary and Legal Studies*, Oxford, Oxford University
   Press, 1990.
11 Pierre Legendre, *Le Désir politique de Dieu*, Paris, Fayard, 1988; and also and most recently,
   Legendre, *Dieu au miroir*, Paris, Fayard, 1994; Costas Douzinas and Ronnie Warrington,
   *Justice Miscarried*, London, Harvester, 1994.
12 David Caudill, 'Freud and Critical Legal Studies' (1991) 66 *Indiana Law Review* 651; Drucilla
   Cornell, *Transformations*, New York, Routledge, 1993; P. Goodrich, *Oedipus Lex*, Berkeley
   and Los Angeles, University of California Press, 1995.
13 This theme is well elaborated in P. Legendre, 'Communication Dogmatique (Hermés et
   la structure)', in L. Sfez (ed.), *Dictionnaire critique de la communication*, Paris, Seuil, 1993.
   See also L. Sfez, *Critique de la communication*, Paris, Livre de Poche, 1992.

law and of its jurists and of questioning the effects of their power of interpretation, the life that law institutes:

> one must not forget that institutions, in the most violent of juridical senses (that of *vitam instituere*), touch the most basic feature of social repro- duction . . . that is to say, the question of the relation of institutions to the unconscious, to an excess or beyond (*au delà*) of that which is said. . . .[14]

That excess or 'beyond' concerns precisely and quite technically the history of legal language, the dogmatic character of the tradition and the power that accumulates over the long term of the institution in its custom, its silence, its unwritten law. What is transmitted, in other words, is too powerful or traumatic to be transmitted in a direct or wholly conscious fashion; it is law and so speaks in the mode of repetition; it is dogma and so speaks in the manner of dream, through symbols, allegories, metaphors and other species of irony or dissimulation.

The general theory of transmission, of its indirection and of the inter- preters or *interpositae personae* that its normativity generates and necessi- tates, can be given a variety of elaborations. Each of the disciplines or jurisdictions that subsist to the side of law could be used to provide a language that would reconstruct the development and the interior mean- ing of the legal form. They would do so, in general, by reconstructing the institutional history of the legal subject, the genealogy of subjectivity corresponding broadly to the biography of psychoanalytic interpretation and the character of literary theory. In the spirit, however, of the classical jurists who propounded the maxim that only the deceitful work in generalities – *dolosus versatur in generalibus* – I will instead use the notion of an institutional unconscious or undisclosed transmission at the root of legal judgment to analyse a specific decision as an instance of transmission. The argument will be that just as in the anecdote of Budé lost in love and in his texts, the case analysed can be interpreted most interestingly and productively in symbolic terms as instituting a hierarchy or series of priorities for the affectivities or addictions of law. Just as Budé's infidelity, his other love, *Philologia*, can be read, behind the elliptical language of study and of literary scholarship (*literarum optimarum studium*), as a wilder delirium or greater passion, as being of considerably stronger interpret- ative significance, than his apparent marriage, so it is equally the case that it is certain incidental and philological features of the case of *James Cundy and T. Bevington . . . Appellants v Thomas Lindsay and Others . . . Respondents*, that will direct interpretation of the law.[15]

The case is a 'difficult' one and is not easily reconciled either with earlier

---

14 Pierre Legendre, *L'Inestimable objet de la transmission: étude sur le principe généalogique en occident*, Paris, Fayard, 1985, at p. 140.
15 *Cundy* v *Lindsay* (1878) 3 AC 459.

or later decisions in apparently similar circumstances.[16] One Alfred Blenkarn hired a room in a house on the corner of Wood Street, Cheapside, and Little Love Lane. Lindsay and Co. were linen manufacturers in Belfast. In late 1873, Blenkarn wrote to Lindsay and Co. making inquiries about purchasing goods – chiefly cambric handkerchiefs. His letters were written as from 37 Wood Street, Cheapside, even though the only access to his room was from Little Love Lane. The name signed to these letters 'was always signed without any initial as representing a Christian name, and was, besides, so written as to appear *"Blenkiron & Co"'*.[17] Lindsay and Co. knew of Blenkiron and Co. of 123 Wood Street, a respectable firm, and sent goods addressed to Blenkiron and Co., 37 Wood Street, Cheapside. These were taken in at once by Blenkarn and were never paid for. The goods were subsequently sold to different persons, and among the goods were 250 dozen cambric handkerchiefs sold to Messrs Cundy, bona fide purhasers. The question on appeal to the House of Lords was whether title to the goods had passed by contract between Lindsay and Co. and Blenkarn or whether the mistake as to the identity of Blenkarn meant that the contract was void and so left title to the property with Lindsay and Co. It was decided that there was no contract between Lindsay and Co. and Blenkarn and in consequence that no title to the property had passed.

The 'difficulty' of the decision is in part doctrinal and in part circum-stantial. In circumstantial terms, the difficulty was simply that of deciding which of two innocent parties should bear the loss for the fraud perpetrated by the now convicted and sentenced Blenkarn. This aspect of difficulty has been much commented by the courts and has been well analysed in relation to more recent cases concerning mistaken identity *inter praesentes*. Narrative analysis or a critical exposition of character can be used convincingly to argue that the courts have tended to resolve the choice between innocent parties by distinguishing desirable and less desirable forms of innocence. 'Narratives come laden with tacit social evaluations' and the courts use those evaluations to determine which forms of inno-cence deserve legal protection.[18] There are, in law, different types of innocence or of fool: 'God's fools, the young, the old, women and artists who are innocent. Their natural stupidity makes them vulnerable and

---

16 G.C. Cheshire, C.H.S. Fifoot and M. Furmston, *Law of Contract*, London, Butterworth, 1991, at p. 254: 'the case is difficult, for the facts admitted of two different inferences'. Hugh Collins, *The Law of Contract*, (London, Butterworth, 1993, at p. 196, suggests that *Cundy* is probably now to be regarded as anomalous.

17 *Cundy* v *Lindsay*, at 460.

18 B.S. Jackson, *Law, Fact and Narrative Coherence*, Liverpool, D. Charles, 1989, at p. 104, discussing *Ingram* v *Little* [1960] 3 All ER; *Lewis* v *Averay* [1971] 3 All ER 907. Of the further literature on this aspect of mistaken identity and the various attempts to resolve the philosophical problems involved, see particularly Glanville Williams, 'Mistake as to Party in the Law of Contract' (1945) 23 *Canadian Bar Review* 271 and 380; A.L. Goodhart, 'Mistake as to Identity in the Law of Contract' (1941) 57 *Law Quartely Review* 228.

worthy of social protection. The experienced and the intelligent, on the other hand, are the real dupes and fools.'[19] Analysis of mistaken identity cases in the narrative terms of the law's 'tender treatment'[20] of certain classes of victim may appear plausible in relation to cases concerning communication *inter praesentes* but this general equitable concern does not explain the development or the 'difficulties' of the doctrine of mistaken identity.[21] Nor is it of great explanatory value in relation to cases involving communication *inter absentes*.[22]

In doctrinal terms, the *ad hominem* or indeed *ad feminam* basis of decisions has tended to complicate the development of principles.[23] The anomalies and anachronisms generated by a case-law more concerned with the reputation or innocence of the litigants than with understanding or interpreting the law can be succinctly stated. In terms of the law of sale, with which the cases are mostly concerned, the general rule of classical law was that a contract could only be treated as void if there was a mistake as to the identity (*in corpore*) or the substance (*in substantia*) of the thing sold.[24] The distinction between mistakes which will and will not make a sale void is illustrated as follows:

> If I think that I am buying a virgin when she is, in fact, a woman, the sale is valid, there being no mistake over her sex. But if I sell you a woman and you think that you are buying a male slave, the error over sex makes the sale void.[25]

While common law has on occasion attempted to claim that it does not follow the civilian doctrine,[26] the case-law on mistake has broadly

19 Costas Douzinas, Ronnie Warrington and Shaun McVeigh, *Postmodern Jurisprudence. The Law of Texts in the Texts of Law*, London, Routledge, 1990, at p. 102.

20 For a recent analysis of the equitable notion of 'tender treatment', see *Barclays Bank plc v O'Brien and another* [1993] All ER 417, at 428–429.

21 The general plausibility of the thesis can be supported by analysis of the main authorities. In *Hardman and Others v Booth* (1863) 1 H & C 803, the criterion of innocence marginally favoured the outcome arrived at by the Court of Exchequer, not only by virtue of the fact that there had been several meetings between the parties to the original agreement, but also because the mistake had arisen originally from a visit by the defrauded sellers to the premises of the company with which they wished to do business. *Lake v Simmons* [1927] AC 487, similarly involved facts in which prior relations between the parties in a sense justified the mistake as to identity and so distinguished the facts from those in *Phillips v Brooks* [1919] 2 KB 243. *Sowler v Potter* [1940] 1 KB 271; and *Newborne v Sensolid (Great Britain)* [1954] 1 QB 45, clearly support the thesis.

22 Most strikingly, *King's Norton Metal Company (Limited) v Edridge, Merrett, and Company (Limited)* (1897) 14 Times Law Reports 98.

23 An argument *ad feminam* means, in logic, an argument as to the thing, but I suspect that we may now be entitled to a more modern usage although it could be noted that in psychoanalytic terms the argument *ad feminam* can plausibly be interpreted as an argument as to maternity or as to the mother. See Jacques Lacan, *The Ethics of Psychoanalysis*, New York, Norton, 1992 at pp. 43ff.

24 *Digest* 18.1.9.

25 *Digest* 18.1.11.1.

26 As, for example, by Lord Denning in *Lewis v Averay* [1972] 2 QB 198.

conformed to the principle set out in terms of requiring mistake to be of such a kind as to 'go to the substance of the whole contract'.[27] In these terms, the problem with cases of mistaken identity is that the identity of the party to whom a sale is made is unlikely to be a term, let alone 'of the essence' of the agreement unless the contract is specifically for personal services, or depends upon some prior agreement.[28]

The doctrinal 'difficulty' of the decision in *Cundy* v *Lindsay* thus comes down to the problem of how the court was to determine that the identity, the name, of the purchaser of goods was fundamental to the sale of such goods. The difficulty can be illustrated most graphically by comparing the decision in the case to that in *King's Norton Metal Co. Ltd* v *Edridge*. In the latter case, the question for the court was explicitly posed as being that of 'which of two innocent parties should suffer on account of the fraud of a third person'.[29] The facts were that one Wallis, for the purposes of cheating, set up in business as Hallam and Co., and got notepaper prepared for the purpose, 'at the head of which was a representation of a large factory with a number of chimneys, and in one corner was a printed statement that Hallam and Co. had depots and agencies in Belfast, Lille and Ghent'.[30] The letter ordered some goods which were sent but never paid for. Lord Justice A.L. Smith had no doubt that there was a contract in these circumstances: 'The question was, with whom, upon this evidence, which was all one way, did the plaintiffs contract to sell the goods? Clearly with the writer of the letters.'[31] The fact that Wallis had used an *alias* did not void the contract, for the simple reason that the identity of 'the entity called Wallis' was not part of the subject-matter of the agreement.

In *Cundy* v *Lindsay* the House of Lords, being, some suppose, difficult, took a different view. The clue to their Lordships' reasoning may be taken from a rather different and seemingly incidental circumstance of the case, namely, the subject-matter of the contested agreement, handkerchiefs made of cloth from Flanders. The initial question to be posed in the broadest literary and analytic sense of interpretation is that of the significance of sending a large quantity of handkerchiefs to the wrong address. It is, of course, a principle of *onirocriticism* or interpretation of dreams that

---

27 *Kennedy* v *The Panama, New Zealand and Australian Royal Mail Co.* (1867) LR 2 QB 580 (per Blackburn J.). *Bell* v *Lever Brothers* [1932] AC 161, talks in terms of 'essential' or 'fundamental' qualities; while, most recently, in *Associated Japanese Bank Int. Ltd.* v *Crédit du Nord* [1988] 3 All ER 902, the doctrine of *error in substantia* has again been explicitly recognised. For a highly informative discussion of medieval theories of mistake, see James Gordley, *The Philosophical Origins of Modern Contract Doctrine*, Oxford, Oxford University Press, 1991, at pp. 57–61; for an interesting discussion of Pothier and the early case-law, see J.C. Smith and J.A.C. Thomas, 'Pothier and the Three Dots' (1957) 20 *Modern Law Review*, 38.

28 As in *Boulton* v *Jones and Another* (1857) 2 H & N 564.

29 *King's Norton Metal*, at p. 99, col. 1.

30 Ibid.

31 Ibid., at 99, col. 2.

'nothing is dreamed of in vain'[32] and a corresponding principle can be offered in interpreting case-law, no fact can be ignored. The handkerchiefs, which are sent to the wrong address in Wood Street, Cheapside, but are taken into a room off Little Love Lane, can be interpreted in a number of ways. Most obviously, the handkerchief is a sign within a series of different codes and the sending of handkerchiefs is a double signification or, in an appropriately baroque terminology, an enfolding of codes. From contemporary gay culture's use of the handkerchief to signal sexual preferences to the courtly code of chivalry, the handkerchief is an essential and shifting sign. Desdemona's dropped handkerchief in *Othello* foretells her death, other handkerchiefs are oracles of other plots or hidden things: the white handkerchief signals surrender, the scented handkerchief love, while other gestures related to the handkerchief portray sympathy or violence, madness or desire. There is no great distance of principle between the handkerchiefs dipped in the blood of the dead Caesar, and the 'Veronique', the handkerchief handed to Christ by Veronica at the seventh station of the Cross and with which he wiped his brow. Each symbolic use of the handkerchief signals an image of desire in the same sense that the knot in the handkerchief seeks to remind the amnesiac that there ought to be something to remember, that it is good or erotic to recall what has already passed, that there must be desire for there to be memory. As to the knot itself it might also be appropriate to recall the relation between memory and repression. Nietzsche writes in a missing fragment of having lost his handkerchief, a fragment which is most usually interpreted in terms of abandonment to pleasure; he lost his handkerchief and so his repression, he lost his monogram and his memory – a loss which should probably be interpreted as the sign of a 'gay science' or 'joyful wisdom'.[33]

The specific rites and rules relating to the different codes and manners of circulation of the handkerchief are too numerous to elaborate. The handkerchief is evidence or proof, it is invitation or seduction, it is a standard or flag, and marks both lust and sorrow, departure and mourning, identity and defeat. The proximity of the handkerchief, on the one hand, to tears, and on the other hand, to the veil or mask is sufficient to indicate the baroque potential and expansiveness of signifying uses to which the humble cambric can be put. Returning to the circumstances of our case, the handkerchiefs that are in some sense spirited away on Little

---

32 H. Cornelius Agrippa, *Of the Vanitie and Uncertaintie of Artes and Sciences*, London, H. Bynneman, 1575, at sig. 52ᵛ. For an important contemporary discussion of such method, see Carlo Ginzburg, *Myths, Emblems, Clues*, London, Radius, 1990, at pp. 96–125.

33 Nietzsche was, of course, a contemporary of the decision in *Cundy* v *Lindsay* and would have interpreted the handkerchief as a sign of repression, a symbolism which is extravagantly and brilliantly exploited by the artist Max Klinger, a contemporary and compatriot of Nietzsche's.

Love Lane, there can no doubt that the handkerchiefs symbolise in a fairly direct sense a sorrow that affects all the parties involved in the narrative.[34] The handkerchiefs represent a double loss, that of the addressee and also of the sign: the letter *and* the handkerchief fail to arrive at their destination.[35] The handkerchief which fails to arrive, the handkerchief as the emblem of transmission, of the passing on of meaning, is almost predestined to loss, bound or ordained to failure. A triple mourning thus ensues upon the duality of loss. In the inverse order of their materiality: there is the mourning appropriate to the failure of meaning; there is that of postal 'destinerrancy', of the letter, envelope, invagination or package that does not arrive; there is finally the absence of the handkerchiefs and so the loss of the means of mouring itself, a reflexive loss which might also be interpreted according to a certain feminist logic in that women were predominantly the bearers or subjects of the handkerchief as sign – men, after all, had moustaches as well as *mouchoirs*.

The handkerchief is predominantly both a figure or sign of sorrow and its means of expression and it is as such a sign that it will play its more important interpretative role. The handkerchief is in this sense a metonymic figure and is most broadly used to indicate emotions, amorous trysts or mournful departures within romantic narratives that could not represent passion or sorrow in any more direct way. The handkerchief thus relays emotions that could not be spoken, it enfolds as a text a series of messages which, due to departure, death or some other physical circumstance or social code could not be directly expressed. The handkerchief imparts its emotive message across a certain geographical or semantic distance: it waves or signals, it absorbs the tears of loss or it passes an illicit message. In each case it is a sign for something absent, a communication *inter absentes*, an essential form or fold of a communication which could not otherwise be sent. Such, of course, is the structure or law of the sign as well as of the handkerchief: the sign signals across the indeterminate and indeterminable space of memory and as such it is always a reminder of death. The sign transmits and so preserves the image or memory, desire or death, which precedes enunciation and informs us

---

34 One of the earliest works directly concerned with the link between mourning and handkerchiefs is Thomas Allestree, *A Funeral Handkerchief*, London, for the author, 1671. This remarkable work places the handkerchief firmly in a theological context and links it to femininity and to weeping. The handkerchief, in a sense, is here supposed to stem the flow of those that 'weep immoderately', or engage in 'irregular' or 'inordinate passion'.

35 On 'destinerrancy' in this context, see Jacques Derrida, 'Pour l'amour de Lacan' (1994) 16 *Cardozo Law Review* 699 ('That too is one of the most common phenomena of destinerrancy which imposes on the destination of the letter an internal drift [*dérive interne*] which may never return, but which always brings us back'). See also on the question of destination, Derrida, *The Post Card*, Chicago, Chicago University Press, 1987, at p. 58 ('Once intercepted – a second suffices – the message [*mouchoir*] no longer has any chance of reaching any determinable person, in any determinable place whatsoever').

that it is never only 'our language' or intention which is passed through speech or writing. The sign as handkerchief, the symbol or name alike inscribe a fate or distant cause upon the individual or subject. It is in this sense the function of transmission to indicate the ephemerality of each instant sign, fragility or defeasibility of every signature, identity or other mark.

The obvious if oneiric relation between subject-matter and law in *Cundy* thus becomes somewhat more apparent. The handkerchief signifies a case concerned essentially with signs. The handkerchief symbolises an emotive and complex message, it is the other text or allegory of the law, the sign of a certain mourning for the past or for the laws that have been handed down from origins or immemorial sources which both exceed and survive the present. The origin is first and is to be viewed in law as *instar omnium*, the source of all. The origin is good and so lost, and what is mourned is thus the virtue of the ancestors and in their place and time the justice that nature or divinity bequeathed to law, a justice enfolded in law and for which the lawyer needs both handkerchief and memory, mnemonic and precedent. The handkerchief is thus a sign also and quite directly of the questions of communication and transmission with which all law is concerned. The handkerchief will return, but for the moment it can provide the first clue as to the doctrinal decision in *Cundy*, namely that the case itself involves a complex transmission of canon and civil law norms in a context in which the concern with the innocence of the parties forces the court to resort to criteria drawn from a much more venerable and mixed tradition of law than simple Anglican precedent. The immediate issue concerns forms of communication between absent parties, and specifically the uses and legal effects of the representation of absent presence, through signature, name and address. The analysis will endeavour to reconstruct the institutional past of these categories and so endeavour to understand the genealogy of a specific rule.

The issue of identity at common law is predicated upon conceptions of presence and of visibility. What is in essence at issue is the differentiation of degrees of presence and correlatively of the various forms of representation of absence. The rules govern both the identity of persons and of documents and things. Some of the earliest cases concerned with mistaken identity were thus concerned with documents and their content rather than directly with persons. The rules relating to *non est factum*, or documents mistakenly signed, were developed around conceptions of capacity, comprehension or vision, rather than being directly concerned with immediacy or presence in its corporeal sense and sentiment. Thus the earliest rules relating to mistake reported in the *Digest* are concerned with blindness and incomprehension:

> what if the purchaser were blind or a mistake over the material were made by a purchaser unskilled (*in minus perito*) in distinguishing

materials? Do we say that the parties are agreed on the thing? How can a man agree who cannot see (*qui non vidit*)?[36]

In reliance on this principle, the blind or illiterate could plead *non est factum* where, incorrectly informed of the contents, they had signed documents whose contents they had not seen or had not understood.[37] So too, if a married woman entered a contract without the consent of her husband, she could also plead *non est factum* as not having the capacity or will to sign the deed.[38]

The notions of blindness and incomprehension, of external and internal vision as the related criteria by which to identify either a document or a thing, both presence and meaning, have a similar role in relation to physical presence. Identity is rooted in the notion of sameness, the person must be *idem*, the same, just as much as the agreement must be *ad idem*, or concerned with the same thing. It is with the various ways in which the sameness underlying identity can be disclosed that the common law tradition has grappled. The first source of rules governing identity is generally taken to be the Lord Chancellor Francis Bacon in *Elements of the Common Lawes of England*.[39] He is cited as authority for the maxim *praesentia corporis tollit errorem nominis* – physical presence erases error by name or, more broadly, 'if the thing be identified, a mistake over its name makes no difference'.[40] The example which Bacon gives is of a gift: 'if I give a horse to I.D. being present, and say unto him, I.S. take this, this is a good gift, notwithstanding I call him by the wrong name.'[41] The logic behind the rule is that of the priority of visibility or presence over other forms of reference. In Bacon's own analysis:

> there be three degrees of certainty: 1. Presence 2. Name 3. Demonstration or reference . . . whereof the Presence the law holdeth of greatest dignitie, the Name the second degree, and the Demonstration or Reference in the lowest, and always the errour or falsitie in the lesse worthy.[42]

In *Cundy v Lindsay* there is no question of presence, but rather the issue is that of the determination of identity *inter absentes* in an agreement reached through the post:

36 *Digest* 18.1.11 (Ulpian).
37 Thus, see *Esthall* v *Esthall* (1313) YB 6 & 7 Ed; 27 Selden Society 21; *Thoroughgood's Case* (1582) 2 Co Rep 9 a; *Foster v Mackinnon* (1869) LR 4 CP 704.
38 Anon., *Baron and Feme: A Treatise of the common law concerning Husbands and Wives*, London, Walthoe, 1700, at p. 4–5: 'If a feme covert enter into bond, non est factum may be pleaded to it.'
39 Thus, for example, the reference in *Ingram v Little* (per Pearce LJ). Reference is to Bacon, *Maximes of the Law*, pp. at 96–101.
40 Digest 18.1.9.1 (Ulpian) 'nihil enim facit error nominis, cum de corpore constat'.
41 Bacon, *Elements* at pp. 96–97.
42 Ibid., at p. 96.

your Lordships are not here embarrassed by any conflict of evidence, or any evidence whatsoever as to conversations or acts done, the history of the whole transaction lies upon paper. The principal parties concerned, the Respondents and *Blenkarn*, never came in contact personally – everything that was done was done by writing.[43]

An agreement made *inter absentes* is of a different degree of certainty than that made by parties present to themselves and to each other. Again following Bacon's *Maximes of the Law*, there is an intermediate category between presence and name:

like law is it, but more doubtfull, where there is not a presence but a kinde of representation, which is less worthie than a presence, and yet more worthie than a Name or Reference . . . . As if I covenant with my ward, that I will tender unto him no other marriage, than a gentlewoman, whose picture I delivered unto him, and that picture hath about it *aetatis suae anno* 16 and the gentlewoman is 17 years old, yet nevertheless if it can be proved that the picture was made for the gentlewoman, I may notwithstanding this mistaking, tender her well enough . . . .[44]

The most relevant feature of the example is the use of a portrait to identify the person: a stolen presence, the face of one absent, may act as the representation of the body and not simply of the name. In an important sense, the body substantiates the name, although the name and indeed the portrait equally legitimate or display the family likeness, the social place of the subject – the English face.[45] The distinction is important in that the name is 'less worthie' and is understood legally as a species of demonstration or description that at its best mimicks the representation of a picture. Unembarrassed by, or in the absence of either presence or a picture, the Court in *Cundy* v *Lindsay* had merely to judge 'the conclusion to be derived from that writing, as applied to the admitted facts of the case'.[46] The writing in question was, as described earlier, a correspondence in which, by means of ambiguous or false signature and address,

Blenkarn, by the mode in which his letters and his applications to the Respondents were made out, and by the way in which he left uncorrected the mode and form in which, in turn he was addressed by the Respondents; by all those means he led, and intended to lead, the

---

43 *Cundy* v *Lindsay*, at 464–465.
44 Bacon, *Elements*, at p. 97.
45 On portraiture as representation of family see Pierre Legendre, *L'Inestimable objet*, at pp. 35–36; for a recent study of portraiture, see Richard Brilliant, *Portraiture*, London, Reaktion, 1991.
46 *Cundy* v *Lindsay*, at 465.

Respondents to believe, that the person with whom they were com-
municating . . . was Blenkiron and Co.[47]

The question, of course, is how to determine the identity of an absent
person. If there is no portrait then the issue becomes one of scriptural
demonstration, of showing or seeing by words, and while a proper name
is the 'most certain' demonstration, it is not immediately apparent that it
differs in kind from other sorts of appellation, additions or notes of the
person, as that someone is 'son of such a man, wife of such a husband; or
addition of office'. The examples which are given of 'demonstration' of the
person, however, distinguish the essential quality of the name from other
accidental features. To make an obligation

> I.S. filio et haeredi G.S. where indeed he is a bastard, yet this obligation
> is good. . . . But, by converse, if I grant land to I.S. filio et haeredi G.S.
> and it be true that he is son and heir unto G.S. but his name is Thomas,
> this is a void grant.[48]

Similarly, a grant of land to the Bishop of London

> who instructed me in my childhood, this is a good grant, although he
> never instructed me . . . but if it was the Bishop of Canterbury who
> instructed me in my childhood, yet shall it be good to the Bishop of
> London and not to the Bishop of Canterbury.[49]

The latter example is a strong one in the sense that it adopts a rigorously
nominalist view of the order and relation of language to things. Mistake
as to the motive of the gift is of less significance than the bond between
name and body or person, word and thing.

The relation of the sign to its referent becomes of the essence of the
decision in *Cundy*. A false signature and a misleading address led to the
misappropriation of handkerchiefs on Little Love Lane. Spared the embarrassment of having actually met or indeed of having been introduced,
the mistake of identity made by Lindsay and Co. turned the contract into
a 'pretence', a 'failure'.[50] The then Lord Chancellor, Lord Cairns, thus
states that there could be no contract because the seller had no intention
of dealing with Blenkarn 'the dishonest man. Of him they knew nothing,
and of him they never thought'.[51] The problem with this view, however,
is that the fact that the seller neither knew nor thought of the identity of
the dishonest man is indicative of the fact that his identity was not a

47 Ibid., at 465. Also at 467: credit was obtained 'by a falsification of the signature of the
   *Blenkirons*, writing his name in such a manner as that it appeared to represent the signature
   of that firm' (Lord Hatherley).
48 Bacon, *Elements*, at p. 102.
49 Ibid.. at pp. 102–103.
50 *Cundy* v *Lindsay*, at 466.
51 *Cundy* v *Lindsay*, at 465.

significant feature of the agreement. What was at issue was the status of a false signature and a misleading address as 'demonstrations' or 'references' to a proper name and so to a dignity or person. In other words, the common lawyers, in this instance, become confused by virtue of failing to understand the doctrinal basis of the issue, that the question of presence and absence is always a question of representation and of the reference of image or face or word to bodies or things. The decision is an instance of what Sir Thomas Ridley ironically termed 'the Midas touch of common law', namely, the bizarre belief that anything named or touched by common law is immediately 'transubstantiated' into a temporal and relative thing without either spiritual or civilian past.[52]

The opposite is the case. In the terms of Bacon's transcription of the classical law, there was, in *Cundy*, an error of both name and demonstration or reference. While *veritas nominis tollit errorem demonstrationis*,[53] the court were happy to find that the name itself was forged or in error. In which case the proper finding should be error on both counts, error of name and reference, or, as Petrus has it 'error of the person one is contracting with prevents a transfer of ownership when it falls on the substance of the person (*circa substantiam persone*)'.[54] Contrary to the logic of the decision in *Cundy* and to that in *King's Norton Metals*, it is not a subjective question of intention but an objective question of name and reference, a question which depends in the end upon complex civilian and canon law norms not simply of designation but also of transmission and inheritance whereby the name is passed in the form of succession from generation to generation. It is a question, as indicated earlier, of genealogy as the form and model of transmission and it is to that issue of transmission at the level of language or structure that I will return by way of conclusion.

## NOMINA OSSIBUS INHAERENT

The case of *Cundy* v *Lindsay* returns us ultimately to Budé's love, to *Philologia*, to the relation of masculine to feminine and, in sum, to the recovery and custody of law and belief in the texts of an ambivalent Roman tradition. The law is classically defined as a name, and similarly the study of law, philology, is the study of the meaning of words and most particularly of nouns or names. In this context it is surprising that the English courts have tried to deal with questions of identity and of the signing of the name in terms of intention. The confusion of the position is most clearly signalled in the incidental remarks which the judges make

52 Sir Thomas Ridley, *A View of the Civille and Ecclesiasticall Law, and wherein the Practise of them is streitened and may be relieved within this land*, Oxford, H. Hall, 1607, at p. 228.
53 Bacon, *Elements*, at p. 96 (truth of the name erases error of demonstration).
54 Petrus de Bellapertica, *Quaestiones vel distinctiones*, Lyons, 1517, q 391.

with reference to the hypothetical version of the same facts as those in *Cundy* repeated *inter praesentes*. As Lord Hatherley put it:

> suppose this fraudulent person had gone himself to the firm from whom he wished to obtain goods, and had represented that he was a member of one of the largest firms in London. Suppose on his making that representation the goods had been delivered to him. Now I am very far, at all events on the present occasion, from seeing my way to this, that the goods being sold to him as representing that firm he could be treated in any other way than as an agent of that firm . . . .[55]

Lord Penzance remarked of the same hypothetical

> I do not think it necessary to express an opinion upon the possible effect of some cases which I can imagine to happen of this character, because none of such cases can I think be parallel with that which your Lordships have now to decide.[56]

The problem faced by the judges is that the issue *inter praesentes* is the same, in substance if not in degree, as that *inter absentes*. It is a question of the representation of identity in the three degrees of body, name and demonstration. The issue, in other words, is one of reference and not of intention and it requires reconstruction according to the laws of reference, according to which even the body is an image or reference, a 'spectacle of things invisible'. The question of representation is tied to genealogy and it can be reconstructed in terms of the hierarchies of appearance or visibility. The handkerchief could indeed again act as the emblem of reference. To the extent that the handkerchief is a veil or shroud or mask, to the extent also that it is a sign and signals, it does so without inscription. Curiously, the significance of the handkerchief as a sign resides in its sending and not in its substance or representation. It is a pure sign, as, for example, in Rousseau's discussion of the salaam, the handkerchief sent, via the eunuch, to a lover in a harem, it speaks to the eye and is more effective for that very reason than language or prose.[57] The handkerchief, according to the earlier testimony of Andreas Capellanus' *De amore*, is a legitimate sign or token of love for a similar reason. It gives nothing away insofar as it does not represent its sender, and yet it says everything in that unlike the word it exists on the border of visibility and marks the reference from image or sign to that which it signifies (*ab imagine ad rem significatem*).[58]

55 *Cundy* v *Lindsay*, at 468–469.
56 *Cundy* v *Lindsay*, at 471. It could be observed here that the extraordinary confusion of the common law in relation to mistaken identity *inter praesentes*, stems largely from the vagaries of this judgment.
57 J.-J. Rousseau, *Essai sur l'origine des langues*, Paris, Nizet, 1970 edn, at p. 22. Discussed in Goodrich, *Languages of Law*, at p. 155ff.
58 Andreas Capellanus, *Tractatus amoris et de amoris remedio*, Havaniae, Gadiana, 1186, 1892 edn, at p. 293.

In this respect the handkerchief itself represents the most perfect form of sign, the *acheiropoietic* image, the sign which signals without the intervention of human artifice or hand, the cloth or linen veil which has imprinted on it the face of the divinity or some other imprint of God without art or brush, as with *Christus dolens* or the Turin shroud.[59]

The *acheiropoietic* image is the visible form of the word, the flesh, and it is equally the purest form of visual symptom or of presentation. To this it can be added briefly that

> the most striking feature of [these images] is that they are in general inscribed on the most trivial, or excessively humble, objects, thus being displayed upon material as simple as rag. Handkerchiefs (*mouchoirs*) of old flax or linen or charred shroud, they exhibit only the assumed – yet exorbitant – privilege of having been touched by the divinity. They are relics as much as they are icons. This is why they have for so long been endowed with the capacity to reveal, despite the fact that they are generally presented as simple veils (*voiles*).[60]

Within the patristic tradition, the *acheiropoietic* image is simply the purest sign, the clearest and closest symptom of a lack, of a reference to an absence. All true images within the Christian tradition are but a form of mourning, they are vestiges or imprints of a loss of presence that dates back to the Fall. And the handkerchief is perhaps as good an emblem of the pure image as could be found within a Protestant or iconoclast tradition: it shows a God which cannot and should not be represented, a God of which there should be neither external nor 'inward images', neither painted representation nor 'phantasm of God in our minds'.[61]

The more secular point to be made is that the legal conception of sign and of reference is theological in its sources or derivation. The word is explicitly an image and its truth relates to its reference or to the imprint of divinity or inheritance that it retains on its surface. Without embarking upon another analysis of the linguistic history of common law it can simply be stated that the secular tradition of law replaced the plastic image by the word, but equally that the word was *imago* or sign of the Father, of 'he who sent us', and should be understood and interpreted in that sense. The word, like the iconic image, is a sign of its prototype:

> what are these prototypes? Very specifically, they are again images (God, the Virgin; the persons of the saints whom humans should

---

59 On the Turin shroud and the Christus dolens, see the discussion in Louis Marin, 'Figurabilité du visuel: la Véronique ou la question du portrait à Port-Royal' (1987) 35 *Nouvelle revue de psychanalyse* 51. See also Louis Marin, *De la représentation*, Paris: Gallimard, 1994, at pp. 62–70.

60 Georges Didi-Huberman, *Devant l'image*, Paris, Editions de Minuit, 1990 at pp. 224–225. See also Alain Boreau, 'Vues de l'esprit' (1987) 35 *Nouvelle revue de psychanalyse* 67.

61 Edward Stillingfleet, *A Discourse Concerning the Idolatry practised in the Church of Rome*, London, H. Mortlock, 1671, at p. 79.

*resemble*); I could equally well say: they are names. *Images and names*, towards which are directed ritual gestures of love (kissing), respect (baring the head), and fear (genuflection), formulations which are themselves legally classified and which, by virtue of this fact, raise a problem of sanction.[62]

The point to be stressed in the context of the present analysis is that body and name are alike images in the strong sense of being representations of an absent source whether that source be formulated as God or father, spirit or unwritten law. In Selden's words, 'the best or first I took always for *instar omnium*'.[63]

The word should be loved, the name respected and the body honoured. Each is an image of a prototype, each represents another scene or further jurisdiction of law. In relation to the case-law and specifically to *Cundy* v *Lindsay*, the contract made under the influence of a mistake as to identity is a hard case. It raises a peculiar and painful issue of justice in the form of the innocence of both the parties at suit. It is, therefore, not unreasonable to view it as a problem not only of law but of equity and to point to the fact that in equity 'the name inheres in the bones'.[64] The issues of justice or conscience force recourse to another law within which the criterion for deciding the reference of the name is predicated upon a genealogical criterion: the name inheres in the bones is the canon law equivalent of a *ius imaginum* which ruled that the *imago*, image or death mask of the face of the ancestor, was both *ossa* and *nomen*, both bone and name, both sign and real entity or body.[65] That the name inheres in the bones refers to the fact that the name is a reference to an honour and obligation, to the fact that *nomen* is *vinculum* or bond, it is a 'title of antiquity', a 'virtue of the fathers', it precedes the subject and in a dual sense is born within and carried throughout a life. Both body and name, bone and sign are in other words related not only to the extant subject but to its cause or destiny, the immediate cause being the family and the mediate or more distant cause being the law of nature or divinity.

Viewed from the perspective of the two laws or *utrumque ius*, the distinction between the apparently conflicting decisions on mistaken identity *inter absentes* can be given a different resolution. In *Cundy* there was error of demonstration, together with a species of error of name. The source of the error of name lay in Blenkarn's 'falsification of the signature of the *Blenkirons*, writing his own name in such a manner as that it

---

62 Legendre, *Le Désir politique de Dieu*, at p. 228.
63 John Selden, *Titles of Honour*, London, N. Stansby, 1614, at fol. C 4 b.
64 This glossatorial maxim is discussed in E. Genzmer, 'Nominis ossibus inhaerent', *Mélanges Melan*, Lausanne, 1963; it is also discussed in Legendre, *L'Inestimable objet*, at p. 337. The reference is to Accursius, *Corpus Iuris Civilis commentariis Accursii*, Lugduni, 1627, gloss to Digest 17.2.3 proem.
65 See Selden, *Titles of Honour*, at fol. a 3 b ff.

appeared to represent the signature of that firm'.[66] The name in this instance, Blenkiron, had a reference but had been manipulated deceitfully or by misprision. The deceit was grounds for voiding the contract, but it is harder to argue that the mistake as to identity could be genuine grounds for finding that the contract was void *ab initio*. It was a case in which a party assumed the name of another but the sign, image or word, manipulated was not an invention and could not be treated as either meaningless or as a nullity. In *King's Norton Metals*, on the other hand, the fraudulent party entering the contract was the entirely fictive entity *Hallam and Co.*, an invented company and hence a fiction of a fiction, a sign which represented nothing.[67] In the latter case, in other words, the argument as regards error of name is much stronger than in *Cundy*. It is, in consequence, much easier to argue that there was no contract in *King's Norton Metals* than it is in relation to the firm that was 'fooled' and sent handkerchiefs to a wrong address, to Little Love Lane, in *Cundy*. In *King's Norton Metals* the plaintiff firm had endeavoured to sell goods to a company that did not and had never existed. The error of name is thus much stronger and indeed comes close to being the nominal equivalent of *res extincta*: how could a contract be formed with a name which referred to nothing? How, in more classical terms, could a court condone the notion of entering a legal relation with an 'improper' name, with dead letters, with an image without either substance or reference, a 'vanitie', an idol, of which the canon law says *idolum nihil representat, quod subsistat*, for the idol is *rei mortua*, a dead thing.[68] In short, the mistake as to identity was much more substantial in the latter case than in the former, a conclusion that can in many senses be supported by later case-law.[69]

It remains, finally, to ask what else can be read in this precedent from the 1870s? What is transmitted by and through this example? Of what is the handkerchief an *acheiropoietic* – and so lawful – sign? The answer, of course, is that the transmission of law is not simply a matter of law but is also a question of genealogy and of the incidental, marginal, symptomatic and circumstantial features of institutional texts. What the analysis of transmission suggests is nothing less than a species of therapy for the

---

66 *Cundy* v *Lindsay*, at 467.
67 The corporation, of course, is described historically as *nomina iuris, a nomen intellectuale*. See Ernst Kantorowicz, *The King's Two Bodies*, Princeton, Princeton University Press, 1957, ch. 2.
68 The definitions are taken from N. Sander, *A Treatise of the Images of Christ and his Saints*, Omers, J. Heigham, 1624, at p. 109. For further discussion, see H. Hammond, *Of Idolatry*, Oxford, H. Hall, 1646, at p. 1–5.
69 It is indeed a conclusion arrived at in the case of *Newborne* v *Sensolid (Great Britain)*, where the name in question was Leopold Newborne (London) Ltd a prospective limited company which had not been registered at the time that its promoter and future director, Leopold Newborne, entered a contract with the defendant. As the company did not exist at the time of the contract, it was held by the Court of Appeal that the contract was a nullity.

self-effacement or erasure of those caught up in or otherwise addicted to the interpretation of law. Such therapy takes the form of tracing the varying identities and differing jurisdictions of law so as to comprehend something of the desire which motivates law's textuality and drives its interpreters. Like all the arts, the practice and interpretation of law involves in no small measure that peculiar delirium which constitutes belief in the object of the art of law, namely, the phantasmatic bridging of the gap between legal rule and legal judgment, precedent and decision. It is that obscure object of judgment, the phantasm, the unconscious of law that can only be studied and understood through the painstaking and often painful reconstruction of the pleasure of the text, of the desires and the phantasms of its interpretation. There is a certain madness or at least infidelity in the study of law and as the anecdote of Guillaume Budé lost in love and lost in texts was designed to illustrate, we forget that madness at our peril.

At the level of doctrine the case of the purloined handkerchiefs is a case concerned with certain exemplary features of identity. The mistaken identity is exemplary of the fragile and misrecognised quality of identity as such. The exception, the difference or dissimulation, precedes and determines the rule. Specifically, through obscuring or forging a signature and using a wrong address, the appropriately named Little Love Lane, the case of the handkerchiefs which do not reach their destination can act as an emblem of all transmission or the passing on of all meaning. More precisely, the loss of the handkerchiefs occurs through the circulation of a false identity, the erroneous representation of a name. I have suggested that this illicit slippage of the signifier was a breach of contract. It was so serious a breach that the Court held that there was no contract at all, that this play with the order of names and the certainty of signs was a modern form of legal sacrilege or offence to meaning as such. What was at stake, and what legitimated the decision in *Cundy* v *Lindsay*, was the monstrous act of assuming the identity of another, stealing a name or purloining an image, both *ossa* and *nomen*. This was classically a form of treason, it was *crimen falsi*, not simply forgery but abuse of the name and so an offence within the order of honour and correlatively of spirit. The soul was harmed by the theft of symbols. More abstractly, the disassociation of signifier from signified was a disrespect and a threat to the order of transmission. The breach of contract, in other words, was in essence a breach of a much deeper order of contract or contraction, that of the social and specifically that of the symbolic. If word and referent, signifier and signified, were to become unattached then the law would fail as also would the order of generations, of meaning and of inheritance upon which law is based. The theft of handkerchiefs threatened to breach the security or legality of the social contract in its deepest substratum, that of meaning. In doing so it threatened the order of names and of laws. It challenged the meaning of words and so too it endangered the destination of laws. For a while the handkerchiefs were lost. Handkerchiefs have been lost and handkerchiefs will be lost. It is, one might conclude, of the essence of handkerchiefs to be dropped and so lost, as also it is their function to signal loss and to help us come to terms – to mourn – that loss.

# Chapter 7

# Fate as seduction
## The other scene of legal judgment

Fate . . . . is a great wooden vessel which among Brewers in London is ordinarily used at this day to measure Mault by, containing a Quarter, which they have for expedition in measuring.[1]

What is law?
Destiny, Sir. Destiny.[2]

The defining feature of legal modernity lies in the attempt to make law self-founding. Unable or unwilling any longer to justify or found law upon nature, justice, right or contract, jurisprudence was forced to seek the legitimacy of law, the justification of judgment and the criterion of legality, within law itself. The science of law was thus predicated upon closure.[3] It sought to replace a jurisprudence based upon theocracy, nature or ethics with a secular conception of a self-regulating system of norms or rules. The crisis of legal modernity and of its hermeneutics, its interminable theories of interpretation, lies in its failure to address the issues that were

---

1 John Cowell, *The Interpreter: Or Booke Containing the Signification of Words*, London, W. Sheares, 1608/1627.
2 Mervyn Peake, *Titus Groan*, Harmondsworth, Penguin, 1976, at p. 202.
3 For a sophisticated introduction to the senses of legal closure, see I. Stewart, 'Law and Closure' (1987) 50 *Modern Law Review* 908; and I. Stewart, 'The Critical Legal Science of Hans Kelsen' (1990) 17 *Journal of Law and Society* 273, at 279, distinguishing practical reason, as the prescriptive function of will, from the Kantian idea of purity as following 'from [a] firm adherence to the logical law of identity, that each thing is what it is and not something else. Any statement of something, therefore, must state it as what it is and without admixture. Such a statement will be pure'. Contemporary European debates around the issue of legal closure have tended to centre around Luhman's conception of autopoiesis, depicted by F. Ewald, 'The Law of Law', in G. Teubner (ed.), *Autopoietic Law*, Florence, European University Press, 1988, as an extension of Kelsen's thesis:

> To be sure it rejects the hypothesis of the fundamental norm in favour of the idea of an interaction, of a correlation, of some solidarity among norms. But this is a secondary proposition by comparison with the reconfirmed thesis that law can have no other reference than itself.

For a recent statement of Luhmann's own view, see N. Luhmann, *Essays on Self-Reference*, New York, Columbia University Press, 1990.

previously posed in terms of nature or ethics, in terms of legal foundation or ultimate canons, causes or reasons.

As the metaphor of closure suggests, a self-regulating science is shut up or enclosed, it is silent or at least cannot speak of foundation but must rather presupppose it.[4] In etymological terms it is not simply a question of circularity: the Latin root of closure, *claudo*, not only means to close, end, terminate or finish – to die – but also refers to something crippled, lame or defective, and so by implication it refers to something approaching its fate or coming towards death. To invoke the problematic of closure is necessarily to address the question of death as the repressed object of institutional structure, as the fate which comes without reason, consideration or pretext, as the law of law. The end, closure or terminus of law refers ultimately to the finality of the institution as the legal structure or limit of personality, the closure of law is here a negative or indirect expression of its finitude. Closure is correlatively, though in more secular terms, a reference to the modern positivised conception of law as an autonomous system of judgment enclosed by its self-appointed criteria of normative legitimacy.[5] It is in this sense a reference to the death of legal interpretation as an ethical practice, as an aesthetic or art. In the ensuing analysis, I will examine first the latter, broader meaning of the death of law in terms of the closure or demise of an institution whose very protocols of interpretation or enactment sever its relation to the lifeworld. Its interpretative closure, it will be argued, is its death precisely because such closure constitutes mundane sociality, its practices and forms of life, as the outside or other of law. It is a question, therefore, of addressing the death of law in terms of the fatality of that institution which represents the call of the dead in the form of the pre-existent structure of historical being and the morbidity of its protocols and other interpretative rules. The image or mask of law is also the fate of individuality as subject to an inevitable progress or call towards a prospective death whose event is masked by the prior death of law.

---

4   On the transcendental logical presupposition, see H. Kelsen, *The Pure Theory of Law*, Berkeley, University of California Press, 1967, at p. 75:

> By defining law as a norm and by limiting the science of law to the cognition and description of legal norms and to the norm-determined relations between norm-determined facts, the law is delimited against nature, and the science of law as a science of norms is delimited against all other sciences that are directed toward causal cognition of actual happenings.

For a different view of foundation in self-reference, see S. Fish, 'Dennis Martinez and the Uses of Theory', in *idem, Doing What Comes Naturally*, Oxford, Oxford University Press, 1990.

5   F. Kafka, 'The Parable of the Law', in *idem, The Trial*, Harmondsworth, Penguin, 1976. See, for jurisprudential commentaries, J. Derrida, 'Prejuges, devant la loi', in J. Derrida, J. Luc-Nancy and J.-F. Lyotard (eds), *La Faculté de juger*, Paris, Editions de Minuit, 1985. P. Legendre, *L'Empire de la vérité*, at p. 107; and also I. Stewart, 'Sociology in Jurisprudence', in B. Fryer (ed.), *Law, State and Society*, London, Croom Helm, 1981.

## DEATH AND LAW

In an immediate and frequently observed sense, the death of law refers to the demise of a particular tradition and meaning of legality, or more specifically of legal judgment.[6] Classical jurisprudence had historically associated law with both an origin and an end or goal, a fatality, which exceeded its merely positive status and norms. The life of law belonged to a reason, art or cause which preceded and survived its mere administration or simple acts of judgment. To separate law from its cause was to separate law from life. More particularly, it was to divest law of the possibility of becoming, of creating new meanings or participating in a politics of interpretation which takes place across the boundaries of disciplines and their institutions. The positivised conception of law as the brute fact of a system of norms was simultaneously a repression of the possibility of the system having any conscious meaning, any indeterminacy, which would relate law as fate, as judgment without reason, consideration or pretext, to its moments of temporal presence or application. In this sense, the death of law was hermeneutic: bereft of reason, cause or essence, legality is without life and can neither be defined nor valued.

To take an example from the early era of modern law, we thus find a proleptic criticism of common law, in the mid-seventeenth century, posed in terms of the exile and abandonment of the reason and art of law. A nation such as England, which casts classical jurisprudence and its conceptions of universal reason and supra-national justice out of its territory, 'plainly puts out the light of [its] own laws, and does abandon and exile that mother, of which [its] own laws, for so much as is good in

---

6  For typical statements of this thesis, see P. Legendre, *Le Désir politique de Dieu: études sur les montages de l'état et du droit*, Paris, Fayard, 1989; F. Ewald, *L'Etat providence*, Paris, Grasset, 1986; J. Donzelot, *L'Invention du social*, Paris, Fayard, 1987. In each case, the death of law refers to the demise of any conception of a law of law:

> *the* law does not exist; that which one calls 'law' is a category of thought which does not designate any essence, but rather serves to qualify certain practices: normative practice, practices of constraint and of social sanction no doubt, political practice certainly, practices of rationality as well. These are capable of being very different from each other; the law is in its entirety, without remainder, in each of these practices, without any possibility of anywhere supposing the permanence of an essence.
> (Ewald, *L'Etat providence*, at p. 30)

Similarly,

> we have shattered the seals of the message of the Laws and established that they contain nothing. God the legislator and Nature have ended by disappearing as a setting, or alternatively, are maintained at a distance in the manner of the founding texts of the American constitution, blurred in the aura of a halo.
> (Legendre, *Désir politique de Dieu*, at pp. 29–30)

For a lengthy elegy, see P. Legendre, *Paroles poetiques échapées du texte*, Paris, Seuil, 1982, especially at pp. 212ff.

them, are but the off-spring'.[7] A law founded upon closure or internal to a nation and its system of positive – and all too human – law, a system of purely municipal regulation, is dead in the sense of being irreversibly estranged from the reason, justice and art of universal law. Common law, by virtue of its particularity and its limited territory, is here depicted as

> fitted for the climate of one people only, and serves for the exigencies and occasions of the state, and varies at times and occasions ... [it] commands rather than teaches ... [and] has an eye more to what is profitable to the public, than for what is just or equitable.[8]

The art of law, by contradistinction,

> understands some more universal law, that is commonly embraced and allowed by the best and most potent nations; that is full of equity and true reason, and being grounded upon dictates of nature and common reason, is unchangeable; whose method is to teach and instruct by certain rules and principles orderly and handsomely digested. . . it is the only necessary art.[9]

Without justice, without the learning and knowledge of a reason of law (*ultima ratio*), judgment depends upon 'the wandering fancies and imaginations of men only: . . . under how many several shapes and forms must it needs appear, when the apprehensions and conceptions of men . . . are as different as their visages be?' In short, law dies in the sense that it ceases to be recognisably law because it lacks any referent, justification or foundation beyond its simple existence or acts of self-positing: 'the professors of municipal law must acknowledge that their Book cases (the only learning of their law) must needs fail them here'.[10]

Closure entails loss, in the sense that death is not only absence but, in its transitive form, it is privation. It is also failure, the breakdown of a system. In its more complex connotation, the death of law is not simply its restriction or self-limitation to the plural and changing needs of municipal regulation, but also its 'shutting up', its failure to speak to the issues of justice and judgment, reason and nature that are historically its principal jurisdictions. In the absence of a criterion by reference to which it is possible to judge or value law and to define its 'lawfulness' it is not

---

7  Sir Robert Wiseman, *Lex legum*, translated as *The Law of Laws: or the Excellency of the Civil Law*, London; Royston, 1664, at p. 167.
8  Ibid., at p. 168. For a similar argument, see J. Bodin, *De Republica*, London, Knollers, 1606, at pp. 555–560.
9  Wiseman, *Law of Laws*, at p. 168.
10 Ibid., at pp. 167–168. For similar views expressed from a perspective external to law, see A. Fraunce, *The Lawiers Logike, exemplifying the praecepts of logike by the practise of the common lawe*, London, W. How, 1588, at pp. 119–120. On the failings of a law bound only to acts of self-positing, see the powerful argument in Gillian Rose, *Dialectic of Nihilism*, Oxford, Blackwell, 1984.

simply impossible to criticise or evaluate law but it is equally impossible to know what law is.[11] The death of law becomes synonymous with the arbitrariness of legal judgment: to the extent that law becomes no more and no less than what lawyers do – or jurists recognise – within any given field of legal regulation, the defining feature of law is its non-definition and correlatively the absence of any constraint or limit upon the content, proliferation or practice of such regulation. The death of law in this sense ironically signifies the hyper-inflation of legal practices or of legal regulation: it signifies the death of judgment, death, in Blanchot's terms, being 'the utterly indeterminate, the indeterminate moment and not only the zone of the unending and the indeterminate'.[12] Indifferent in terms of value, purposeless in terms of need and irrational or merely technical in terms of practice, the death of law here refers to the absorption of legality into a series of pragmatic, actuarial and disciplinary administrative practices. Legal judgment is 'crippled' and the value of law subordinated to a series of overriding bureaucratic and normalising concerns: 'nothing can any longer claim identity for itself. Everything changes, unceasingly. The social bond can no longer have the form of an original contract, whose terms would be invariable; these terms can only be continually negotiated and renegotiated'.[13]

In the discussion which follows, I will be concerned less with the positivity of legal closure, the various specifications of legal normativity in terms of theories of sources of law, systematicity or auto-regulation, than with the loss of meaning and the repression of sensibility or judgment that such closure entails. In a stronger and more specific sense, I am concerned with the problematic of judgment which legal modernity repressed and so too with reconstructing such a problematic or form of

11 This point is taken up at great length by Ewald, *L'Etat providence*, at pp. 33–43, 433–437; see, at 433–434, discussing the failure of justice to any longer define or constrain law:

> The law (*loi*) was [historically] judged in the name of a law of law (*droit*); as if one conceived the possibility of a control of law (*loi*) by the law of law (*droit*). That has disappeared entirely now: the law of law (*droit*) is now confounded utterly with positive law; in place of the classical delimitation of the law of law we find substituted a study of sources of law. That is law which is stated as law. A formalism which implies that in place of the control of law by a law of law there is substituted a control of the constitutionality of laws and the jurist is forbidden any critical attitude in the name of law. With regard to the statement of the law, jurists become technicians, practitioners of a law which itself becomes ever more technical. Their task is simply to put the indefinite proliferation of a more and more complex legislative and regulatory arsenal into order. But it is no longer their task to orientate us as to the definition of a politics of law. They are no longer the guardians of law.

12 M. Blanchot, *The Space of Literature*, Lincoln, Nebr., University of Nebraska Press, 1982, at p. 99.

13 Ewald, 'The Law of Law', at p. 44. For an introduction to the logic of risk management, see J. Simon, 'The Ideological Effects of Actuarial Practice' (1988) *Law and Society Review* 111; see further F. Ewald, 'Insurance and Risk', in C. Burchell, C. Gordon and P. Miller (eds), *The Foucault Effect*, Hemel Hempstead, Harvester Wheatsheaf, 1991.

discourse in the languages of fate and destiny, cause and chance, in which they received their classical expression. As will become clear, the motive or deceit underlying such a reconstruction relates to the possibility that the reformulation of the discourses of judgment or the speech of the Fates can serve to reinstate the question of justice, the question of absolute indeterminacy, as the essential and explicit question of the history and practice of law. The function of law is in this respect bound to death as the limit and constraint represented by the image of law as the expression of human fatality. It is bound also to that indeterminacy which speaks the failure of law and so the possibility of life. To represent that indeterminacy is not to reinvoke a lost universal but rather to recognise an absent object of desire, a law of indecision, of that failure, gap or lapse which marks all closure as provisional.

## LAW AND FATE

The thesis of the death of law can be posed either in terms of the twilight of legal ideals, and so characterised in terms of the loss of legal *universalia*,[14] or alternatively it can be approached as a question relating to the decay of legal reason, and specifically to the demise of certain forms of speaking about or invoking legal judgment.[15] In either case, it is first a matter of death and of what it means for an institution to die. Hermeneutically, it is initially a paradox insofar as institutions are by definition legal fictions that do not die: institutions such as religion, law or economics are deep structures embedded in the *longue durée*, they are the forms of (social) life and as such they cannot die: individuals or those who hold offices may die, but structures, offices or forms of sociality are passed on in the indefinite and durable time of tradition.[16] In consequence, to speak of the death of law is to appropriate a metaphor which is contradicted by the classical principle of *lex aeternitas* and the maxim *dignitas [ius] non moritur*. It is also, however, and as a consequence of this paradox, a matter of mixing genres: to speak of the death of law is not only to raise the question of the relation of law to temporality but also to juxtapose law and literature, symbolic and imarginary, and to

---

14 The *universalia* of law are classically associated with laws of nature: 'they are not discovered by stress of arguments or logical demonstrations, but . . . by induction, by the assistance of the senses and the memory', per Sir J. Fortescue, *De Laudibus Legum Angliae*, London, R. Gosling, 1460, at pp. 13–14.

15 On the conception of a rule of judgment, see Ewald, *L'Etat providence*, at pp. 33–40; also F. Ewald, 'Norms, Discipline and the Law', in R. Post (ed.), *Law and the Order of Culture*, Berkeley, University of California Press, 1991. See also J. Boyd White, *Justice as Translation*, Chicago, Chicago University Press, 1990, on a comparable theme, namely the absence of an ethics of judgment, the emergence of a purely technical jurisdiction which exists simply to order regulation without reference or recourse to the rhetorical arts of judgment as translation, character and communal speech.

16 F. Braudel, *On History*, Cambridge, Mass., Harvard University Press, 1980.

suggest that there is a very precise relation of repression between the two genres.

Death is the object and end of literary discourse, it is the subject of poetics and the aesthetic principle of philosophical writing: to the extent that each literature in its turn endeavours to produce an impossible staging or image of the other, of that which cannot be represented because it does not yet exist, it attempts to present the unpresentable in an imaginary (phantasmatic) or symbolic (legal) form. Literature precedes law and subsists within it, marking its history as a narrative of choices or exercises in the language of power and the expression of the choices of fate. Yet law cannot recognise the literary without confronting the possibility of its own demise. Death belongs in this sense to the biography of law and as a literary or metaphoric figure or attribution it is to be understood not as an external force threatening legality but as an internal quality, as an active principle of disintegration, which would be formulated in rhetorical (or aesthetic) terms as *vanitas* or decadence and in psychological terms as an instinct or drive negating both pleasure and reproduction. Philosophically it would be the death of the soul, an extinction which in metaphysical terms is represented as closure or the failure to create, and in mundane terms as injustice in the precise sense of *ressentiment*, passivity or existential inauthenticity, namely a being in flight from death.[17] Literature, in short, threatens law by recognising the play of language to which law is also subject and by virtue of which it is possible to imagine worlds other than that of the unitary jurisdiction of the modernist juristic institution. Literature imagines an end of law, a death already signalled by the impermanence of legal forms and the ambiguities of their transmission. Before examining these various terms in detail, it is necessary to establish a more diffuse relation between law, death and *amor fati*.

It has been suggested so far that the theme of the death of law necessarily engenders a problematic which exceeds the closure of law and evokes the language of poetry, literature and the philosophy of aesthetics. These are simultaneously the first forms of law and the first objects of regulation. For the western tradition, language is the primary institution and is classically aligned with nature as the condition for any contract or for the earliest species of civility. Language is the first institution held in common; it the universal law prior to Babel; it is the invisible writing of law in the heart prior to the invention of writing; it is the only inscription of law which can escape the idolatry of other signs. These facets of language form the exemplar or origin of that commonality which later gains expression in conceptions of unwritten custom, common law or immemorial practice as the natural though hidden basis of legality as such. These are primary

---

17 For a lucid account of *ressentiment*, see G. Deleuze, *Nietzsche and Philosophy*, London, Athlone Press, 1988, at pp. 111–119.

affinities and they can be rendered more specific by examining the cross-cutting values of necessity and chance, interiority and exteriority, tradition and accident, pleasure and suffering, to which both poetry and law would speak through their death or *in articulo mortis*.[18]

In immediate logical terms, law masks death in the sense that the institution of tradition is concerned precisely with the passing on of structures across and against the blandishments of time. To the extent that law constitutes and transmits traditions as meanings, as persons, things and actions,[19] it establishes the very form of survival as repetition and in a stronger sense as eternal recurrence. In passing on – and it is not accidental that passing on is also a metaphor for death – the deep structures or forms of social reproduction, the legal tradition is bound classically to expressing or imagining death as the incident of inheritance, as the structure of sociality. Death is what passes, what succeeds, un-acknowledged, from father to son. Death, which, as an event, cannot be contained and so cannot have a value or price,[20] is that which makes containment possible. Death is the condition of possibility of sociality, precisely because it limits and so also delimits the subject and in con-sequence displays the necessity of the social. In historical terms, the imaginary status of death, its unassimilable quality or irreducibility, made the event or meaning of death the repressed reality of the symbolic or legal form. In that it was imaginary – without reason, consideration or pretext – it was associated, like all images, with the literary and with the feminine: it was feminine in this sense not simply by virtue of its futurity, but also because being defined by the soul or *anima*,[21] it was associated with a being which both sows and reaps and is in consequence the appropriate gender and metaphor for creativity as both birth and death, production and destruction of a life which will be over soon.[22] In theological terms death confuses meaning and sense, spirit and flesh. The great fear associated with death in the western tradition of repressed materiality is precisely a fear of the feminine, of contingency, contact and the irreducibility of

18 On the concept of speech *in articulo mortis*, see P. Legendre, *L'Empire de la vérité*, at pp. 106–110.

19 For discussion of such a point, see particularly D. Kelley, *The Human Measure: Social Thought in the Western Legal Tradition*, Cambridge, Mass., Harvard University Press, 1990; T. Murphy, 'Memorising Politics of Ancient History' (1987) 50 *Modern Law Review* 384. For attempts to classify and systematise common law according to such divisions, see Sir Matthew Hale, *The Analysis of the Law: Being a Scheme or Abstract of the Several Titles of the Law of England, Digested into Method*, Savoy, J. Nutt, 1713; J. Cowell, *The Institutes of the Laws of England, Digested into the Method of the Civil Law*, London, Roycroft, 1605; H. Finch, *Law or a Discourse Thereof in Foure Bookes*, London, Society of Stationers, 1627.

20 In classical Roman law, there was no civil liability for death, on the ground that a life in its entirety could not be valued. A similar position obtained in common law until reforming legislation of the late nineteenth century.

21 On the duality of *animus* and *anima*, see G. Bachelard, *The Psychoanalysis of Fire*, New York, Harper, 1984; and S. de Beauvoir, *The Second Sex*, Harmondsworth, Penguin, 1975.

22 On the femininity of fate more generally in its relation to philosophy, see Boethius, *The Consolation of Philosophy*, London, Elliot Stock, 1897, book 1.

corporeal habitus. In Christian terms, death destroys the inessential, the egotistical, the ornament or shell of living, it shatters the image and so disassociates the soul from the mundane capture of mortal forms. Femininity is thus either essential to the realisation of undying forms or it distracts from a spirituality that can only ever be confused by the false representations and pleasures of the flesh.

In historical terms, the paradoxical relation between law and the feminine gender is tied to images of justice and of judgment which express that which exceeds, mitigates or abrogates, and so defines legal rule. The necessity of law is matched classically with the accident of an indefinable justice conceived as harmony, mercy or lesbian rule.[23] Even or especially within the common law tradition justice is a woman and the origin of law is represented in the Furies, the Goddesses of a fateful justice derived from the *Oresteia*.[24] The Furies, or *Semnai-theia* (venerable Goddesses), are referred to by Selden as the first law-givers. The avenging Goddesses

> sit upon the skirts of the wicked: but the Eumenides, that is, the kind Goddesses . . . do attend the good and such as are blameless or faultless . . . [whereby] we see out of the most ancient Divine among the Heathens, how judges and the Dispensers of law pass under the notion of these venerable Goddesses.[25]

In Britain, Selden, following Camden, finds evidence of the *semnai* as the original judges of English law in references and inscriptions addressed to mother Goddesses or *Deis Matribus*, to which he adds 'nor let it be any hindrance, that so splendid and so manly a name is taken from the weaker sex, to wit, the Goddesses'.[26] The figures of a vengeful and unconscious femininity, the Justices who are also the daughters of night, the harbingers of death, represent the political fates whose task is to assure that in life as in death, judgment will take place according to the indefinable, feminine and fateful, will of the divine Justices. The Furies inscribe the dictates of fate upon the human soul. It is a fate which kills but it is also a figuration of truth, an affective representation of necessity as a law to which the soul, the emotions, are bound.

Remaining with the historical relations between law and death, justice and fate, the tradition runs from the Stoics to Cicero and Boethius. Law conceived as necessity or nature is ideally aligned to the tragic pronouncements of the Fates, the *moirai* or *fata*, which are born with, and dictate each

23 For legal commentaries on Aristotle's conception of justice as lesbian rule, see W. Lambard, *Archeion or Discourse upon the High Courts of Justice in England*, London, Seile, 1591, at pp. 68–72; J. Bodin, *De Republica*, London, Knollers, 1580, at pp. 760–765 (1606 edn).
24 Aeschylus I, *Oresteia*, Chicago, Chicago University Press, 1953 edn. See also, J. Hogan, *A Commentary on the Complete Greek Tragedies*, Chicago, Chicago University Press, 1984.
25 J. Selden, *Jani Anglorum Facies Altera*, London, T. Bassett, 1610/1683 edn, at pp. 4–5.
26 Ibid., at p. 5. See also W. Camden, *Britannia sive florentissimorum regnorum, Angliae, Scotiae, Hiberniae chorographica descriptio*, London, F. Collins, 1586/1695 edn.

human life from beginning to end. The Fates are the figures of the judgment and justice of providence, they represent in legal terms the speech of irreversible necessity or of ultimate causes which link past (*Lachesis*), present (*Clotho*) and future (*Atropos*) from a temporal perspective (eternity) external to them.[27] In one sense the space of legal speech is thus coincident with a series of 'inaugural' or prescient discourses, and the founding act of law is to appropriate the human expression of fate to the representatives of law. The founding definition of law is one which distinguishes law from divination, soothsaying, magic, astrology and witchcraft not because the speech of law differs from those discourses or practices in terms of its concerns or objects, but precisely because it belongs to the same order and is the only socially legitimate expression of them.[28] Law enacts the symbolic form of human relationship and gives effect to those unconscious forces which would otherwise remain in the hands of the magician, the soothsayer, the diviner or the evil women who invoke the powers of Satan to perform impossible acts or to represent an invisible order of past or future causes. Law claims to be the sole legitimate representation of the order of fate; it is the human speech of providence and knows that no science can fully apprehend the plenitude of absolute causes or the preordination of causal relations.

Fate, in Cicero's depiction of Chrysippus' argument, is providence, namely the pre-existent but unknowable order of absolute and unchanging causes: to the extent that phenomena and events are said to have causes 'you are bound to admit either that everything takes place by fate (*fato*) or that something can take place without a cause'.[29] So too future events are fated in that they will in retrospect be seen to have had causes:

> is it possible for anything to have happened that was not previously going to be true? For just as we speak of past things as true that possessed true actuality (*vera fuerit instantia*) at some former time, so we speak of future things as true that will possess true actuality (*vera erit instantia*) at some following time.[30]

Fate predetermines irrevocably but it does so through the medium of

27 Plato, *Republic*, Baltimore, University of Princeton Press, 1963 edn, book X, at 617 c–d:

> And there were three others who sat round about at equal intervals, each one on her throne, the Fates, daughters of Necessity, clad in white vestments with filleted heads, *Lachesis*, and *Clotho*, and *Atropos*, who sang in unison with the music of the Sirens, Lachesis singing the things that were, Clotho the things that are, and Atropos the things that are to be.

28 P. Legendre, *Le Crime de caporal Lortie: traité sur le père*, Paris, Fayard, 1989, at pp. 29–30. See also P. Goodrich, *Languages of Law: From Logics of Memory to Nomadic Masks*, London, Weidenfeld and Nicolson, 1990, at pp. 139–142.

29 Cicero, *De Fato*, London, Heinemann, 1942 edn, at 223 (Bk xi, line 26).

30 Ibid., at 223 (Bk xi, lines 27–28).

causes and their interconnection.[31] The event is predetermined as the consequence of preceding causes, but the unity of those causes is unknown, an argument formulated by Boethius in terms of a distinction between

> providence [which] embraces all things, however different, however infinite; [and] fate [which] sets in motion separately individual things, and assigns to them severally their position, form, and time ... providence is the fixed and simple form of destined events, fate their shifting series in order of time.[32]

It is thus the task of those who would know or love their fate, the task also of lawyers who apply the dictates of the Fates, to understand and interpret the interconnection of causes. It is an unknowable providence which determines the movements of all manifest causal series, for it is this underlying series or unitary providence

> which renews the series of all things that are born and die through like successions of germ and birth; it is its operation which binds the destinies of men by an indissoluble nexus of causality, and, since it issues in the beginning from unalterable providence, these destinies also must of necessity be immutable.[33]

On the other hand, such destinies, or such interconnectedness of all things, are unknowable, they are the accidents of a fate which is without reason, consideration or pretext. To love fate, to act fatefully, is to accept chance: 'Thou deemest *fortuna* to have changed towards thee; thou mistakest. Such were ever her ways, ever such her nature. Rather in her very mutability hath she preserved towards thee her true constancy.'[34] The crucial question in existential terms is thus between chance and choice, the one implying the other in the irrevocable choice, the necessary fate invoked and imposed by acting in the world, by living according to the ethical or aesthetic dictate of making something of one's lot.

Fate, in assigning to individuals their manifest place, their position and time, assigns human destiny in the form of a structure or place, and in legal terms it dictates the institutional form of social existence. To speak of destiny or fate is to talk of the institution of life (*institutere vitam*) in the precise sense of the pre-assignment of individual and social places. It is to speak of the predetermined familial and political places that await an individual before their birth. In Freudian terms, fate constitutes *the other scene* of human life, the unconscious, in the form of the juridical categories

---

31 A. Schopenhauer, *The World as Will and Idea*, London, Kegan Paul, 1906 edn, vol. 1 at pp. 389–390; G. Deleuze, *Logic of Sense*, London, Athlone, 1990, at pp. 169–170, 270.
32 Boethius, *Consolation of Philosophy*, at p. 201.
33 Ibid., at pp. 204–205.
34 Ibid., at p. 44.

of father and son, or familial fate, and claim and due, or political fate.[35]
These categories give form to the unconscious and to its demands: far from
being accidental, or a veneer imposed upon human reality, these categories stake out the structure of human life, its destiny, namely its place
and its truth. Two features of fate deserve particular comment in this
context. Formulated in terms of the unconscious as the 'discourse of the
other', and in legal terms as the will of the sovereign Father in whose name
law judges, fate is exteriority. It is that into which the individual is born
and in relation to which the individual acquires an identity: it is, in
Lacanian terms, the figure of the mirror phase,[36] while in more classical
terms it is the structure of narcissism, the prohibition through which the
individual enters the genealogical line.[37] Conceived as exteriority, the *Fata*

> are the speeches of foundation, they take hold of life, they are the
> speeches which make (*fabriquent*) us, as is suggested by the word *tyche*
> used by Sophocles, and translated as destiny. Consider also the Greek
> *daimon*, the other equivalent of destiny, some inner demon: by this word,
> Oedipus addresses himself in uncovering his parricide.[38]

The exteriority of the Fates represents the exteriority of the order of
institutional causes and of political organisation, 'humanity is spoken in
advance, it enters an instituted life'.[39] Such exterior institution, which
bewitches or fascinates, which fabricates subjectivity as a place of predetermined possibilities or common destiny, is also, however, the place of
interiority. The external law of the institution is at the same time the law
of interiority, the institution of a personality adjusted to its culture.[40] In
this second sense, the Fates or *moirai* are depicted as a foreign will within,
an interior exteriority.[41] What is at issue is a process of identification or
internalisation; it is the function of law to make necessity recognisable as
limitation:

> these received determinations are themselves synthetic and internal,
> since they are always directed to a future end, and they represent a
> constant enrichment and an irreversibility of time, they proceed not
> from analytical Reason or the laws of exteriority but, if one is not to
> prejudge them, from an external law of interiority . . . this law might of

35 Papageorgiou-Legendre, 'Analecta', in A. Papageorgiou, *Filiation: fondement généalogique
   de la psychanalyse*, Paris, Fayard, 1990, at pp. 216–217. See also, G. Deleuze and F. Guattari,
   *Anti-Oedipus*, New York, Viking Books, 1977, at pp. 12–16, 51–56.
36 J. Lacan, *Ecrits*, London, Tavistock, 1977, at pp. 2ff.
37 See Papageorgiou-Legendre, *L'Inestimable objet de la transmission: étude sur le principe
   généalogique en occident*, Paris, Fayard, 1985, at pp. 55–56.
38 Papageorgiou-Legendre, *Le Crime de caporal Lortie*, at p. 29.
39 Ibid., at p. 51.
40 See Papageorgiou-Legendre, *Filiation*, at pp. 56–59.
41 On fate as a foreign will within, see E. Levinas, *Totality and Infinity*, Pittsburg, Duquesne
   University Press, 1969, at pp. 226ff.

course be referred to as destiny, since an irresistible movement draws or impels the ensemble towards a prefigured future which realises itself through it.[42]

Necessity is experienced as contingency, as accident or chance, the distribution of lots. It is the function of law to intimate the irreversibility of such predeterminations. As a discourse of foundation, law makes the individual – the persona – as exteriority, the legal subject enters the social as other to herself, as a signification of self in the objectivity of destiny: 'all of us spend our lives engraving our maleficent image on things, and it fascinates and bewilders us if we try to understand ourselves through it, although we are ourselves the totalis[ing] movement which results in *this* particular objectification'.[43] In short, we meet our fate, again and again, in each and every image that we inscribe in the world.

## FATE AND JUDGMENT

The space of legal judgment or of the art of law is predicated upon an ignorance: 'the *Fata* are the echo of the abyss (*l'abîme*) and, at the same time, to take up a formulation of Seneca's defining destiny, they are the will of the sovereign Father'.[44] In representing necessity or the force of exteriority, the speech of the Fates is intrinsically tied to law in both its objective and its subjective dimensions. One and the same discourse of fate speaks both to the institution of the subject and to the institution of sociality. At the level of the subject,

> the discourse of the *Fata* can be defined as the discourse of foundation, that is to say, as that discourse which should provide the young subject with the subjective means of surviving the horror of a subjective division inaugurated by its separation from the first incestuous object, that is to say from the mother – from the biological mother, but above all from the mythological Mother of the order of representation. . . . No one escapes the law of separation, to which the biological father, himself also a child of the mythological Mother, is also a subject. . . .[45]

Within this Lacanian paradigm the father remains subject to a pre-Oedipal attachment until by means of 'symbolic permutation' he identifies himself with, and takes up his place as, the image of the Father and transposes biological paternity into the role of transmitting social fate through the image of the Father, through entry into the symbolic. Once the infant enters

---

42 J.-P. Sartre, *Critique of Dialectical Reason*, London, New Left Books, 1976, at pp. 179–180, and at 551–552.
43 Ibid., at p. 227.
44 Papageorgiou-Legendre, *Le Crime de caporal Lortie*, at p. 29.
45 Ibid., at p. 81.

into the parental discourse she finds herself subject to its law, a law which requires the child to detach herself irrevocably from her physical reality as a surface of pleasure and excitation, and to identify herself with the signifier which carries her into discourse and so also into law.[46] The institution, as that which has always already fabricated human existence, engenders the human as a 'speaking being' through both an interior and an exterior governance. The institution establishes legitimacy in the dual form of the father (*patria potestas*) and of sovereign (*regia potestas*). The institution institutes both a familial and a political relation to others and to exteriority:

> The law is the word of the father. The father intervenes to counter the phantasm of maternal omnipotence with the potency of his word. Its force is not that of the pain of a real fear effectively produced. Subjection to the word of the father . . . [is subjection to a] speech [which] is not only indicative but also imperative: speech itself orders. . . . It functions to put a sign in the place of reality – the phallus in the place of the penis. It makes the infantile surfaces into signs.[47]

The discourse of fate is the oracular representation of a life which will be over soon. It is a life which must in consequence be governed by laws of reproduction: the Fates must bring each child before the law and inscribe, in conscious and unconscious forms, upon the body and upon the soul, the narratives of the *longue durée*, of a before, during and after which both comprehend (include) and survive the individual life: 'all production, creative or symptomatic, cultural or pathological, only ever emerges at the point of the opening of the structure, which is also the point of its failure'.[48] What is crucial to an understanding of fate as judgment is the indissoluble tie between interiority and exteriority, the commonality of destiny in an institutional existence that is both outside and within:

> the most private, the most intimate, that which is at the heart of the concept of a subject, to know the fantasm, is already marked by the seal of the genealogical order. All subjects carry with them, if I can express myself in this way, the institutional under the primary form of familial institution.[49]

The first myths or representations of fate are thus narratives of a necessity which captures the subject for law, for transmission across the generations, for reproduction. That which until recently did not exist, has to be inscribed with individuality and with personality or citizenship. It

---

46 Papageorgiou-Legendre, 'Analecta', at p. 218.
47 A. Lingis, *Deathbound Subjectivity*, Bloomington, Indiana University Press, 1989, at p. 79.
48 Papageorgiou-Legendre, *Filiation*, at p. 33.
49 Ibid., at p. 56.

is in this respect no accident that the inaugural narrative of law takes the emblematic form of a legend of the family expressed in terms of genealogical forms. The story of Oedipus thus recounts the tragic unravelling of a subjectivity which defied genealogical prohibition, in which the subject who infracts the rules of kinship, and specifically the interdictions of parricide and of incestuous descent, pays the absolute price first of madness and then of annihilation.[50] In the *Oresteia*, divine vengeance in the form of the Furies (the repulsive maidens) is visited again upon one who does harm to their kin. Apollo orders Orestes to kill his mother, Clytaemnestra, and must then protect Orestes from the Furies.[51] These are the Goddesses who punish all crimes against kin, of which murder of the parent is the most absolute and sacrilegious in that it steals the power of the Gods and puts it into human hands.[52] The first and principal crime is precisely one which challenges fate by attempting to arrogate destiny and, in specifically legal terms, to expedite the speech of the Gods (*fata properaverit*).[53] Those who commit such a crime against the genealogical order are pursued by the Furies, Goddesses who are invisible to all but their victims and whose approach drives the victims mad. They strike, in other words, at the soul.

Death, in Heidegger's terms, is not extinction without recompense, but the condition for the possibility of every significance and every value.

> Death then is nowhere else than in the world, and in throwing ourselves into the world we are casting ourselves into death; death is the world as pure openness or clearing in which beings are distinguishable and phosphorescent, [it is a] reservoir of possibility for beings and for nothingness.[54]

The institutional form of reproduction is one which inscribes a pattern of repetition upon the unconscious of the subject: 'there is transmission, because there is repetition';[55] indeed Freud specifically designates instinct as an urge for repetition, for the restoration of 'an earlier state of things', and fate is likewise defined as the repetition of infantile experiences which are explicitly depicted as possession by a 'malignant fate' and as an

---

50 The Freudian account of the Oedipus tragedy takes it as an instance of the founding murder of the father. See S. Freud, *Moses and Monotheism*, London, Constable, 1962 edn; see also Freud, *Totem and Taboo*, London, Hogarth, 1936, for the earlier version of that thesis. For criticism of this interpretation for its failure to recognise the underlying figuration of a principle of blood, see Legendre, *Le Crime de caporal Lortie*.

51 *The Eumenides*, at lines 66–93.

52 See, on sacrilege, Sir Henry Spelman, *The History and Fate of Sacrilege*, London, J. Hartley, 1632/1695 edn.

53 Justinian, *Code*, 9.17, under the title: *De his qui parentes vel liberos occiderunt* (Of those who have killed their parents or their children).

54 Lingis, *Deathbound Subjectivity*, at p. 185.

55 Pagageorgiou, *Filiation*, at 49.

internal 'daemonic power'.[56] Fate refers, in other words, to the inscription of a pattern upon the empty space of the unconscious and at a collective level it refers to what Heidegger terms destiny (*geshick*), the historicisation of being. Dasein has fate (*schicksal*) inscribed in it; it is fate to the extent that it is authentic to its destiny, to the recurrence of inherited possibilities: repetition hands down, it is the means of historicality, for 'in repetition, fateful destiny can be disclosed explicitly as bound up with the heritage which has come down to us. By repetition, Dasein first has its own history made manifest'.[57] Fate is here the handing-down of inherited possibilities, and particularly the anticipation of the events of birth and death as the implicit object, the other scene, of all transmission. It is, in Heidegger's terms, being-towards-death or the finitude of temporality, that joins the subject to history and so also to repetition as the means of entering history, as *amor fati*: 'when historicality is authentic, it understands history as the recurrence of the possible, and knows that a possibility will recur only if existence is open for it fatefully . . . in resolute repetition'.[58]

A final step in the argument is taken in the conception of *amor fati* as the manner in which possibility is realised, and necessity lived as chance. Where Shopenhauer suggested quiescence in the face of fate, and Kierkegaard offered redemption as the end product of repetition, poststructuralist thought – which is itself the expression of a certain contemporary sense of fatality – addresses the active principle of *amor fati* as the precondition of all creativity or becoming.[59] It derives its inspiration from Nietzsche's conception of eternal recurrence as the principle of becoming predicated not upon causality but upon chance, not upon law but upon judgment as the justice of play and the will to affirm fortune or *fortuna* as she stands. The authentic thought of finitude, of being towards death, is predicated upon an historical conception of fatality as the irreversibility of chance:

> my formula for greatness in a human being is *amor fati*: that one wants nothing to be different, not forward, not backward, not in all eternity. Not merely bear what is necessary, still less conceal it – all idealism is mendaciousness in the face of what is necessary – but *love* it.[60]

It is the irreversibility of the past, of the dice-throw of necessity, that

---

56 S. Freud, *Beyond the Pleasure Principle*, London, Hogarth Press, 1961, at pp. 30–31 and at 15–16.

57 Heidegger, *Being and Time*, Oxford, Basil Blackwell, 1962, at p. 438.

58 Ibid., at p. 444.

59 Sartre, *Critique*, at pp. 551–552, offers conceptions of praxis and of groups in fusion as the realisation of an interiority which can transcend the practico-inert. A history which is conscious of itself can be critical to the extent that it can make and unmake an exteriority which is otherwise perceived as a serial and necessary exterior totality. If the law of exteriority escapes us, we are powerless to act upon it. In this respect, Sartre's *Critique* comes close to Nietzsche's conception of *amor fati*.

60 F. Nietzsche, *Daybreak*, Cambridge, Cambridge University Press, 1881, 1982 edn, at p. 258.

dictates both the circumstance and the *persona* or identity of present action. Neither could be other than they are because history – necessity as chance – has made them such as they are: 'becoming must be explained without recourse to final intentions; becoming must appear justified at every moment', and similarly, 'the present must absolutely not be justified by reference to a future, the past by reference to the present'.[61]

Formulated in Nietzsche's terms, destiny or providence takes the form of eternal return as the structure of all action, the repetition of life or more specifically of action in the form of the unique coupling of chance and necessity or chance and destiny. It is the fate of law to act 'as if' each act will return eternally, 'as if' each judgment were unique. The necessity or law that governs each decision is precisely the necessity of judging; it is the fate of law to have to decide, to be decided upon deciding while knowing that nothing can be absolutely determined. Necessity imposes choice. Chance dictates the conjunction of discrimination and decision, feeling and rule. Law, in short, expresses the need to act upon the circumstances, the facts which fate flings, without reason, consideration or pretext, to be judged. In one sense, the eternal return is the categorical imperative of each act of judgment. Destiny produces both the necessity – the historical circumstances – and the person who acts and they must act or judge in the knowledge that their act will return eternally, namely that no rewriting of the past, nor future intention nor afterlife will ever change that action. The categorical imperative of judgment expresses both the irreducibility of judging and the universality of judgment. In Nietzschean terms, *amor fati* refers both to the positive force that affirms the uniqueness of each act of judgment – that closure creates openness – and to a responsibility, that each act determines the fate of the soul. It is of the essence of judgment as fate that while the impact of judgment – of eternal recurrence – may escape codification and may indeed be inexpressible, it is nonetheless remembered and inscribed. The soul of the judge is marked by judgment. While others may not perceive or judge the act of judging, the judgment is indelible nonetheless: judgment (discrimination and taste) trace and define the subject that judges and the body carries the corpus or product of judgment.

The eternal return is thus the return of the same in the substantive form of becoming or difference.[62] In this respect, the eternal return

> is not the effect of the Identical on a world which has become the similar (*semblable*), it is not an exterior order imposed upon the chaos of the world, the eternal return is, on the contrary, the internal identity of the world and of chaos ... it is not the same which returns, it is not the

61 F. Nietzsche, *The Will to Power*, New York, Vintage, 1882–1888, 1968 edn, at p. 377.
62 See Deleuze, *Nietzsche and Philosophy*, at pp. 25–29.

similar that returns, but the Same is the return of that which returns, that is to say of the Different, the similar is the return of that which returns, that is to say of the Dissimilar . . . of simulacra.[63]

The history of return is thus the history of the image, of the representation or simulation of the same, the image of resemblance conceived as if the return of the same was an exterior force, a trace of a vanished difference or division. At an ontological level, the return of the same is the motive principle of closure, the image of the same is conceived juridically in terms of a reference to an absolute cause (*causa causans*) or vanished unity towards which human judgment endeavours to approximate or refer. In this respect, closure is a principle of passivity or reaction to a determinant exteriority or law which has already decided, already judged and already spoken the way. Closure is the history of an infinitely extended error in which finite representation is predicated upon an eternal principle of correspondence to exterior identity. It excludes the force or active principle of becoming in which it is simply the return that both returns and passes on, returning is the being of that which becomes: 'that everything recurs is the closest approximation of a world of becoming to a world of being'.[64] The eternal return is being as becoming, a principle of passage or synthesis of past, present and future states, of diversity and its reproduction. In Nietzsche's later writings, the same principle of return is expressed existentially and politically in terms of an aesthetic of judgment, a theory of affectivity as the object of ethics and of justice. *Amor fati* is an aesthetic principle of judgment and of action: the aesthetic is the criterion of ethical action insofar as authentic being survives the truth – fate or law – through artistic endeavour, through dramatising and transfiguring an inexorable yet unknown order of providential fate into an act of will. The ecstasy of authenticity is the necessity of self-determination and its pleasure or its play lies in the ethical and in many senses theatrical will to become the appropriate expression or vehicle of that which fate dictates.

## JUDGMENT AND LAW

The concept of the eternal return, of fatality or destiny as law, is also an application of the concept of judgment to all genres or aspects of existence and of care of the self. It should be recollected that 'Dionysus is a judge'[65] and that the jurisdiction of judgment is a singularity which is connected in Stoic terms to all being. The eternal return indicates precisely the relation of destiny to finitude and imposes the necessity of judgment upon

63 G. Deleuze, *Différence et répétition*, Paris, Presses Universitaires de France, 1968, at pp. 382 and 384.
64 Nietzsche, *Will to Power*, at p. 617.
65 Ibid., at p. 541.

every act, the inescapability of a choice between reaction and affirmation, *ressentiment* and *amor fati*, in relation to all discourses:

> the overriding aim is to combat the historical and philosophical effacing of the connections between law and morality. . . . Instead a text is designed which makes explicit and visible the historical connection between law and morality for the sake of 'justice' (*die Gerechtigkeit*). Zarathustra's discourse is the jurisprudence of this law beyond the opposition of the rational versus revealed.[66]

For Nietzsche too it transpires that law is dead in the sense that it has lost its value, that in its closure as scientific jurisprudence it has embraced an internal principle or logic of separation. Through denying connection as fate, as the operation of very distant causes, it has consequently been forced also to deny its relation to judgment and to destiny as the interconnectedness of ethics and law. It has ceased to judge, it has ceased to be of value, it remains as no more than passivity, lethargy or brute repetition: a law or *logos* without *nomos*, namely a law which no longer produces value.

The distinction between *logos* and *nomos* refers to two opposed conceptions of legality. In terms of classical law, *logos* refers to that speech which lies at the basis of the legal bond, to *legere* or that which ties a being to its proper form. By extrapolation, *logos* can be viewed as the basis of symbolic order, of law in its most general sense of enforcement or prohibition, as word of the Father or oracular speech. *Logos* within the Christian tradition of law is precisely the word as substance, as the impossible unity of two natures, as the law of law. *Nomos*, by contradistinction, refers to the qualitative principle of measure; it is law but it is also movement in the sense of nomadism, of that transhumance or itineration that marks out territories according to the contingent criteria of seasons and foods or the availability of markets.[67] In Nietzschean terms, it is a question of two different principles of theoretical organisation, spelled out in Nietzsche's most jurisprudential work, *The Birth of Tragedy*, as the Apollonian and the Dionysian.[68] The Apollonian is the legal model, it is scientific and operates upon the basis of extracting constants or of establishing invariant forms for variable matter. The Apollonian offers order for flux, morality for hedonism, law for life, seriousness for play. Its foundation lies in calculability in the sense that the essential feature of legal science lies in reproduction, in iteration and reiteration within defined territories. *Logos* formalises and separates so as to reproduce the same:

66 G. Rose, *Dialectic of Nihilism*, Oxford, Basil Blackwell, 1984, at p. 90.
67 On the relation of geographical law to markets, see Fernand Braudel, *The Mediterranean World*, New York, Viking Books, 1976.
68 Nietzsche, *The Birth of Tragedy*, Edinburgh, Foulis, 1905.

'reproducing implies the permanence of a fixed point of view that is external to what is reproduced';[69] it searches for a form, a constancy, which law itself will extract from variation. *Nomos*, by way of distinction, is expressive of individuation and heterogeneity. It is founded upon difference and itinerancy, it is what Deleuze terms 'an ambulant science',[70] that is, one which does not reproduce but rather follows singularities. Where the ideal of reproduction pervades the science of law and reduces difference to variation, the nomadic science searches for 'the singularities of a matter, or rather of a material . . . that consist in following a flow in a vectorial field across which singularities are scattered like so many accidents'.[71] It expresses forces, which come like fate, without reason, consideration or pretext. In its singularity and heterogeneity it suggests another justice, another movement, another space, another time.

Translated into jurisprudential terms, the distinction between *logos* and *nomos* as principles of science is loosely equivalent to that between authority and practical reason, law and justice.[72] The legalistic model seeks reproduction and self-reproduction within a defined territory, an autonomous sphere or field. The surrealistic principle of nomadism is different in that it follows the particularity of the event. More specifically, the legal model charts the calculability of rule and extracts the constancy of norm or of principle from the variability of rule application or precedent. In either case, the form of law remains separate from its matter or particular instances. The destiny of law becomes unspeakable or closed in the sense that questions of form, of the immutability of law, are conceived as strictly distinct from those of the circumstances of its expression. In its positive formulation, law follows rules and not events, norms and not values. The event of judgment escapes law, it is the point of its failure. It is also the moment of excess, of a variability which exceeds the stability of a system and faces the judge with the aporia of judgment, with facts which appear like fate, without reason, consideration or pretext. A logic or science which follows the irreducibility of the event is a nomadic science of shifting

---

69 G. Deleuze, *Mille Plateaux*, translated as *A Thousand Plateaux*, London, Athlone, 1988, at p. 372.

70 Ibid., at p. 372.

71 Ibid., at pp. 372–373.

72 J. Derrida, 'Force of Law: The Mystical Foundation of Authority' (1990) 11 *Cardozo Law Review* 920, at 955:

> One must be *juste* with justice, and the first way to do it justice is to hear, read, interpret it, to try to understand where it comes from, what it wants of us, knowing that it does so through singular idioms (*Dike, Jus, justitia, justice, Gerechtigkeit* . . .) and also knowing that this justice always addresses itself to singularity, to the singularity of the other, despite or even because it pretends to universality.

For a distinctive manipulation of a comparable theme, see D. Cornell, 'From the Lighthouse: The Promise of Redemption and the Possibility of Legal Interpretation' (1990) 11 *Cardozo Law Review* 1687.

jurisdiction or theoretical openness. The competence to speak of the event is based upon the ability to move from a field of reproduction or of law to a field which is demarcated around the event and which by virtue of its externality shatters the pre-existent sentence or competence.

In classical jurisprudential terms, awareness of the event to be judged was theorised in terms of an opposition between judgment and law, *nomos* and *logos*. Law was perceived to err where it rested upon no more than prior sentence or precedent: 'those that do succeed, may be by many degrees more eminent in wisdom, reason, knowledge and experience, than those that sat in the same tribunals before them; for there is in this world an undoubted wheeling in all things'.[73] That wheeling, *fortuna*, chance or accident, is formulated in terms of an aporia of judgment to the effect that *argumentum ductum a simili est multum fragile et infirmum; nec procedit, quando datur dissimilitudo etiam parvai.*[74] The maxim founds the rule in the Justinian Code that judges are bound to pursue strictly Truth, Justice and the Laws and 'not in judging to take their example from the most solemn sentences of the highest and most eminent judges in the whole Empire'. The principle upon which such an ordinance of judgment is based is nomadic and predicated at first upon the simple perception of the eternal return of difference:

> in so many ages, and in such multitude of cases that have occurred, there has not been found one wholly like another, for indeed the dissimilitude and difformity that is amongst ourselves and the whole off-spring of man not in outward form, visage, lineaments, or stature only, but even in our natures, tempers, inclinations, and humours, also makes all the matters we deal in, and the actions that flow from us, disagreeing too. Also in other productions of nature, and the accidents that are commonly ascribed to chance and fortune, there is such a strange and wonderful variety, that nothing is acted, produced, or happens like another, but that in some circumstance or other that does diversify it and make it differ.[75]

From fate, which is without reason, consideration or pretext, there flows difference and no amount of law can erase that difference save by evacuating the otherness of justice and abandoning the event. Again,

> the Emperor makes it a strange and unwonted thing in Rome that judgments had between other parties should either profit or prejudice those who were neither present then in court, nor ever called. . . . Neither will any likeness of one case to another, involve an absent person in such accidents as have fallen upon the men . . . though the cases are never so

---

73 Wiseman, *The Law of Laws*, at p. 39.
74 (An argument drawn from a like case is very weak and fragile; it falls to the ground when the smallest dissimilitude is found.) Quintilian, *Institutio Oratorio*, 5.2.
75 Wiseman, *The Law of Laws*, at p. 41.

much the same, yet a third person that never was a party, shall sustain no detriment by what hath been done between those that were.[76]

The itinerant singularity of judgment, or the face-to-face quality of justice, leads to the appointment of the Roman judge being made subject to a rule of indeterminacy; he is to have equity always before his eyes: *semper aequitatem ante oculos habere*. By *Code* 1.8 the point is repeated: in all things there ought to be a greater consideration of right and equity than of strict and exact rule: *placuit in omnibus rebus praecipuam esse justitiae aequitatisque quam stricti juris rationem*. Finally, it might be added, a further patristic principle states *corde creditur ad iustitiam*, that he who believes in the heart will always do justice.

The principle of judgment elaborated in terms of the indeterminacy of the event to be judged should be read in an extreme way. Nature binds destiny to death and faces the judge with a choice. The judge either acts reactively with a resentful passivity towards death and so reproduces a past state of affairs according to 'grave sentences' already handed down, or the judge acts affirmatively and creatively and suspends those sentences so as to do justice in the face of fortune. The nomadic judgment is the expression of *amor fati* and remakes the law in each judgment. It is a quality of judgment which is curiously captured by Schopenhauer in linking fortune to *synderesis*. In this conception the conscience of the judge belongs to the one who dreams or at least imagines a future which will ever repeat his judgment in its singularity, who recognises that each judgment is the last judgment for those that are judged.[77] To judge is to discern, to discriminate, to move:

> *synderesis* is a natural power or motive force of the rational soul . . . moving and stirring it to good and abhoring evil . . . this *synderesis* our Lord put in men to the intent that the order and connection of things should be observed. . . . And this *synderesis* is the beginning of all things that may be learned by speculation or study.[78]

What is learned is an openness to the irresistibility of fate, to a fate which since the Stoics has been inscribed in human conscience as the interconnectedness of all things or phenomena, an interconnectedness that is only apparent through the failure of scientific systems and of legal reproduction. Fate is the operation of extremely distant causes and it is the manifestation of those causes, without reason, consideration or pretext, that destroys science and rule. Exigency of singularity, event or accident cannot be treated by science but only by a species of differentiation or nomadism, a law by other means or of the heart.

---

76 Ibid., at p. 43.
77 A. Schopenhauer, *Counsels and Maxims*, London, Allen and Unwin, 1890, at p. 113.
78 The citation is from St German, *Doctor and Student*, London, Selden Society, 1528, 1974 edn, at p. 81.

Law, as the discourse of fate as judgment, becomes a discourse of seduction. Fate seduces in the form of singularity and it is the task of an itinerant judge to follow that which fate has presented to be decided. To judge, in this perspective of *nomos* in excess or transgression of *logos*, is to follow the eccentric logic of matter and to recognise that the judge 'finds himself therefore in the pagan situation of having a kind of "fate" inflicted upon him by his utterance'.[79] The judge is seduced by his fate, his role is to love fate, to create a law that is ethical, which is to say, a law which is appropriate to its circumstance. Where literary theory has suggested that rhetorical figures be interpreted according to the language of the genre from which they are drawn, that floral figures require recourse to botanical vocabularies, metaphors of light to discourses of optics, the judge must render judgment that is adequate to its circumstances. In Derrida's depiction, the philosophical is 'carried away' each time that one of its products – in this instance, the concept of metaphor – attempts to include under its own law the totality of the field, namely rhetoric, to which its product belongs:

> one then would have to acknowledge the importation into so-called philosophical discourse of exogenous metaphors, or rather of significa- tions that become metaphorical in being transported out of their own habitat. Thus, one would classify the places they came from: there would be metaphors that are biological, organic, mechanical, technical, eco- nomic, historical, mathematical.[80]

As Derrida's argument progresses it becomes apparent that metaphor is both the seduction and the fate of philosophical discourse; it cannot escape figuration save by abandoning language. It is in consequence fated either to police arbitrarily the boundaries of proper and non-proper metaphors or to follow the logic of metaphor itself.

In jurisprudential terms a similarly ethical reading of the legal text would be equally 'carried away' by the irreducible connections, the sensibility and the excess, of events themselves. Legal memory, or prec- edent in such a context, is no more than an image (*phantasiai*) of desire (*epithumia*): in Platonic terms the representation, the image or the memory of the thing, gives pleasure and so activates the soul.[81] In medieval terms *affectus* or emotion is bound to *intellectus*, and *memoria* to *cogitatio*: 'desire begins the ascent to understanding by firing memory, and through

---

79 J.-F. Lyotard and J.-L. Thebaud, *Just Gaming*, Manchester, Manchester University Press, 1985, at p. 42. See further, Derrida, 'Force of Law', pp. 935–943.

80 J. Derrida, 'The White Mythology', in *idem*, *Margins of Philosophy*, Brighton, Harvester Press, 1982, at pp. 219–220. For further discussion, see M. Le Doeuff, *The Philosophical Imaginary*, London, Athlone Press, 1989.

81 Plato, *Philebus*, 34b ff. See also the discussion in M. Foucault, *The Use of Pleasure*, New York, Pantheon, 1985, at pp. 38–47.

memory's stored-up treasures the intellect is able to contemplate'.[82] The phantasms of memory provide both the stimulus, the desire, that will move the will to action and also the images of likeness (*simulacrum*) that will guide reason from one scene to the other. Both memory and desire appertain to the soul or in a more recent terminology to the unconscious and are the phantasmatic motive forces of what Bodin terms the 'execution' of law, namely its fateful acts of judgment, its soul.[83] In the same text, indeed, we are taught that

> the law without equity, is a body without a soul, for that it concerns but things in general, and leaves the particular circumstances, which are infinite, to be by equality sought out according to the exigence of the places, times and persons.[84]

The ethical judge pursues precedent as the lingering memory of past desires, as the images or phantasmata of value, as *amor fati* or the laws (*nomoi*) which, without reason, consideration or pretext, the singular judgment must connect.

## THE END

Legal closure may be addressed finally as a nihilism which refuses fate. In more specific terms it is an account of judgment which denies the value, force, desire and art of judgment. While it is undoubtedly ironic to reinvoke a classical or indeed medieval conception of judgment as an antidote to the closure of law, it is precisely the hermeneutic significance of the tradition, the place of history, which is in question. In a striking variety of forms and metaphors, the medieval reception of Roman law attempted both to accommodate and to revise the inheritance of universal law. Theories of 'harmonicall judgment',[85] geographical variation of constitutions,[86] lesbian artifice[87] and of a precedence of desire[88] all served a comparable function of providing a supplement for laws which 'experience and time doth beger'.[89] The science of the supplement can be interpreted as a science of *nomos*, a postmodern pursuit of the simulacrum, a path paved by memory and by desire, by fateful speech and an art of

---

82 M. Carruthers, *The Book of Memory: A Study of Memory in Medieval Culture*, Cambridge, Cambridge University Press, 1990, at p. 201. She subsequently cites Gregory the Great: 'We devour the book when with eager desire we clothe ourselves with the words of life' (ibid.: 201).

83 Bodin, *De Republica*, at p. 760.

84 Ibid., at p. 763.

85 Ibid., at p. 760; Lambard, *Archeion*, at p. 72.

86 Bodin, *De Republica*, at pp. 547ff.

87 Lambard, *Archeion*, at p. 70.

88 Bodin, *De Republica*, at p. 559.

89 Lambard, *Archeion*, at pp. 66–67.

smooth spaces, vague essences and singular indeterminacies. The integrity of law lies in a logic of disintegration, in the paradoxes and aporia that inevitably accompany the pursuit of similitude, likeness or the 'semblable' into the infinite variety or change of circumstances, of persons, places, times and their connections. It is a singularity beyond the jurisdiction of any laws, it follows circumstances or events 'which [in their] infinite varieties can in no laws, no tables, no pandects, no books, be they never so many or so great, be all of them contained or comprehended'.[90] The pursuit of the supplement extends beyond both rule and jurisdiction; it is a quest for images of particularity, for an ethics of the singular, for an impossible justice.

In consistently contemporary terms we may speak of an aesthetic of judgment as the being of law towards the indeterminacy of living forms. The historicisation of law first presents judgment with the requirement of an ethics. A judgment which is embedded in the world and appropriate to the event necessarily follows singularity and much as the leaden rule of the 'lesbian artificer' would 'bow to every stone of whatever fashion',[91] it loves its fate sufficiently to judge according to the historical possibilities of the matter before it. In Aristotelian terms it is an ethics or practice of virtue, 'an energy of the soul according to reason, or not without reason', a transformation which establishes character and happiness, and expresses *synderesis*.[92] It is second a species of responsibility, which at a political level denies that it is possible to judge within the closed framework of an autonomous law or to think law without justice. Its injunction is that the judge should not

> remain enclosed in purely speculative, theoretical, academic discourses, but rather [should] aspire to something more consequential, to *change* things and to intervene in an efficient and responsible though always, of course, very mediated way, not only in the profession but in what one calls the city, the *polis* and more generally the world.[93]

The irony of *nomos* as a science of law is that it is fated to a tradition which it inherits without reason, consideration or pretext. It is equally fated to love and to change that world or tradition in ways which it cannot predict or foresee. Judgment in this respect is Kant's 'law without law',[94] it is an aesthetics, sensibility or style. It is both the fate and the face of history as judgment. To be ethical or to be just it must respond to the plurality of faces and fates which history confronts it with. It must follow so as to direct, or more simply it must both seduce and be seduced.

90 Bodin, *De Republica*, at p. 766.
91 Lambard, *Archeion*, at pp. 72 and 70.
92 Aristotle, *The Nicomachean Ethics*, Oxford, J. Vincent, 1846, at pp. 19–20.
93 J. Derrida, 'Force of Law', p. 919 at pp. 931–933.
94 I. Kant, *The Critique of Judgment*, Oxford, Oxford University Press, 1952 edn, at ss. 22, 76.

# Chapter 8

# Sleeping with the enemy

## On the politics of critical legal studies in America

> The task of extremist writing is to put through the call for a justice of the future. Henceforth, Justice can no longer permit itself to be merely backward looking or bound in servility to sclerotic models and their modifications (their 'future'). A justice of the future would have to show the will to rupture.[1]

There seems little doubt within the contemporary American legal academy that critical legal studies represented the emergence of a left intelligentsia in law.[2] While there are indeed few other intellectual criteria by which to demarcate either a critical movement or position within legal theory, there remains the basic common denominator of a commitment to a radical political position both within and without the legal institution.[3] Critical

1 Avital Ronell, *Crack Wars: Literature, Addiction, Mania*, Lincoln, Nebr., University of Nebraska Press, 1992, at p. 21.
2 The expression is taken from D. Kennedy, 'Critical Labour Theory: A Comment' (1981) 4 *Industrial Relations Law Journal* 503, 506. It is reiterated in D. Kennedy, 'Cost Reduction Theory as Legitimation' (1981) 90 *Yale Law Journal* 1275 and confirmed in A. Hutchinson and P. Monahan, 'Law, Politics and Critical Legal Scholars: The Unfolding Drama of American Legal Thought' (1984) 36 *Stanford Law Review* 199. See further A. Hunt, 'The Theory of Critical Legal Studies' (1986) 6 *Oxford Journal of Legal Studies* 1; M. Tushnet, 'Critical Legal Studies: A Political History' (1991) 100 *Yale Law Journal* 1515; J. Schlegel, 'Notes Toward an Intimate, Opinionated, and Affectionate History of the Conference on Critical Legal Studies' (1984) 36 *Stanford Law Review* 391; D. Kairys (ed.), *The Politics of Law*, 2nd edn, New York, Pantheon Books, 1990.
3 Peter Gabel introduced the session at which this paper was delivered in terms of critical legal studies being 'the most radical show in town'. While there are several radical connotations to the carnivalesque, to festivals, circuses and travelling shows, the metaphor also suggests a transience and abnormality restricted to theatre or to the stage. The recourse of critical legal studies to metaphors drawn from theatre, drama, cinema, rock music and indeed jazz as well as a more general strain of popular culture, has been remarked upon frequently and will not be engaged with here. See J.P. Oetken, 'Form and Substance in Critical Legal Studies' (1991) 100 *Yale Law Journal* 2209 at 2214–2216; A. Chase, 'Toward a Legal Theory of Popular Culture' (1986) *Wisconsin Law Review* 527; or G. Frankenberg, 'Down by Law: Irony, Seriousness, and Reason' in C. Joerges and D. Trubek (eds), *Critical Legal Thought: An American–German Debate*, Baden-Baden, Nomos Verlag, 1989, p. 315. Alternately the most stylistically frightening and bemusing example of such style probably remains A. Hutchinson, *Dwelling on the Threshold: Critical Essays on Modern Legal Thought*, Toronto, Carswell, 1988.

legal studies is the 'leftist' inheritor of legal realism; it is a 'political location', 'subversive', 'deviationist' and on occasion even 'nihilistic', the extremist political position of a critical movement which ironically no longer believes in critique.[4] The movement or network thus both defines itself in terms of an oppositional practice and is in its turn criticised by its detractors for its commitment to fundamental change if not abolition of the extant rule of law.[5]

This chapter is dedicated ironically to the proposition that critical legal studies in America has failed in its radicalism: it has neither gone to the roots of the tradition, in the sense of philosophical radicalism, nor pursued any consistent commitment to fundamental change, in the sense of political radicalism. It is in many respects unsurprising to observe that the left in law shares the 'disintegrative' fate of its European counterparts,[6] that in conditions of political seclusion and existential isolation it treads the same path as western Marxism, towards philosophical idealism focused upon questions of method applied, if at all, to the field of aesthetics in a vein of speculative pessimism.[7] At the level of specifically American culture, the movement expresses an instance of the failure or evasion of philosophy in America, while at a political level it confirms the absorption of the left and of the literate dialogue of the public sphere into the institution, the mass university and the 'ruminations' of higher education.[8]

---

4   The aspersion or attribution of nihilism seldom achieves this level of philosophical coherence, but such a theme is implicit in Joseph Singer, 'The Player and the Cards: Nihilism and Legal Theory' (1984) 94 *Yale Law Journal* 1; Peter Gabel and Duncan Kennedy, 'Roll Over Beethoven' (1984) 36 *Stanford Law Review* 1; Gary Peller, 'The Metaphysics of American Law' (1985) 73 *California Law Review* 1151. See, for a discussion of this point in relation to the French left, the excellent Vincent Descombes, *Modern French Philosophy*, Cambridge: Cambridge University Press, 1979, pp. 110–131; also Peter Dews, *Logics of Disintegration*, London, Verso, 1987, at p. xvi: 'the fundamental issue here, of course, is the sense in which a philosophical position which assumes the foundations of the classical forms of critique to be necessarily and oppressively identitarian can itself continue to perform a critical function'.

5   Paul Carrington, 'Of Law and the River' (1984) 34 *Journal of Legal Education* 222; O. Fiss, 'The Death of Law?' (1984) 69 *Cornell Law Review* 1; *idem*, 'The Law Regained' (1989) 74 *Cornell Law Review* 245; Charles Fried, 'Jurisprudential Responses to Legal Realism' (1988) 73 *Cornell Law Review* 331; Neil Duxbury, 'Some Radicalism about Realism? Thurman Arnold and the Politics of Modern Jurisprudence' (1990) 10 *Oxford Journal of Legal Studies* 11.

6   The notion of disintegrative reason comes from Theodor Adorno, *Negative Dialectics*, London, Routledge, 1973; see also Dews, *Logics of Disintegration*. Further development of this theme can pursued through Norman Geras, *Prophets of Extremity*, London, Verso, 1990; Ernesto Laclau, *New Reflections upon the Revolution of Our Times*, London, Verso, 1991.

7   Perry Anderson, *Considerations on Western Marxism*, London, New Left Books, 1976, at p. 93, concluding a magisterial account of the western left aphoristically: 'Method as impotence, art as consolation, pessimism as quiescence: it is not difficult to perceive elements of all these in the complexion of Western Marxism.' See further, P. Anderson, *In the Tracks of Historical Materialism*, London, Verso, 1983.

It offers little more than a politics of pragmatism, disjunctive theories of practice and the analysis of a reality whose object is defined by the citation of other critical legal texts.[9]

In common with the European left and with the broader critical tradition located in a rapidly changing public sphere, critical legal studies is faced by numerous contradictions of institutional circumstance and existential compromise – an unhappy consciousness which has become the condition and privilege of postmodern intellectual culture.[10] At its best critical legal studies is a species of neo-scholasticism, and like its scholastic forebears it faces the geopolitical or translational risks of reviving or receiving an alien, imported or borrowed discipline and its accompanying tradition.[11] Far more frequently it appears closer to the dogma of patronage, the fashionable pedagogy of an institutional elite or high clergy, concerned not so much with a culture of the left as with the preservation and reproduction of its own institutional place and status.[12] In both aspects, it will be argued, the political survival of critical legal studies depends upon the development of an institutional radicalism which both recognises the specific

8  The most striking version of this argument is to be found in Russell Jacoby, *The Last Intellectuals*, New York, Noonday Press, 1987; see also Jon Wiener, *Professors, Politics and Pop*, London, Verso, 1991, especially pp. 339–347 ('Footnote or Perish'); Cornel West, *The American Evasion of Philosophy*, Madison, University of Wisconsin Press, 1989. See also Paul Buhle, *Marxism in the United States*, London, Verso, 1990; Régis Debray, *Critique of Political Reason*, London, Verso, 1983. Cf. Allan Bloom, *The Closing of the American Mind: How Higher Education has failed Democracy and Impoverished the Souls of Today's Students*, New York, Viking Books, 1987; also Alisdair MacIntyre, 'Reconceiving the University as an Institution and the Lecture as a Genre', in *idem, Three Rival Versions of Moral Inquiry*, London: Duckworth, 1990.

9  This is the modest programmatic conclusion arrived at, for example, in Alan Hunt, 'The Big Fear: Law Confronts Postmodernism' (1990) 35 *McGill Law Journal* 507, 533. See also, Rosemary Coombes, 'Toward a Theory of Practice in Critical Legal Studies' (1989) *Law and Social Inquiry* 69; Hutchinson, *Dwelling on the Threshold*; J. Boyle, 'The Politics of Reason: Critical Legal Theory and Local Social Thought' (1985) 133 *University of Pennsylvania Law Review* 685.

10 For a political analysis of this Hegelian term, see Jean-Paul Sartre, 'The Concrete Universal', in *idem, Between Existentialism and Marxism*, London, New Left Books, 1974. The theme is philosophically central to the unjustly overlooked J.-P. Sartre, *Critique of Dialectical Reason: Theory of Practical Ensembles*, London, New Left Books, 1976. On the conditions of postmodern intellectual life, the 'locus classicus modernus' is Jean-François Lyotard, *The Postmodern Condition*, Minneapolis, University of Minnesota Press, 1984; together with Hal Foster (ed.), *Postmodern Culture*, London, Pluto Press, 1986.

11 For an historical account of critique in law, see Peter Goodrich, 'Critical Legal Studies in England: Prospective Histories' (1992) 12 *Oxford Journal of Legal Studies* 195; also Peter Goodrich, 'A Short History of Failure: Law and Criticism 1580–1620', in *idem, Languages of Law: From Logics of Memory to Nomadic Masks*, London, Weidenfeld and Nicolson, 1990.

12 See Arthur Jacobson, 'Modern American Jurisprudence and the Problem of Power' (1985) 6 *Cardozo Law Review* 713. For an implicit recognition of this point, see Duncan Kennedy, 'Psycho-Social CLS: A Comment on the Cardozo Symposium' (1985) 6 *Cardozo Law Review* 1013. J. Schlegel, 'American Legal Theory and American Legal Education', in Joerges and Trubek (eds), *Critical Legal Thought*.

character and limitations of the scholarly field and in turn commits itself to the intellectual values which constitute the place, the institution and the social force of scholarship.

The argument will proceed in three stages. First, I will address the paradox of success and failure within American critical legal studies. I will argue that the success of critical legal studies, its high profile in the media, its demonic yet phantasmatic (and often ephemeral) presence in the faculty, and its satirical role within the law review are also the signs of its failure – its absence from institutional practice, its marginal status in relation to the reproduction of lawyering through educational rites. Second, I will suggest that the institutional politics of critical legal studies is in practice a politics of translation, of disciplinary borrowings, of cultural importations and of fashionable gestures. The politics of institutional populism, of media profile or of oppositionist bravado does not constitute any real threat to the established forms of doctrinal scholarship or pedagogic practice. Third, I will set out certain preconditions for a radical legal scholarship, a politics of legal academic reproduction rather than repetition, of the criteria of licit writing and of a radicalised rhetoric of law.

## SHOOTING ON LOCATION

It is the function of scholarship both to remember and to reproduce, to repeat and to transmit. The role of the scholar – who has historically incorporated the cleric, the scribe and the priest – is thus an admixture of curator, lector, tutor and visionary. At the centre of the intellectual project was the institutional recollection and passing on of tradition, of the bonds of identity and community that are signalled by the very term religion, *re-ligare*, to bind again.[13] On the margins of scholarship there are historically the poets, the artists and those other heretics or critics 'whose discourse wavers';[14] while on the periphery within the institution there are those who seek to devote their professional careers entirely to research and to writing. Here too, however, the reverie of the transcendent, the romanticism of vision or the narcotic aura of textuality can scarcely hide the positive pedagogic mission or frequently the celebrity status of marginal or 'critical' intellectuals. They too seek to convert, to expose, to pontificate and to persuade. Even the modest clerical message of doubt, of irony, of transcendental uncertainty or epistemic indeterminacy is programmatic

13 For an extensive discussion of this etymology and function, see R. Debray, *Critique of Political Reason*, London, Verso, 1983, at pp. 184–217. In one etymology the word 'law' can also be traced to *ligare* as well as to *legere* (to read) and *legein* (to speak). For a brief discussion, see G. Rose, *The Dialectic of Nihilism*, Oxford, Blackwell, 1984; P. Stein, *Regulae Iuris*, Edinburgh: Edinburgh University Press, 1966; and more extensively, E. Benveniste, *Le Vocabulaire des institutions Indo-Européenes*, Paris, Minuit, 1969.

14 P. Legendre, *Paroles poétiques échapées du texte*, Paris, Seuil, 1982, at p. 12.

and performative, it seeks to bind its audience, to move its constituency or identify and cohere its community. Nihilists have often been the most successful orators, the most charismatic of religious figures, the most purposive of clerics.[15] Nor should the homonymy of spirit and spirit, of phantasm and alcohol be entirely ignored. Narcotic free association slides easily into messianic vision, hallucinatory insight into intellectual dogma or doctrine, yet spirit also produces stupor, inertia and the stupidity of the inebriate.

Whatever the self-perception of critical legal studies in America, whether marginal or central to the academy, its most striking attribute from a sociological perspective is its media status and international profile. In superficially descriptive terms, critical legal studies had all the glamour of schism within the Vatican, dissent among the synod or Teresa among the Spanish nuns. It also has had the high visibility of foreign fashion, of the importation of European trends, new vocabularies and a commitment to political culture which for once extended far beyond the cloisters of the legal academy. To the extent that the movement represented an intellectual departure from the earlier theory of legal realism, it did so not least by virtue of its neo-scholasticism, its return to the philosophical tradition and its importation of European social theory.[16] While copious reference to the translated works of continental philosophy are no guarantee of any substantial theoretical genealogy,[17] they do have the elite function of identifying a community and of legitimating an esoteric marginality in relation to traditional doctrinal scholarship. In terms of the sociology of intellectuals, however, there is an undoubted irony in the opposition between the critics' claim to an outsider status, to a leftist marginality and the elite hubris or kudos of continental theory. Critical legal studies as an imported phenomenon, as a politics of intellectual credentials, also finds

15 Thus the myth of Hegesias, according to which Hegesias preached the valuelessness of life so successfully that his audiences would regularly commit suicide, leading Ptolemy to ban him from Egypt. See George Puttenham, *The Arte of English Poesie*, London, Field, 1589, at p. 118. The various heretical traditions of gnosticism and nihilism have seldom refrained from building communities or organising groups. See, for examples in a religious context, N. Cohn, *The Pursuit of the Millennium*, London, Paladin 1970, and Marcel Gauchet, *Le Désenchantement du monde: une histoire politique de la religion*, Paris, Gallimard, 1985; see also R. Debray, *Cours de médiologie générale*, Paris, Gallimard, 1991; R. Debray, *Le Scribe*, Paris, Grasset, 1980; J. Derrida, 'Scribble (Writing-Power)' (1979) 58 *Yale French Studies* 116.
16 See particularly J. Boyle, 'The Politics of Reason' (1985) 133 *University of Pennsylvania Law Review* 685; Drucilla Cornell, 'Institutionalization of Meaning, Recollection, Imagination and the Potential for Transformative Legal Interpretation' (1987) 135 *University of Pennsylvania Law Review* 1135; and more recently, D. Cornell, *The Philosophy of the Limit*, New York, Routledge, 1992. Generally, see D. Carlson, D. Cornell and M. Rosenfeld (eds), *Hegel and Legal Theory*, New York, Routledge, 1991; *idem* (eds), *Deconstruction and the Possibility of Justice*, New York, Routledge, 1992.
17 This point is made extensively in relation to English critical legal studies in W.T. Murphy, 'The Habermas Effect: Critical Theory and Academic Law' (1990) 42 *Current Legal Problems* 135.

itself bound to the patronage of the Ivy League law schools and the media decor that those schools attract. The defining criterion of high intellectual culture in mediatic terms is simply the 'ability to gain access to the means of mass communication',[18] and that, more than anything else, defines the power of the elite institutions.

One interpretation of this phenomenon would be to argue that the postmodern path to intellectual success, to star status and political preferment does not lie in the traditional route through the academic institution. Critical legal studies may in this sense represent the first moment of an intellectual 'mediology' within the legal academy.[19] It would be in one sense a method of bypassing the established institutional route to preferment, while in a more substantial sense it would reflect the changed political and technical context of intellectual work. Empirical studies of European intellectual culture indicate that the social space of intellectual success and of international recognition does not stem from institutional academic conformity but rather from marginal disciplines and from the polemical work of the institutional outsider, the researcher or writer who defines their social identity in terms of writing rather than in terms of academic commitment or institutional service.[20] While the American media may still reserve the full focus of publicity for intellectuals associated with the highest status schools, the role and transhumant career of the media intellectual is an established fact of an electronic culture of 'paratexts', graphic simulations and liquid crystal transmission.[21]

18 R. Debray, *Teachers, Writers, Celebrities: The Intellectuals of Modern France*, London, Verso, 1981, at p. 32 (translating R. Debray, *Pouvoir intellectuel en France*, Paris, Editions Ramsay, 1979).

19 For the development of mediology, see Debray, *Teachers, Writers, Celebrities*; and Debray, *Cours de mediologie*, where mediology is defined as the study of 'the mediations by means of which an idea becomes a material force, mediations of which the "media" are simply a particular belated and overgrown prolongation' (ibid., p. 14). Mediology traces the political genealogy of the contemporary intellectual from the cleric and the scribe but also has the more substantial and technical role of studying the materiality of thought, 'the technically determined material ensemble of supports, rapports and means of transmission which assures thought [*la pensée*] its social existence in each epoch.' (ibid., p. 17) This comes close to a grammatology as spelled out in J. Derrida, *Positions*, Chicago, University of Chicago Press, 1986; and in *idem*, *Of Grammatology*, Baltimore, Johns Hopkins University Press, 1976. In somewhat more conventional historical terms, see D. Kelley, *The Beginning of Ideology*, Cambridge, Cambridge University Press, 1981.

20 This is one of the principal findings of P. Bordieu, *Homo Academicus*, Cambridge, Polity Press, 1988, ch. 3. It is also a central theme of Debray, *Teachers, Writers, Celebrities*. On the legal 'field', see P. Bordieu, 'The Force of Law: Toward a Sociology of the Juridical Field' (1987) 38 *Hastings Law Journal* 814.

21 On paratexts in law, see Ronald Collins and David Skover, 'Paratexts' (1992) 44 *Stanford Law Review* 509; and for a more general critique, in addition to works cited, see Avital Ronell, *The Telephone Book: Technology, Schizophrenia, Electric Speech*, Lincoln, Nebr., University of Nebraska Press, 1989; Jean Baudrillard, *La Transparence du mal: essai sur les phénomènes extrêmes*, Paris, Galilée, 1990; Jacques Derrida, *The Post Card: From Socrates to Freud and Beyond*, Chicago, Chicago University Press, 1987. As regards the secondary literature, see Mark Poster, *The Mode of Information: Poststructuralism and Social Contexts*, Cambridge, Polity Press, 1990; Gregory Ulmer, *Teletheory: Grammatology in the Age of Video*, New York, Routledge, 1989.

The media intellectual is frequently presented as a figure of inauthenticity and of an active immorality. The move from text to paratext, from the linearity of script to the nodal constellation of video text, is viewed ethically as a move from a world of reference to a world of simulation, from substance to fantasy, from signs that signal something to signs that signal nothing beyond themselves: 'a degree xerox of culture'.[22] The irony to be observed in the present context is not that of the essentially puritanical or properly Protestant rejection of images and of the intellectual imaginary but rather the mediological proposition that there is a massive overproduction of texts and, in more technological contexts, of signs. While this argument has been levelled generally at the self-referential culture of the contemporary university and at the academicisation or co-optation of the left, it has been encountered also in relation to criticisms of the style and jargon of critical legal studies.[23] The new legal intellectuals, it is argued, write for themselves in an esoteric and exclusory rhetoric which circulates internally within the academy and signifies nothing much more than the fact of having been published. Such publication confers a certain symbolic credit within the institution but it has no wider significance beyond that of creating a class of *nouveau riche* intellectuals whose publications represent a constant aspiration towards upward mobility.[24]

There is a further significance to the critical aspirations of the more visible or prominent of the movement scholars, the patrons, merchants and middlemen of the new legal art. Without entering the debate on the politics of rhetoric or the institutional consequences of legal academic style, it is still appropriate to point out that the reproductive function of scholarship, its institution of an order of succession, is predicated upon production. In mediological terms, the positivity of critical legal studies must be viewed in terms of its literary produce, in terms of its material output and the institutional consequences of its graphematic substance, its

22 Baudrillard, *La Transparence du mal*, at p. 82. For a comparable argument made from a more properly sociological perspective, see Jacques Donzelot, *L'Invention du social: essai sur le declin des passions politiques*, Paris, Fayard, 1984; and in a literary critical context see Edward Said, *The World, the Text and the Critic*, London, Faber and Faber, 1989; E. Said, 'Opponents, Audiences, Constituencies and Community', in H. Foster (ed.), *Postmodern Culture*, London, Pluto, 1985. More broadly, see the historical analysis of intellectuals – though primarily literary critics – in Frank Lentricchia, *After the New Criticism*, Chicago, Chicago University Press, 1980; Terry Eagleton, *Literary Theory*, Minneapolis, Minnesota University Press, 1983; Tzvetan Todorov, *Literature and its Theorists*, Ithaca, NY, Cornell University Press, 1987. See also, Bruce Robbins (ed.), *Intellectuals: Aesthetics, Politics and Academics*, Minneapolis, University of Minnesota Press, 1987; Frederic Jameson, *The Political Unconscious*, London, Methuen, 1981; Michel Foucault, *Power/Knowledge*, New York, Pantheon Books, 1990.

23 For criticisms of obscurity, pretention and fraudulence, see Carrington, 'Of Law and the River', pp. 222–223: Fried, 'Jurisprudential Responses'; O. Fiss, 'The Death of Law?'.

24 Said, 'Opponents'; Baudrillard, *La Transparence du mal*.

writing. Here the politics of critical legal studies becomes more opaque. The claim to being a 'political location', 'subversive', 'oppositional' or simply leftist does not appear to necessarily carry to the alternately febrile and flippant produce of its harbingers. Aside from an early and now dated Marxist sociology of law which has been largely abandoned and which was itself imported,[25] the defining feature of the critics was arguably that of a naive and somewhat bowdlerised translation of continental social theory into an American legal idiom.[26] One consequence of such a characteristic of the literature was the limited audience which such a product or positivity was likely to have in the legal academy itself. Its success was its failure, its external visibility was its strongest form of internal secession, its text was its context. More interestingly and ironically, however, a literature bent upon importation and translation across languages, continents and jurisdictions has only an indirect relation to the immediate politics of the institution or practice of law. Such may yet, however, be the critics' greatest strength: not only does the repressed return,[27] but those that are either literally or figuratively expelled can use the rupture of institutional place as the most striking of emblems of injustice, and as the strongest of ethical gounds for the call to change. This is certainly one aspect of the critical movement's biography but it is not yet a defining feature of its politics.

In a bureaucratic age, the scholar is by profession a teacher. What is

25 Jacoby, *The Last Intellectuals*, at p. 167:

> As in many American industries, imports dominate the Marxist academy – for roughly the same reasons as with cars. Although the final product is sometimes assembled in the United States, foreign Marxism seems snappier, better designed; it accelerates more easily. It is more finished and polished.

See, for an example, Martin Jay, *Marxism and Totality*, Berkeley and Los Angeles, University of California Press, 1984; and David Lehman, *Signs of the Times*, London, Deutsch, 1991 at pp. 22–24.

26 For a recent and by and large sophisticated example of this project, see Matthew Kramer, *Legal Theory, Political Theory and Deconstruction: Against Rhadamanthus*, Bloomington, Indiana University Press, 1991, at pp. 2–3:

> For those not familiar with the more arcane pathways of recent French philosophy, the preceding paragraphs may be somewhat obscure. It is the aim of this introductory chapter, and indeed of this whole book to start to gain wider currency for the insights of French scholars among jurisprudes and political theorists in the Anglo-American tradition.

The work, in common with the bulk of American critical legal theory, is one of importation, translation and appropriation. For some interesting observations on this theme from a feminist perspective, see Suzanne Gibson, 'Continental Drift: The Question of Context in Feminist Jurisprudence' (1990) 1 *Law and Critique* 173. Cf. Alice Jardine, *Gynesis: Configurations of Woman and Modernity*, Ithaca, NY, Cornell University Press, 1985, ch. 1.

27 On the return of the repressed in law, see Austin Sarat and Tom Kearns (eds), *The Fate of Law*, Ann Arbor, University of Michigan Press, 1991, at p. 12: 'perhaps it is the ironic fate of law to be reconstructed or revitalized by those very ideas, for example, compassion, engagement, even politics, that law has for so long tried to exclude'.

striking about the literature of critique is its almost complete absence of relation to teaching practice and so to the immediate politics of the institution which it otherwise supports and publicises. It could be termed 'critique without copula' in the sense that it offers an order of succession of academics, a transmission of a self-referential and so exclusory form of symbolic capital which refers only by way of the most distant signals to the lifeworld of the legal pedagogue. If critical legal studies purportedly offers a local politics[28] it is not at all clear what or where the locale is; if it offers a 'relational politics' it is equally hard to discern with what or to whom the relationship is made.[29] It would seem to be divided at best between heterotopias of literature and difference on the one hand, and the moralism of the outsider seeking domicile on the other. While both projects may well have an ethical value, such a value or ethics is not yet connected to the life or practice of the academic institution. The most striking facet of American critical legal studies is its failure to penetrate, subvert or deviate from the established norms of legal educational practice. With only occasional exceptions[30] – and these exceptions do not involve substantially changing the syllabus or the classificatory grid of educational practice – the casebook and the Socratic method reign supreme. In an observational or empirical sense, critical legal studies has nothing to do with legal education, it has nothing to do with the teaching practice of legal scholars, it has only the most marginal of relations to the academic disicipline of law, if that discipline is defined in doctrinal or pedagogic terms. It rather obeys a mediological law:

> for the media, the objective world – the thing there is something to speak of – is what other media are saying. Be it hell or heaven, from now on we are going to have to live in this haunted hall where mirrors reflect mirrors and shadows chase shadows.[31]

The radicalism of American critical legal studies does not appear to extend to the lives of its practitioners. It does not threaten the institutional safety, tenured security, economic comfort or frequently elite status of the critics. Were its product not so frequently intellectually tawdry, it would be tempting to regard the movement as a form of designer chic within the legal academy, an imported fashion, the latest in pre-packaging 'from the shelf to you' without need for alteration. At one level it can simply and

28 James Boyle, 'Politics of Reason'; Mark Tushnet, 'Some Current Controversies in Critical Legal Studies', in Joerges and Trubek (eds), *Critical Legal Thought*. Also A. Sarat and T. Kearns, 'A Journey through Forgetting: Toward a Jurisprudence of Violence', in *idem* (eds), *The Fate of Law*, especially pp. 253–265.
29 The theory of a relational account of law is best expressed in A. Hunt, 'The Critique of Law', in Alan Hunt and Peter Fitzpatrick (eds), *Critical Legal Studies*, Oxford, Blackwell, 1987.
30 See particularly the essays collected in Kairys (ed.), *The Politics of Law*.
31 Debray, *Teachers, Writers, Celebrities*, at p. 118.

cynically be argued that legal academics in America were long ago bought out by the size of their professional salaries, that they suffer 'an enlightened false consciousness', a thoroughgoing cynicism or modern form of 'unhappy consciousness'.[32] Such unhappy consciousness is a species of pseudo-critique in which critical stances are subordinated to professional roles, the immediate politics of the institution to totalising theories of the particular, conflicts of value in the workplace to the exigencies of privatised therapies which order happiness, good relations with colleagues, or at least a realistic deference to the mechanisms of institutional advancement.

I will be more specific as to the features of the counter-revolution. The American law professor is too well paid to be politically committed, too status conscious to be intellectually engaged and too insular – too bound to the parochial and monolingual culture of the law review – to be scholarly. These are the progeny of mass legal culture, of the stupefaction which passes for legal education and at best produces a blend of intellectual naivety and doomed political enthusiasm. Its history appears from the outside to have been one of therapeutic self-confirmation hiding behind a legitimatory romanticism which views political radicalism as a species of patronage: critique is in pragmatic terms no more and no less than the essentially liberal yet nonetheless imperialistic desire to embrace and to include any stranger, any other, any nomad, any political infant or any woman who can plausibly represent an outside within the academy. These, however, are the tokens of radicalism, the coinage of hubris, whereby an inauthentic and uneasy bureaucratic elite salvages its conscience by buying in representatives of repressed, marginalised or disadvantaged groups.

More than that, however, the American translation of European social theory – of the 'new philosophies' and the 'new politics' – seems predicated upon the belief that by supporting the marginal, the foreign, the peripheral or the outsider, the intellectual within the institution becomes, presumably by projection, marginal or foreign – and so *ipso facto* politically radical himself. As if the greatest injustice known to the world were the indignity of being fired from Yale, refused tenure at Harvard or barred from promotion at Stanford or Pennsylvania. As if a political biography which ends at the law school in Georgetown, Washington or in Madison, Wisconsin or Cardozo, New York or Hampshire College, Amherst or the New School, San Fransisco or Amsterdam, Earth, Mars or Kansas somehow spelled out the injustice of the American polity, of the marginal, the unloved or the ignored, in its entirety. In these terms the time of critique

32 For development of these and related themes, see Peter Sloterdijk, *Critique of Cynical Reason*, Minneapolis, University of Minnesota Press, 1987, chs. 1 and 2. See further, G.W.F. Hegel, *Phenomenology of Spirit*, trans. A.V. Miller, Oxford, Oxford University Press, 1977; Jean-Paul Sartre, *What is Literature?*, London, Methuen, 1984 edn.

has surely run out, for critique is a matter of distance, of prospect and perspective, whereas the network or the group is altogether too close for comfort or at least too close for criticism.

It seems almost appropriate that Mark Tushnet, in a most unpolitical 'political history' of critical legal studies should propose a rather anodyne yet peculiarly telling emblem or, more properly, icon for the movement: it is a place, a location, a heading, an umbrella.[33] This place or location is in the law school and it is interesting to contemplate further and from a variety of perspectives why an umbrella might be useful in law school. First, and most interestingly, from the perspective of the social moralist Stevenson we learn that 'it is the habitual carriage of the umbrella that is the stamp of Respectability. The umbrella has become the acknowledged index of social position'.[34] It is tempting to prolong and emphasise the metaphor of moral place that the umbrella offers: it is the icon of bound space as well as of transient refuge or mobile structure. Yet it is also, as Stevenson does not fail to recognise, a portable icon and constitutes a mystical space.[35] From the perspective of those that do not believe, it is potentially duplicitous or mendacious.[36] In Stevenson's moralistic terms the duplicity of the network, movement or place lies in a critique or critical stance which seeks little more than institutional respectability or a place within the hierarchy for the radical and the marginal, but also – it might be suggested – for the naive and the incompetent; the tired, the masculine, the white and the obscure.

The same point could be made by reference to the symbolism of the umbrella. It is in Freudian terms a phallic symbol, the pleated gingham or silk hides, veils or secrets away 'an organ which is at once aggressive and apotropaic, threatening and/or threatened'.[37] There is a certain modesty to the symbol but there is also an ideology or a paranoia which pitches

---

33 Tushnet, 'Critical Legal Studies', particularly at pp. 1515–1519. On the 'umbrella' movement of critical legal studies, see also Peter Rush, 'Killing them Softly with his Words' (1990) 1 *Law and Critique* 21, at 23.

34 Robert Louis Stevenson, 'The Philosophy of Umbrellas', in *idem, Lay Morals*, London, Chatto and Windus, 1911 edn, at p. 151. He argues further 'that we . . . are almost inclined to consider all who possess really well-conditioned umbrellas as worthy of the Franchise . . . they carry a sufficient stake in the commonweal below their arm' (ibid., p. 153).

35 In orthodox Christianity, the church (*ecclesia*) is constituted by the collapsible presence of the icon; where an icon is raised or installed, the secular space becomes sacred, the profane spirited. For general accounts, see: Alexandre Schmemman, *L'Eucharistie*, Paris, SCM, 1985; Yngve Brilioth, *Eucharistic Faith*, London, Dent, 1990.

36 Having argued that 'umbrellas, like faces, acquire a certain sympathy with the individual who carries them; indeed they are far more capable of betraying his trust ', Stevenson, concludes that 'a mendacious umbrella is a sign of great moral degredation' ('Philosophy of Umbrellas', at p. 154).

37 Jacques Derrida, *Spurs: Nietzsche's Styles*, Chicago, Chicago University Press, 1979, at p. 129. For extensive further analysis, see Dominique Noguez, *Sémiologie du parapluie et autres textes*, Paris, Editions de la Difference, 1990, pp. 11–29, developing a neo-logistic science of 'parahyetology'. He remarks at one point – of the symbolism of the umbrella – 'the phallus is . . . at one and the same time desire and repression, the blind continuity of a plenitude and the yawning sight of the void'.

artifact against nature, culture against tempest, style against expression. Nietzsche forgets his umbrella,[38] which is possibly to say that in a life devoted to the proximity of thought to nature, of mind to body, it was impossible to hide from either fate or thunder, destiny or storm, by the artifice of the umbrella. Nor did Nietzsche hide his writing behind the artifice or conventions of genre or of style: for the philosopher as aesthete, the style *was* the thought, a life lived as art – 'like a woman or like writing, it passes itself off for what it passes itself off for'.[39] Writing does not need to shelter, it is rather the institution and the law which imposes a standardised rhetoric, a writing for essays, trials, tests and examinations, a writing for bureaucracy, a prose for conformity and for defeat.[40]

Nor, finally, should one fear to be wet. The umbrella suggests a place that is dry, a liberal location which keeps nature and fluid at bay. As Drucilla Cornell has observed, 'wetness' is associated with femininity, with bodily fluids and occasionally with uncleanness.[41] Fluid – pluvial, aquaeous, oceanic, vaporous or internal – is the allegory of femininity, for fluid dissolves and escapes, it is inconsistent, disequilibriated and changing, *'fluid* has to remain that secret *remainder'*.[42] Could the umbrella keep these aquarian phenomena away? Is it appropriate to be 'stiff' and dry, to erect barriers against nature and against the writing or thought of the body? Again there is a potential duplicity or at least an irony, the umbrella is not a utopian instrument, it is at most heterotopic and as such should be used only occasionally and terroristically. It need simply be reiterated that in psychoanalytic terms this particular symbolism of critique is tied to aspirations of acceptance, to the desire to be accepted, to the desire for proximity or to be close and incorporated. Nor does the emblem of the umbrella exhaust itself in the metaphor of community. As a reference to the carapace of style, it can be argued further that it is precisely in relation to writing that law is most directly and disturbingly threatened. It is precisely in challenging the normativity of genre or the rhetoric of writing that

38 'I have forgotten my umbrella.' Fragment classified no. 12,175 in the French edition of *Joyful Wisdom*, p. 147, cited and discussed at length in Derrida, *Spurs*, pp. 123–140.
39 Ibid., at p. 127. On art, language and life, see particularly F. Nietzsche, *The Will to Power*, Edinburgh, Foulis, 1909, on writing, and particularly the writing of the body, see Hélène Cixous, *Coming to Writing*, Cambridge, Mass.: Harvard University Press, 1991; Luce Irigaray, *Marine Lover: Of Friedrich Nietzsche*, New York, Columbia University Press, 1991; Derrida, *The Post Card*; Susan Sellers, *Women and Writing*, London, Macmillan, 1991. For a fascinating historical relation of the sins of flesh and language, see Carla Casagrande and Silvano Vecchio, *Les Peches de la langue*, Paris, Editions de la Cerf, 1991.
40 Reference is particularly to the informatic prose of technological massification. For critiques of information, see Baudrillard, *La Transparence du mal*; Legendre, *Paroles poétiques échapées du texte*.
41 See Drucilla Cornell, *Beyond Accommodation*, New York, Routledge, 1991, ch. 1; also D. Cornell, 'What Takes Place in the Dark', in *idem*, *Transformations*, New York: Routledge, 1991.
42 Luce Irigaray, *Speculum of the Other Woman*, Ithaca, NY, Cornell University Press, 1985 at p. 237 (emphasis in original). See further, L. Irigaray, *This Sex Which is Not One* Ithaca, NY, Cornell University Press, 1985, ('The mechanics of fluids').

critical legal studies can find a space that awaits its appropriate politicisation.[43] Writing differently or writing otherwise are far more threatening to the academic institution and indeed to bureaucracy generally than many more overtly radical strategies or politically subversive messages.[44]

## NO PARTICULAR PLACE TO GO

The politics of form is necessarily accompanied by substantive effects. Indeed it is arguable that the two cannot be differentiated but rather are dialectically bound.[45] In that respect critical legal studies continues the ancient war of texts.[46] It goes further than the Romanists, the glossators, the commentators or the common lawyers – the Anglican legists – by recognising that the gloss is also an intervention rather than a simple or neutral repetition, précis, concordance, paraphrase or rephrasing. It obscurely recognises that what is at stake in the text, namely the constitution of legal subjectivity, is a matter of textual politics as well as of a linguistic inhabitation of the text.[47] More so, for a politics located in the academy it should not be hard to recognise that the text is the normative territory of legal life, and the discourse of law the constitution of the sociality – the civility – of legal subjects, 'the children of the text'.[48] Here then there can be no question but that discourse and text are themselves a politics, or in more formal terms that the ontology – the being – of law and so too of

43 Again the principal proponent of this thesis is Derrida, *The Post Card*; and again in J. Derrida, *Dissemination*, Chicago, Chicago University Press, 1981. See also the remarkable discussion of writing and law in A. Jacobson, 'The Idolatry of Rules: Writing Law According to Moses' (1990) 11 *Cardozo Law Review* 1079; and for further discussion, P. Goodrich, 'Contractions', in *idem*, *Languages of Law*; C. Douzinas and R. Warrington, 'Posting the Law: Social Contracts and the Postal Rule's Grammatology' (1991) 4 *International Journal for the Semiotics of Law* 115. For futher discussion of the postal rule, see Peter Goodrich, *Oedipus Lex: Psychoanalysis, History, Law*, Berkeley and Los Angeles, University of California Press, 1995.

44 This point is made at length in Michel Foucault, *Power/Knowledge*, New York, Pantheon Books, 1982; M. Foucault, *Language, Memory, Counter-Practice*, Ithaca, NY, Cornell University Press, 1977. See also, J. Derrida, 'Response', in N. Fabb, A. Durant and C. Mcabe (eds), *The Linguistics of Writing*, Manchester, Manchester University Press, 1989. The theme is also present in Roberto Unger, *The Critical Legal Studies Movement*, Cambridge, Mass., Harvard University Press, 1986.

45 For an interesting example of this thesis put into practice, see P. Schlag, 'Cannibal Moves: An Essay on the Metamorphoses of the Legal Distinction' (1988) 40 *Stanford Law Review* 929. For another example, see Rush, 'Killing them Softly'.

46 For a history of the 'war of texts', see P. Legendre, *Le Désir politique de Dieu: étude sur les montages de l'état et du droit*, Paris, Fayard, 1988. More broadly, see P. Legendre, *Jouir du pouvoir: traité sur la bureaucratie patriote*, Paris, Editions de Minuit, 1976; P. Legendre, 'The Lost Temporality of Law' (1990) 1 *Law and Critique* 3.

47 In American critical legal terms, this thesis returns to Karl Klare, 'Law-Making as Praxis' (1979) 40 *Telos* 123. For further discussion, see A. Hunt, 'Theory of Critical Legal Studies', at pp. 37–43; and Hunt, 'The Big Fear', p. 507. For further discussion in a European context, see Goodrich, *Languages of Law*, ch. 8 ('Law's Emotional Body').

48 On which, see P. Legendre, *Les Enfants du texte*, Paris, Fayard, 1992. In the American context, see the excellent P. Schlag, 'Le Hors de Texte, C'Est Moi: The Politics of Form and the Domestication of Deconstruction' (1990) 11 *Cardozo Law Review* 1631.

legal subjectivity is located in the material circulation, access to, storage of and transmission by texts.[49] While, in a strictly schematic sense, the ensuing analysis moves from form to substance, from place to purpose and from style to intellectual circumstance, it is not intended to imply anything more than a descriptive account of philosophical and political oppositions identified with critical legal studies. If the umbrella is an unfortunate emblem for a putatively radical movement, it may be more effective to seek an intellectual identity or political space in the conflictual trajectory of the academic literature produced by and descriptive of the movement, network or place of critique.

The discourse of identity is most usually the product of denial, the unitary identity of legal subjects in particular being the positive consequence of the negation of the fragmentary *personae* and fractured experiences of institutional biography and collective belonging. Our group or individual identity is a product of the claims we make to difference, we are by virtue of what we claim we are not.[50] In this respect an intellectual and political cartography of American critical legal studies could well begin with the attribution of nihilism to the critical stance: this designation is both an exemplar of negation and an instance of ethical mistranslation.[51] It is further the most obvious space of political conflict within the legal academy: in a reprise of certain of the denunciations of the legal realists, those that were deemed neither to believe in the enterprise of law nor to express adherence to the values of established doctrine, were to be labelled nihilists and irrationalists and were explicitly and implicitly invited to leave the legal academy.[52]

49 For an historical analysis of this point, see Peter Goodrich, 'Literacy and the Languages of the Early Common Law' (1987) 14 *Journal of Law and Society* 422. More broadly, see M. Foucault, 'The Discourse on Language', in *idem, The Archaeology of Knowledge*, New York, Pantheon Books, 1972; Julia Kristeva, *Revolution in Poetic Language*, New York, Columbia University Press, 1984; P. Goodrich, *Legal Discourse*, New York, St Martin's Press, 1990.

50 Sigmund Freud, 'Negation', in *idem, General Psychological Theory*, New York, Macmillan, 1963; Homi Bhabha (ed.), *Nation and Narration*, London, Routledge, 1990; Benedict Anderson, *Imagined Communities*, London, Verso, 1983; Peter Goodrich, 'Poor Illiterate Reason' (1992) 1 *Social and Legal Studies* 7.

51 I have analysed and criticised this debate previously, in Peter Goodrich, *Reading the Law*, Oxford, Blackwell, 1986, at ch. 7. On the philosophical genealogy of the concept of nihilism, of which American critical legal studies seems so easily ignorant, see Nietzsche, *The Will to Power*; Martin Heidegger, *Nietzsche: Nihilism*, New York, Harper and Row, 1982; Gianni Vattimo, *The End of Modernity*, Oxford, Polity, 1990.

52 Paul Carrington, 'Of Law and the River' (1984) 34 *Journal of Legal Education* 222, responding to the closing remarks of R. Unger, 'The Critical Legal Studies Movement' (1983) 96 *Harvard Law Review* 563, 675; P. Carrington, 'Butterfly Effects: The Possibilities of Law Teaching in a Democracy' (1992) 41 *Duke Law Journal* 741; Fiss, 'The Death of Law?'; O. Fiss, 'Objectivity and Interpretation' (1982) 34 *Stanford Law Review* 739. For the more general debate as to nihilism in legal studies, see Singer, 'The Player and the Cards'; John Stick, 'Can Nihilism be Pragmatic?' (1986) 100 *Harvard Law Review* 332; and the literature reviewed in David Chow, 'Trashing Nihilism' (1990) 65 *Tulane Law Review* 221. On irrationalism and nihilism, see Georg Lukacs, *The Destruction of Reason*, London, Lawrence and Wishart, 1980; Dews, *Logics of Disintegration*; Norman Geras, *Prophets of Extremity*, London, Verso, 1989; Ernesto Laclau and Chantal Mouffe, *Hegemony and Socialist Strategy*, London, Verso, 1986; Thomas Docherty, *After Theory*, London, Routledge, 1991.

## NIHILISM OR NOWHERE LEFT TO GO

The antirrhetic,[53] polemical as opposed to philosophical, character of the aspersion of nihilism deserves momentary emphasis. In its negative connotation it would appear to mean – if such is not too strong a term – a combination of existential hopelessness, doctrinal libertinism, political anarchism, philosophical amoralism, irrationalism, immodesty and faith-lessness. In its positive connotation, it would appear rather as a varied and eclectic advocacy of what is inelegantly termed anti-foundationalism, a combination of philosophical pragmatism and political romanticism. Neither field of connotations accords with any recognised historical or philosophical sense of nihilism, a term deriving from *nihilum*, signifying nothing or nil, of no value or without value, but taken philosophically by Nietzsche to mean negation, the will to annihilation of fixed and sedent-ary values.[54] Nihilism was not the coincident or generic expression of *ressentiment* or passivity but rather an active political and historical force engaged with preparing a post-theistic secular world for recognising that being was without foundation, and that the absence of foundation was constitutive of the human condition.[55] Being, in Heidegger's terms, was not foundation but rather the site of disappearance, of the *mise en abyme* of thought.[56]

In political terms the European philosophical tradition which develops from Nietzsche has tended to argue for an 'accomplished' or positive perception of nihilism. The nihilist recognises the death of the highest values – of a particular Judaeo-Christian order of corporeal and spiritual repression – as a point of ethical and political opportunity, as the meeting of history and destiny, as the inauguration of a novel 'mobility of the symbolic',[57] as the beginning of a secular social world which can only ever begin, only ever aspire to becoming. The pertinent point is that

53 The antirrhetic is the rhetorical form of discourses of denunciation, archetypically discourses against iconoclasts. For an extended historical account of the antirrhetic, see P. Goodrich, 'Antirrhesis: The Polemical Structure of Common Law Thought', in A. Sarat and T. Kearns (eds), *Law and Rhetoric*, Ann Arbor, University of Michigan Press, 1993. In a strictly rhetorical sense the critical legal studies movement could be designated nihilistic insofar as the iconodules would of rhetorical or antirrhetical necessity paint an anti-portrait of the iconoclast as sacrilegious, irrational and against nature.
54 See Gilles Deleuze, *Nietzsche and Philosophy*, London, Athlone Press, 1983, for an interesting account of this sense of nihilism in Nietzsche. See also Rose, *Dialectic of Nihilism*, at pp. 172–173.
55 Albert Camus, *The Nihilists*, Harmondsworth, Penguin, 1969; Vattimo, *End of Modernity*, ch. 1.
56 See M. Heidegger, *What is Metaphysics?*, New York, Harper and Row, 1976. Also, Paul Virilio, *The Aesthetics of Disappearance*, New York, Semiotexte, 1991; J. Baudrillard, *Simulations*, New York, Semiotexte, 1983; J. Derrida, *Writing and Difference*, New York, Routledge, 1978; J. Derrida, *The Truth in Painting*, Chicago, University of Chicago Press, 1987.
57 Vattimo, *End of Modernity*, at p. 28.

however the concept of nihilism is interpreted there is little sense in which critical legal studies could be designated intelligently as nihilistic in either a positive or a negative connotation.

Critical legal studies has neither the philosophical acumen to know what nihilism designates nor the political will to rupture, reappropriate or translate a being without foundation into an historical constellation of legal or counter-legal values.[58] Critical legal studies refers at most to a hermeneutic nihilism, a specific loss of faith first in the constitutional text and subsequently in the determinacy of all legal meanings. While the seemingly interminable lucubrations of the critics and others on the method and theory of interpretation may come close to a species of textual nil or nothingness, to the circulation of texts that have become 'empty speech' or 'gray on gray',[59] the specific problems of the legal consequences of semantic indeterminacy are hardly the same thing as a fully fledged philosophical nihilism to which critical legal studies neither approaches nor in all probability aspires.[60] More than that, the assertion of an absolute indeterminacy could only express the alienation, estrangement or distance of critical legal studies from institutional legal acts, sentences and en-forcement: judgment, after all, occurs within a terrain of inscriptions of pain upon the body.[61] As Lacan once remarked, the real may be elusive, yet 'when we bang our heads against a stone wall, we are struggling with the real' and in that context it might be added, the real leaves us dazed, either delirious or unconscious.[62]

The question surrounding critical legal studies is not that of any direct, conscious or substantial adherence to nihilistic philosophical positions. The most that can be said is that the strategy of self-identification pursued by the movement – presumably so as to indicate the points between which movement or (e)motion occurred – is predicated upon a species of

58 This argument is made most strongly by J.-P. Sartre, *Critique of Dialectical Reason*.
59 The concept of 'empty speech' (*parole vide*) is taken from Jacques Lacan, *Ecrits: A Selection*, London, Tavistock, 1980, at pp. 40–56; the 'gray on gray' comes from Jacoby, *The Last Intellectuals*, at p. 236. For an emotive version of this argument applied to the legal academy, see James Boyd-White, *Justice as Translation*, Chicago, Chicago University Press, 1990, especially ch. 1. In a different tone, there is also Stanley Fish, 'Dennis Martinez and the Uses of Theory', reprinted in *idem, Doing What Comes Naturally*, Oxford, Oxford University Press, 1990.
60 For a critical appraisal of the indeterminacy debate, see Charles Yablon, 'The Indeterminacy of the Law: Critical Legal Studies and the problem of Legal Explanation' (1985) 6 *Cardozo Law Review*; Cornell, *Philosophy of the Limit*, pp. 91–95.
61 An observation made most forcefully in the history of imprisonment, see Michel Foucault, *Discipline and Punish*, Harmondsworth, Pelican, 1978; Michael Ignatieff, *A Just Measure of Pain*, London, Allen Lane, 1980. In an American context, see Robert Coover, 'Violence and the Word' (1986) 95 *Yale Law Journal* 1600. See also the powerful analysis in Costas Douzinas and Ronnie Warrington, 'A Well-Founded Fear of Justice' (1991) 2 *Law and Critique* 115.
62 Cited in Sherry Turkle, *Psychoanalytic Politics: Freud's French Revolution*, London, Deutsch, 1979, at p. 243. See further, Catherine Clement, *Lives and Legends of Jacques Lacan*, Princeton, Princeton University Press, 1985.

negation or denial: the critics cluster around a series of portentous negations: they do not believe in objectivity, (semantic) determinacy or neutrality as attributes of legal judgment.[63] The identificatory thesis is most usually developed around the concept of indeterminacy, the proposition that in all rule application there is an element of variation or uncertainty, choice or discretion. The interesting question to be posed, however, is not that of the degree of variation nor of the extent of uncertainty – these are antique and unexceptionable jurisprudential themes – but rather the form of denial of certainty itself. The claim of the indeterminacy thesis is that of negation of determinacy. It initially can be argued that this negation simply retains the determinacy thesis in an attenuated form:

> the subject-matter of a repressed image or thought can make its way into consciousness on condition that it is *denied*. Negation is a way of taking account of what is repressed. . . . The result is a kind of intellectual acceptance of what is repressed, though in all essentials the repression persists.[64]

More interestingly, however, it is possible to endeavour to pursue the image of indeterminacy and to ask what is at stake in an apparently vague or essentially uncontroversial realist claim. How does the recollection of the function of judgment – of discrimination, taste or political choice – lead so suddenly to aspersions of nihilism, to allegations both of a life and of a law deprived of meaning? No more than a partial answer can be offered.

The etymological root of determinacy is *terminus*, connoting both boundary and conclusion or end. The question becomes what is it that ends in the law? What is it that ends with the law? With this law? A question of the intellectual history of jurisprudence and of doctrine that takes the analyst deep into the unconscious structures of law. First, however, the notion of boundary and of going beyond the pale: it is not the by and large conscious semantic indeterminacy of law that immediately threatens the citadel, it is the mixing of genres, the conflation, non-recognition or transgression of boundaries, texts and territories, that engenders a terror of criticism. What happens when the law is treated as literature or worse when literature plays the law and fiction becomes the

---

63 Chow, 'Trashing Nihilism', at p. 224–225, summarising Singer, 'The Player and the Cards'. See also Gary Peller, 'The Metaphysics of American Law' (1985) 73 *California Law Review* 1151; also G. Peller, 'Reason and the Mob: The Politics of Representation' (1987) 2 *Tikkun* 28.

64 Freud, 'Negation', at p. 214. For discussion, see Kristeva, *Revolution in Poetic Language*; Mikkel Borch-Jacobsen, *Lacan: The Absolute Master*, Stanford, Stanford University Press, 1990; G. Deleuze, *Différence and Répétition* Paris, Presses Universitaires de France 1968.

figure of the truth?[65] At one level the response may be that the literature of legal criticism is of little aesthetic interest, that it is beyond the pale of good or discriminating taste.[66] Perhaps it ceases to be literature.[67] Such a response, however, misses the point. The degree to which the proponents of the indeterminacy thesis seek determinacy or ineffectively mourn its loss is symptomatic of a greater stake than that of simple jurisdiction. At an analytic level the question of the boundary marked by law is that of the separation and opposition of pleasure and pain, life and death, *eros* and *thanatos*.[68]

The indeterminacy thesis exposes the mystical foundation of law.[69] It suggests a level or depth of uncertainty that affects not simply legal judgment but equally the prejudices or prejudgments of law. It asks the question of tradition and of the traditionality of law: if this is common law, to whom is it common? It was not, after all, common to the peasant who stood before the law, who died before the law, for whom the law was ever a secret. But even this is not the stake. The stake is death itself and the lie which suggests that through law, through the law as an order of succession, death may in some measure be evaded. Death is the zone of an absolute and never-ending indeterminacy. It is in Blanchot's terms 'the utterly indeterminate, the indeterminate moment and not only the zone of the unending and the indeterminate'.[70] The residual Christian sensibility embodied in doctrine, in established modern jurisprudence, is appalled

---

65 The question is asked most forcefully in J. Derrida, 'Préjugés: Devant la Loi', in J. Derrida, Jean-Luc Nancy and J.-F. Lyotard, *La Faculté de juger*, Paris, Editions de Minuit, 1985, at p. 134:

> Literature has perhaps come to occupy, in these specific historical conditions which are not only linguistic, a space which remains open to a certain subversive legality (*juridicité*) . . . it makes the law, it comes into view in the place where the law makes itself . . . in the elusive instant where it plays the law, literature passes literature. It finds itself on both sides of the line which separates law from the outside of law. . . .

More broadly on the medieval maxim *fictio figura veritatis*, see Ernst Kantorowicz, *The King's Two Bodies*, Princeton, Princeton University Press, 1956; P. Legendre, *L'Empire de la vérité*, Paris, Fayard, 1983; and Lacan, *Ecrits*, pp. 74–75, 305–306.

66 As, for example, remarked of Singer by Hunt, 'The Big Fear', at p. 528: 'Singer's edifying legal theory of opposition to cruelty, misery, hierarchy and loneliness is just too mushy and indeterminant for my tastes.'

67 As could be remarked, in a different context, of the final chapter of C. Douzinas, R. Warrington and S. McVeigh, *Postmodern Jurisprudence: Texts of the Law in the Law of Texts*, London, Routledge, 1991.

68 Deleuze, *Différence et répétition*; S. Freud, *Beyond the Pleasure Principle*, London, Hogarth Press, 1961.

69 On the mystical foundations of law, see F. Nietzsche, *Birth of Tragedy*, Edinburgh, Foulis, 1905, at p. 174: 'the state itself knows no more powerful unwritten law than the mythical foundation which vouches for its connection with religion and its growth from mythical ideas'; also J. Derrida, 'Force of Law: The Mystical Foundation of Authority' (1990) 11 *Cardozo Law Review* 919.

70 M. Blanchot, *The Space of Literature*, Lincoln, Nebr., University of Nebraska Press, 1982, at p. 99.

by indeterminacy, by the prospect of eventually becoming an indeterminate element in a zone of unending indifference. And yet that is our fate,
such is human destiny: historical being is necessarily being towards
death.[71] The question posed by the indeterminacy thesis is the question of
closure. What is it that law excludes? What is it that law represses? What
is it of which the law will not speak?

One answer, offered by recent strands of critical legal studies – if, as is
I believe possible, feminist jurisprudence and critical race theory can be
aligned with the movement – is autobiographical. The literature and
politicisation of autobiographical accounts of law is in philosophical terms
an attempt to respect the facticity, the historicality and finitude of being.[72]
In recognising the exigency of being towards death, the literature of legal
autobiography engages with a legality of the contingent, an historical and
social as well as literary law, a linguistically and politically constructed
governance or rule of law. In terms of intellectual history, the return to the
'voice' of law (*viva vox iuris* or *lex loquens*), to a bodily writing or bio-graphy
(*bios-graphien*), is a return to (though also projection of) an earlier discourse
of law, that of the fates or *fata*, the daughters of necessity who would
predict or foretell – like the oracles at Delphi – the structure if not always
the events of human existence. Here the law is directly called into question.
The issue is that of the legitimacy of the legal construction of the
institution: if the institution is our fate then the law is the medium and
manner of our resistance to, accommodation of, or love for it.[73] It is in this
sense of law as a response to fate, as an aspect of the discourse of the fates,
that critical legal concern with indeterminacy – with the issues of openness
and closure – can be politicised in terms of hedonism or nihilism, *eros* or
*thanatos*, nascence or nemesis. To which it should be added that only the
most fervently puritanical, complacently ignorant or deeply pessimistic

---

71 M. Heidegger, *Being and Time*, Oxford, Blackwell, 1962; A. Lingis, *Deathbound Subjectivity*,
Bloomington, Indiana University Press, 1989. Generally, Cicero, *De Fato*, London,
Heinemann, 1942 edn; Boethius, *The Consolation of Philosophy*, London, Elliot Stock, 1897
edn.

72 R. Delgado, 'The Imperial Scholar: Reflections on a Review of Civil Rights Literature'
(1984) 132 *University of Pennsylvania Law Review* 561. See also Derek Bell, *And We are not
Saved: The Elusive Quest for Racial Justice*, New York, Basic Books, 1987; Patricia Williams,
*The Alchemy of Race and Rights*, Cambridge, Mass., Harvard University Press, 1991; David
Kennedy, 'Spring Break' (1985) 63 *Texas Law Review* 1377.

73 For a particularly powerful expression of this thesis, see Alexandra Papageorgiou,
*Filiation: fondement généalogique de la psychanalyse*, Paris, Fayard, 1990. See also Debray,
*Critique of Political Reason*, and on *amor fati*, see Nietzsche, *Daybreak*, Cambridge, Cambridge
University Press, 1881, 1982 edn, at p. 258:

my formula for greatness in a human being is *amor fati*: that one wants nothing to be
different, not forward, not backward, not in all eternity. Not merely bear what is
necessary, still less conceal it – all idealism is mendaciousness in the face of what is
necessary – but *love* it.

can propose that hedonism is either apolitical or amoral.[74] Hedonism is nothing less than the political expression of *amor fati*, of fate as character,[75] or at a collective level of an active and dramatic historical and ethical gnosticism. In a more aphoristic and more potent vein, it may simply be observed that the critique of law is the philosophy of its history.

## TRANSLATION OR NOTHING LEFT TO HOLD ON TO

The question of law as a question of fate or fortune, of destiny as the external force which historical being defines itself against, leads to a further consideration and a second identificatory feature of critical legal studies. It was Gadamer who perhaps most clearly posed the question of death as being at the hermeneutic basis of tradition.[76] For Gadamer all institutional speech is a matter of translation, transmission, across the temporal, geographic and linguistic boundaries that separate generations, cultures, communities and institutions.[77] Translation was the always desired and constantly impossible goal of all speech, though its archetype was writing and the textual corpus of tradition. Tradition was the stranger whom the present must come to know; tradition was *nomos* as language and as law. The problem of translation is in that sense also the question of justice: 'that which is here named Babel: the law imposed by the name of God which simultaneously both prescribes and prohibits translation in both showing and hiding the limit'.[78] It is impossible to

74 Slavoj Zizek, *For They Know Not What They Do: Enjoyment as a Political Factor*, London, Verso, 1991. The literature on hedonism is of varied quality, but it is possible to recommend particularly Sloterdijk, *Critique of Cynical Reason* (arguing for a philosophy of disinhibition or classical cynicism); F. Nietzsche, *Ecce Homo*, Edinburgh, Foulis, 1911 edn; Herbert Marcuse, 'On Hedonism', in *idem, Negations*, London, Allen Lane 1976; Paul Feyerabend, *Against Method*, London, New Left Books, 1975.

75 Walter Benjamin, 'Fate as Character', in *idem, One Way Street*, London, New Left Books, 1979, at p. 124, at p. 125: 'the system of signs of character is generally confined to the body'.

76 H.-G. Gadamer, *Truth and Method*, London, Sheed and Ward, 1979. For further accounts of legal hermeneutics, see 'Symposium: Interpretation' (1985) 58 *Southern California Law Review*; 'Symposium: Law and Literature' (1982) 60 *Texas Law Review*; and in a European context, P. Goodrich, *Reading the Law*, at ch. 5; Douzinas, Warrington, and McVeigh, *Postmodern Jurisprudence*, ch. 2. See also, D. Michelfelder and R. Palmer (eds), *Dialogue and Deconstruction*, New York, New York University Press, 1989.

77 Gadamer, *Truth and Method*, at p. 489: 'Everything that is set down in writing is to some extent foreign and strange, and hence it poses the same task of understanding as what is spoken in a foreign language.'

78 J. Derrida, 'Des Tours de Babel', *idem*, in *Psyché: inventions de l'autre*, Paris, Galilée, 1987, p. 234. The literature on the impossible philosophy of translation is extensive but mention should at least be made to W. Benjamin, 'The Task of the Translator', in *idem, Illuminations*, New York, Schocken, 1969; G. Steiner, *After Babel*, Oxford, Oxford University Press, 1975; Paul de Man, *Resistance to Theory*, Minneapolis, University of Minnesota Press, 1986; J. Derrida, *The Ear of the Other: Octobiography, Transference, Translation*, Lincoln, Nebr., Nebraska University Press, 1988. Andrew Benjamin, *Translation and the Nature of Philosophy*, London, Routledge, 1989. On the stranger, see J. Kristeva, *The Stranger*, New York, Columbia University Press, 1991.

translate, and yet justice requires translation as the only available means of accounting, of taking account of, the native, the slave, the foreigner, the stranger, the aegyptian, the nomad, the woman, the other that comes before the law.

As is well known, to translate connotes both to carry over or across, to move from one place to another, *trans-latum*, and, more remotely, to give up, hand over, transmit or betray, from *tradere*, which lies also at the root of tradition. In a direct sense, to translate is to figure, simulate or trope, to move or transfer a meaning from one place to another, where in classical rhetorical terms it does not naturally or properly belong.[79] It is to simulate, to act 'as if' the borrowed word or phrase belonged, or were no longer alien or strange. The translation posts, it sends on, it sends something borrowed, perhaps at a certain rate of interest or loan. Its relation to its source is one of transference, conscious or unconscious, it cannot let go, it betrays by remaining bound to an origin, a sovereign, a law.[80] The geopolitical metaphor of translation, of transfer and transference, of the tradition that traduces, is of considerable – though arguably unwitting – significance to critical legal studies. It may be addressed either geogaphically or temporally in terms of those purloined letters, those languages, posted from Europe to America and returned unopened or in inverted form. The question in geopolitical terms must be simply stated as 'what is America?' What is America to the critique of law? An unanswerable question perhaps, for America is a place one passes through.[81] The United States are after all most obviously a series of relations, of imaginary boundaries and imaginary communities. Their relation to Europe must be as various and several as their relation to themselves. How, in legal terms, could American critical legal studies be bound by an acceptance posted in Europe?

As a preliminary observation, might it not be the case that the prehistory of critical legal studies drew much, if not all, of its radicalism from the translation of European sources? The more iconoclastic realists turned to

79 Thus Quintilian, *Institutio Oratorio*, Cambridge, Mass., Harvard University Press, 1966 edn, book IX. 1: 4–5: (defining trope) 'the transference (*translata*) of words and phrases from the place which is strictly theirs to another where they do not properly belong.'
80 See particularly Derrida, *The Post Card*, pp. 339–347, 384–390. Arguing, *inter alia*, that transference is the mechanism whereby the analyst reduces or overcomes the patient's 'resistances' (ibid., p. 334).
81 See the brief remarks on America in J. Derrida, *Memoires for Paul de Man*, New York, Columbia University Press, 1986, pp. 12–20. Additionally, see J. Baudrillard, *America*, London, Verso, 1989; and in a more sociological vein, J. Baudrillard, *In the Shadow of the Silent Majorities . . . Or the End of the Social*, New York, Semiotexte, 1983. The tradition of French letters home from America goes back to Alexis de Tocqueville and is continued quite strikingly by Sartre and Foucault. In terms of self-description see P. Venturi and D. Scott-Brown, *Learning from Las Vegas*, Boston, MIT Press, 1977; F. Jameson, *Postmodernism or the Cultural Logic of Late Capitalism*, Durham, NC, Duke University Press, 1990; M. Davis, *City of Quartz: Excavating the Future in Los Angeles*, London, Verso, 1990.

Freud, Nietzsche and to Marx.[82] It may be, of course, that these figures are simply those that are recognisable to Europeans, that the real radicals were Peirce, Dewey, James, Morris or even Rorty – 'he created a space in American philosophy in which former New Leftists could go continental'[83] – as sources of legal realist critique and its critical progeny.[84] Yet it seems unlikely in the context of their future, for critical legal studies developed from a European left associated with Lukacs, Heller, Althusser, Foucault, Adorno and Habermas, but also and more improbably from the work of Lévi-Strauss, Ferdinand de Saussure, Jacques Lacan, Julia Kristeva, Jacques Derrida and most recently (in law) Niklas Luhmann. And their attraction was also their otherness, that they were continental, their language foreign, their ideas opaque. It is necessary to ask whether this importation represents an exotic escape from politics? A co-opted deferral of engagement? Lapsed commitment or a politics of apostacy, of the outside, of transgression, of fear? Is it simply a question of the subordination of jurisprudence to broader cultural trends within the academy? Is it rather that American jurisprudence is neither autonomous as a discipline nor free of the legal profession as a practice? That it was never intended as a form of scholarship but rather as a form of technical–practical service?

The dominance of European theory, of the phenomena of importation, translation and visitation, is marked by several ironies.[85] While American critical legal studies returns to Europe as a peculiarly American phenomenon concerned with a peculiarly American jurisdiction, its history is nonetheless that of displaced continental theory, its philosophy one of a

---

82 For an interesting analysis of the 'house radicalism' of realism, see John Brigham and Christine Harrington, 'Realism and its Consequences: An Inquiry into Contemporary Sociological Research' (1989) 17 *International Journal of the Sociology of Law* 41. See also D. Livingstone, 'Round and Round the Bramble Bush: From Legal Realism to Critical Legal Studies' (1982) 95 *Harvard Law Review* 1670; Frankenberg, 'Down by Law', at p. 338ff; D. Kennedy, 'A Rotation in Contemporary Legal Scholarship', in Joerges and Trubek (eds), *Critical Legal Thought*, p. 353; and G. Binder, 'On Critical Legal Studies as Guerrilla Warfare' (1987) 76 *Georgia Law Journal* 13. Cf. Duxbury, 'Some Radicalism about Realism?', 11.

83 N. Fraser, *Unruly Practices*, Minneapolis, University of Minnesota Press, 1989, p. 5.

84 See T. Grey, 'Holmes and Legal Pragmatism' (1989) 41 *Stanford Law Review* 787; R. Summers, *Instrumentalism and American Legal Theory*, Ithaca, NY, Cornell University Press, 1982; F. Kellogg, 'Legal Scholarship in the Temple of Doom: Pragmatism's Response to Critical Legal Studies' (1990) 65 *Tulane Law Reveiw* 15; and as an implicit theme see R. Kevelson, *Law as a System of Signs*, New York, Plenum Press, 1988. Richard Rorty is the last in the line of an indigenous American pragmatism, yet his work and certainly his fame are largely products of his continental connections. Cf. P. Goodrich, 'Law and Modernity' (1986) 49 *Modern Law Review* 545.

85 The debate as to the relationship between European philosophy and American theory can be followed in its various phases in J. Weiner, *Professors, Politics, and Pop*; Lehman, *Signs of the Times*; West, *American Evasion of Philosophy*; A. Bloom, *The Closing of the American Mind*, New York, Viking Books, 1987; Jacoby, *The Last Intellectuals*; and A. MacIntyre, *Three Rival Versions of Moral Inquiry*, London, Duckworth, 1990.

thoroughgoing eclecticism and its method a combination of précis, para-phrase and circumlocution. On one level this could be deemed a wholly postmodern phenomenon, a politics of the marginal and the fragmentary in which the student edited Law Review revels in new possibilities: Derrida applied to law and economics, Lévi-Strauss to torts cases, Lacan to contractual gap-filling, Luhmann to the constitution.[86] It is a one-way street and arguably a transcendental politics repeating old errors in new forms.[87] Yet this is no greater a sin of overconsumption than any other aspect of the American commodity market, it is indeed relatively liberal, pluralistic and free of the xenophobia whereby the English (legal) acad-emy steadfastly resists the incursions of foreign or otherwise 'unsound' theories. At the same time, however, there is a sense of ironic dis-orientation that accompanies much of this work. The translation of continental theory is market led and subjects critical scholarship to a breathless journalism which follows the immediate fashions one after another like papparazzi. One name gives way to another while cultural memory dissolves into the immediacy of the limelight: we can all be critical scholars for fifteen minutes.

The root of the problem in all probability lies somewhere in the subcultural character and conventions of legal scholarship. The Law Review is a steadfastly monolingual institution: what has not been translated does not yet exist.[88] Such an editorial norm is symptomatic of two separate problems. One is the obvious limitation of scholarship to those works which it is commercially viable to translate, while more legally relevant yet more specialist work in, for example, 'Critique du

---

86 D. Carlson, 'On the Margins of Micro-Economics: Price Theory as Logocentrism', in D. Carlson, D. Cornell and M. Rosenfeld (eds), *Deconstruction and the Possibility of Justice*, New York, Routledge, 1992, ch. 8; D. Kennedy, 'A Semiotics of Legal Argument', in R. Kevelson (ed.), *Law and Semiotics III*, New York, Peter Lang, 1990; J. Balkin, 'Ideological Drift', in R. Kevelson (ed.), *Action and Agency*, New York, Peter Lang, 1991; J. Boyle, 'The Anatomy of a Torts Class' (1985) 34 *American University Law Review* 1003; on Lacan and contracts, see D. Caudill, 'Lacan and Legal Language: Meanings in the Gaps/Gaps in the Meanings' (1992) 3 *Law and Critique* 169; and on Luhmann, see the symposium in volume 13 *Cardozo Law Review* (1992); also G. Teubner (ed.), *Autopoietic Law*, Florence, European University Press, 1987.

87 An argument forcefully made in N. Fraser, 'The French Derrideans: Politicising Deconstruction or Deconstructing the Political', reprinted in *idem, Unruly Practices*, pp. 69–93; and see also the analysis of the psychoanalytic left in Turkle, *Psychoanalytic Politics*; and also in E. Roudinesco, *Jacques Lacan and Co*, Chicago, University of Chicago Press, 1990. See further J. Jenson, 'Representations of Difference: The Varieties of French Feminism' (1990) 180 *New Left Review* 127. See also Rose, *Dialectic of Nihilism*. For further discussion, specifically related to law, see W.T. Murphy, 'Memorising Politics of Ancient History' (1987) 50 *Modern Law Review* 384.

88 I cannot resist observing that when this chapter was originally published in *New York University Law Review*, the editors insisted that I bring with me, on a prearranged visit to New York, copies of all non-English language books and articles cited.

Droit',[89] philosophy of law or the cultural history of European law remains in the obscurity of its native tongues.

The monolingual limitation of citation and reference in the Law Review points to a further problem: to what public sphere does the critique of law speak? The restriction of scholarship to the vernacular would have a justification if its political design were to foster a specific public discourse or dialogue as to legal change. Such is far from the case. The stylistic criterion has nothing to do with the vast glut of over-lengthy Law Review articles being read by any but professional academics. The critics speak to and write for the critics within the relative privacy of the law school. Their circle of acquaintance can be reconstructed in large measure from the frequency of citation of other American critical authors.[90] Put differently, if the theory translated, summarised, examined and explained in the Law Review article belongs initially to a European dialogue and corresponding public sphere, its legal significance is likely to be attached in some measure to that jurisdiction and its institutions.

Not only is available theory constrained by the economics of publishing but the potential practice or advocacy of legal change aligned to such theories is limited to continental jurisdictions which are procedurally and substantively different to American law. The irony is deepened once it is realised that it is most often legally harmless texts that are translated: if critical lawyers were to act on the political implications of the theoretical works which are most often cited, they would end up designing different housing, filming according to new theories of cinematography, reforming the practice of literary criticism, developing designer jeans, scribble-

89 'Critique du Droit' is the title of an untranslated series of critical legal work in France, published by an established Parisian publishing House, François Maspero. The early volumes in the series, particularly M. Miaille, *Une introduction critique au droit*, Paris, Maspero, 1976, are discussed in I. Stewart, 'Critical Legal Studies in France' (1981) 9 *International Journal of the Sociology of Law* 225, but the work has otherwise met with silence. I. Stewart, 'Pour une science critique du Droit' (1985) 23 *Annales de Vaucresson* 201; I. Stewart, 'Law and Closure' (1987) 50 *Modern Law Review* 908, provide some interesting and important comparative analyses of critique in law. See also W. Paul, *Marxistiche Rechtstheorie als Kritik des Rechts*, Frankfurt, Verlag, 1974; and the German essays in Joerges and Trubek (eds), *Critical Legal Thought*. In relation to French critical legal thought see also F. Ost and M. Van de Kerchove, *Jalons pour une theorie critique du droit*, Brussels, Presses Universitaires de Bruxelles, 1987; also the earlier work, J. Lenoble and F. Ost, *Droit, mythe et raison*, Brussels, Presses Universitaires de Bruxelles, 1980. It is also something of a scandal that F. Ewald, *L'Etat providence*, Paris, Grasset, 1987; and none of the work of Pierre Legendre have yet been translated. See for recent reviews of the latter, Y. Hachamovitch, 'One Law on the Other' (1990) 3 *International Journal of the Sociology of Law*; A. Pottage, 'Crime and Culture: The Relevance of the Psychoanalytical' (1992) 55 *Modern Law Review* 421. See also P. Goodrich and Alain Pottage (eds), *Law and Desire: Readings in the Jurisprudence of Pierre Legendre*, London, Macmillan, 1996.

90 I owe this melancholic observation to Professor Arthur Jacobson who has developed an elaborate and entertaining theory of the 'citation condominium', a self-circulating group of cross-references, a network of mutual citations inhabiting a largely hermetic or self-enclosed sphere of its own, an autopoietic system of (eternally) recurrent names.

writing or body-building. The relation between translated cultural and literary criticism and an American public sphere of legal reform or of radical legal change is complex, diffuse and to date remote.

In one respect this is a reflection of the decline of the public sphere as a site of intellectual or scholarly dialogue. In another sense it may yet reflect a politics by other means. In either case, it is necessary to ask 'what can intellectual life be, if it is subject to the phenomena of fashion?'[91] Is the everyday world of fashion the only access to politics, to the public sphere, that remains within the institution? Is it the only escape available from a dogmatic theology of law? Is it rather a sign of the loss of intellectual authenticity, of a market led scholarly journalism in which the dedicated academic follower of fashion is subjected to repeating traditions to which they do not belong, translating ideas which they do not understand and more generally instituting an idolatry or romanticism of great theorists, great names and great men.

## ABSTRACTIONIST THEORY: NEW LEFT OR OLD RITE

The preceding remarks may appear unduly negative: the political and cultural pluralism from time to time engendered by American pragmatism has in its way been a virtue. Nor is the left in Europe in any very competent or ethical position to criticise or chastise its American counterpart. The easy *ad hominem* arguments that have pursued the political compromise of Nietzsche, Heidegger or Paul de Man have seldom been predicated upon any reasoned political position nor has the critique of postmodernity generally been impeded by any very closely defined conception of the object – period, space or position – subjected to criticism. Like most intellectual novelties, critical legal studies provokes fear and dogma in equal measure. It is in that respect at least postmodern and on occasion post-scholarly as well. Its plural or diffuse identity – a feature it also shares with legal realism[92] – is not necessarily a commitment either to simple confusion or to a politics of parody, perplexity, pessimism or passivity. The deconstruction of identity, the denial of a unitary form or cause which is reflected among other things in theoretical eclecticism, is simply a denial of identity as foundation or ground of being: 'deconstruction ... establishes as political the very terms through which identity is articulated'.[93]

The identity of the legal critic or critical movement is dialectically tied

91 Debray, *Teachers, Writers, Celebrities*, at p. 8.
92 See, most obviously, K. Llewellyn, 'Some Realism about Realism – Responding to Dean Pound' (1931) 44 *Harvard Law Review* 1222; and the discussion in W. Twining, *Karl Llewellyn and the Realist Movement*, London, Weidenfeld and Nicolson, 1985.
93 J. Butler, *Gender Trouble: Feminism and the Subversion of Identity*, New York, Routledge, 1990.

to or parasitic upon that of the legal or juridical field itself.[94] While the movement of the critics may be contrasted to the stasis of the establishment or of doctrinal scholarship, the two cannot be separated in either political or conceptual terms. If it is the closure of legal doctrine that criticism seeks to subvert, it may well be that it proffers for law a wider cultural and political significance but that significance, that politics and culture are nonetheless bound to or derivative from a practice of law.[95] The political goal of exposing legal doctrine to cultural analysis, the history of legal practice to theoretical reconstruction, is threatening because it challenges the boundaries of the discipline and particularly the seclusion – the innocence – of its practice. At the risk of repetition, or at least of returning to the starting-point of this chapter, a third feature of critical legal studies is the distance between its theory and the discipline of law as a practice. More particularly, the abstractionism of the theory disengages critical legal analysis from the politics of what is primarily or at least in the first instance an educational practice, a politics of the discipline of law in an academic age.

It is perhaps the ironic fate of the postmodern intellectual to be tied to a specific institution and its practice. It is certainly as yet unclear what the consequences or limitations of that position are likely to be. In the meantime, critique still refers to scholarship and to a species of enlightenment although it may well be an ambiguous and contradictory enlightenment, a double agency or *double entendre*, illumination designed to preclude illumination and to subvert the institution.[96] In the meantime it remains a question of the extent, direction and audience or public sphere of the critique of dogmatic reason, of the relationship between the inside and the outside of the institution and of conceiving of discourse 'as a violence that we do to things'.[97] In particular critique must address the question of tradition that underpins so much of the confusion or despair associated with the question of identity: 'our inheritance, because of the manner of its textual survival and the spasmodic mode of its reconstruction, is a conspicuously muddled one'.[98] The inheritance or specific tradition of western left intellectual culture is further both disorientated

---

94 For an analysis of the legal field, see P. Bordieu, 'The Force of Law'; and more generally his contributions to D. Young (ed.), *Knowledge and Social Control*, Milton Keynes: Open University Press, 1976.

95 On which point, see particularly Donald Kelley, *The Human Measure: Social Thought in the Western Legal Tradition*, Cambridge, Mass., Harvard University Press, 1990.

96 Sloterdijk, *Critique of Cynical Reason*, ch. 4; Debray, *Critique of Political Reason*, ch. 7.

97 Foucault, 'The Order of Discourse', in *idem, Archaeology of Knowledge*, New York, Pantheon Books, 1972.

98 Murphy, 'Memorising Politics of Ancient History', at p. 405, and remarking earlier 'there are some things on which it is so hard to make up one's mind' (ibid., p. 393). See further, Derrida, *Writing and Difference*; P. Legendre, *L'Inestimable objet de la transmission*, Paris, Fayard, 1985.

by events and confused by long-term stasis if not outright failure. Our inheritance, however, is two-thirds of our identity, genealogy our first character or fate. In this sobering yet salutary sense it needs to be reiterated that the demarcation of the disciplines, the disciplinary canon, the subject, the treatise, casebook or textbook, is the object language of law and the site of critical legal practice.

One example will suffice. The preface to the much commented and much used Dawson, Harvey and Henderson, *Contracts*,[99] makes the striking assertion that it is not the function of the textbook to merely convey a technical knowledge. Neither is it the purpose of the course in contracts – which the book, needless to say, represents – simply to inculcate the analytic skills of the intellectual discipline of contracts. The work is dedicated to a higher end, one which acknowledges that 'there is a language and a culture to be passed on'.[100] There, in an explicit and direct yet nonetheless overlooked form, is the stake of critique. The question at issue is that of how one would pass on, disseminate or diffuse another language and a different culture, or simply other texts, other portraits, other promises.

The first stage of critique must be to reconstruct the history of that discipline, that language and culture of contracts, to ask what or who was contracted over the long time span of historical and institutional structures, over the *longue durée* of contractual language.[101] There are in these historical terms at least three discernible stages in the development of critique in the specific context of a subdiscipline such as contract. Somewhat idiosyncratically they will here be labelled laconically in terms of grammatology, judgment and representation.[102] Considerable work has

---

99 John P. Dawson, G. Harvey and D. Henderson, *Contracts: Cases and Materials*, Foundation Press, 1985 edn. For a feminist commentary, see Mary Joe Frug, 'Re-Reading Contracts: A Feminist Analysis of a Contracts Casebook' (1985) 34 *American University Law Review* 1065. For further essays on related themes, see *idem*, *A Postmodern Feminist Legal Analysis*, New York, Routledge, 1993.

100 Ibid., at p. xxiii.

101 The term derives from the work of Fernand Braudel. See F. Braudel, *On History*, Cambridge, Mass., Harvard University Press, 1980; and for an example, F. Braudel, *The Mediterranean and the Mediterranean World*, New York, Viking, 1972. See further Murphy, 'The Oldest Social Science?'; D. Kelley, 'Gaius Noster: Substructures of Western Social Thought' (1979) 84 *American History Review* 619.

102 I here respond in part to comments of N. Duxbury, 'Postmodernism and its Discontents' (1991) 11 *Oxford Journal of Jurisprudence* 589. More generally on the theoretical context of critical legal histories, see R. Gordon, 'Critical Legal Histories' (1984) 36 *Stanford Law Review* 57; Hunt, 'The Theory of Critical Legal Studies', pp. 37–43; P. Hirst and P. Jones, 'The Critical Resources of Established Jurisprudence' (1987) 14 *Journal of Law and Society* 21; N. Rose, 'Beyond the Public/Private Division: Law, Power and the Family' (1987) 14 *Journal of Law and Society* 61; P. Goodrich, 'Ars Bablativa: Ramism, Rhetoric and the Genealogy of English Jurisprudence', in G. Leyh (ed.), *Legal Hermeneutics: History, Theory and Practice*, Berkeley and Los Angeles, University of California Press, 1992; G. Rubin and D. Sugarman (eds), *Law, Economy and Society*, Abingdon, Professional Books, 1984; J. Minson, *Genealogies of Morals*, London, Macmillan, 1985.

been done in the history of Anglo-American contract law. A.W.B. Simpson, whose philosophical position would be better described as that of hedonist and cynic rather than as self-conscious critic, among other things has traced the history of assumpsit as the prehistory of contract and has related the development of the doctrine of mistake to an early version of the futures market,[103] as well as indicating the civilian basis and borrowings of English contract doctrine.[104] James Gordley has provided a meticulous account of the medieval glossatorial conceptualisation of contracts and traces the mailbox rule to the *Digest*.[105] P.S. Atiyah has written an extensive and largely critical history of the concept of freedom of contract, while the approach of the major American treatise writers, and of Dawson, Harvey and Henderson in particular, is structured by extensive historical extracts and by the archaisms of American contracts law.[106] It is perhaps for this reason that many of the more interesting works in critical legal studies have engaged with aspects of contract law and with the problems of teaching it.[107] To suggest something more than a simple history or politics of contract law may in this context seem perverse. On the other hand, instrumental histories of the effects of contract doctrine or internal histories of the structure of contractual relations provide only a very partial opening of the discipline.

The second stage of critique endeavours to address the forms of criticism that have shaped the development of the field. In contract law, there have been three discernible forms which, laconically (and somewhat idiosyncratically), are here labelled grammatology, judgment and representation.

103 A.W.B. Simpson, *A History of the Law of Contract*, Oxford, Oxford University Press, 1978; idem, 'Contracts for Cotton to Arrive' (1987) 8 *Cardozo Law Review* 287.
104 A.W.B. Simpson, 'Innovation in Nineteenth Century Contract Law' (1977) 91 *Law Quarterly Review* 247.
105 J. Gordley, *Philosophical Origins of Modern Contract Doctrine*, Oxford, Oxford University Press, 1991, citing Bartolus and the *Digest*.
106 P.S. Atiyah, *The Rise and Fall of the Freedom of Contract*, Oxford, Oxford University Press, 1976; A.L. Corbin, *Corbin on Contracts: A Comprehensive Treatise on the Rules of Contract Law*, St Paul, West, 1950.
107 Unger, 'Critical Legal Studies Movement'; C. Dalton, 'An Essay in the Deconstruction of Contract Doctrine' (1985) 94 *Yale Law Journal* 997; M.J. Frug, 'A Feminist Analysis of Contracts Casebooks' (1984) 35 *American University Law Review*; idem, 'Impossibility in Contract Doctrine' (1992) 140 *University of Pennsylvania Law Review*; P. Gabel and J. Feinman, 'Contract Law as Ideology', in Kairys (ed.), *The Politics of Law*; M. Rosenfeld, 'Contract and Justice: The Relation between Classical Contract Law and Social Contract Theory' (1985) 70 *Iowa Law Review* 769; M. Rosenfeld, 'Hegel and the Dialectic of Contract' (1989) 10 *Cardozo Law Review* 1199; H. Collins, *Law of Contract*, London, Weidenfeld and Nicolson, 1989; P. Goodrich, 'Contractions', in A. Carty (ed.), *Post-Modern Law*, Edinburgh, Edinburgh University Press, 1990; C. Pateman, *The Sexual Contract*, Oxford, Polity Press, 1985; B.S. Jackson, *Law, Fact and Narrative Coherence*, Liverpool, Deborah Charles, 1989; R. Abel, 'Torts', in Kairys (ed.), *The Politics of Law*; Hutchinson, *Dwelling on the Threshold*, at chs. 6 and 10. It is interesting also to note in this context that E.B. Pashukanis, *Law and Marxism*, London, Ink Links, 1978, developed a Marxist theory of law specifically predicated upon the historical linking of modern law to contractual relations. See further, Robert Fine, *Democracy and the Rule of Law*, London, Pluto Press, 1984.

The philosophy of contractual history is initially and at its best a grammatological endeavour.[108] The legal concept of contract develops through the materiality of the signs of contract: the *symbolon* was classically a thing divided, then a creed or literal inscription or enunciation of faith, an ecclesiastical and social pact, and latterly an instrument, tract, deed or obligation, a confession of will.[109] Contract, tract or treatise, is both literally and figuratively a species of writing, of memory and inscription but also of law. Arthur Jacobson develops this theme in an argument that translates the Judaeo-Christian tradition, and specifically the decalogue, into a theory of writing law. The commandments or laws are written three times in a narrative that centres around the destruction of a false image, an idol:

> the struggle over writing in *Names* – between Elohim and Yahweh, between Yahweh and Moses – rescues it from idolatry. The struggle supplies the necessary collaborations. To write is to rewrite. To rewrite is to erase. To erase is to rescue writing from idolatry.[110]

Writing in this tradition is not simply, immediately or only the speech of or 'in the name of' the father.[111] It is a complex negotiation, at base an agreement not only to respect the text or to follow the law according to the later maxim of *pacta sunt servanda*, but also it is a contract as to words and as to language itself. In short, the complex combination of writing and erasure, speech, record and interpretation, that make up the law – its instruments, its deeds, its faiths – impose a duty of interpretation on the ground that law can always change, that a theistic conception of creation

108 On, or of, grammatology, see Derrida, *Of Grammatology*, where grammatology is depicted as the study of systems of inscription: if writing signifies inscription and especially the durable institution of the sign ... writing in general covers the entire field of linguistic signs' (ibid., p. 44). Grammatology proposes an interrogation into the significance of the fact that law is written. More than that, 'the science of writing should ... look for its object at the roots of scientificity. The history of writing should turn back toward the origin of historicity. A science of the possibility of science? A science of science which would no longer have the form of *logic* but that of *grammatics*? A history of the possibility of history ...?' (Ibid, pp. 27–28). See also Derrida, *Positions*. For an analysis of grammatology in terms of the history of legal writing, see P. Goodrich, 'Rhetoric, Grammatology and the Hidden Injuries of Law' (1989) 18 *Economy and Society* 167.
109 On which, see particularly William West, *Symbolaeography: The Art or Description or Image of Instruments, or the Paterne of Presidents or the Notarie or Scrivener*, London, Society of Stationers, 1590/1603 edn; also Thomas Phayr, *A New Boke of Presidentes, in Manner of a Register*, London, E. Whytchurche, 1544. On the use of icons and objects as signs of donation, contract and law, see Michael Clanchy, *From Memory to Written Record*, London, Arnold, 1979; Jack Goody, *Writing and the Organisation of Society*, Cambridge, Cambridge University Press, 1987.
110 Jacobson, 'The Idolatry of Rules', at 1095.
111 As in Plato, on which see Derrida, *Dissemination*. See further, J. Lacan, *Four Fundamental Concepts of Psychoanalysis*, London: Pelican, 1978; J. Lacan, *Seminaire V: l'éthique de psychanalyse*, Paris, Seuil, 1985; P. Legendre, *Le Crime de caporal Lortie: traité sur le père*, Paris, Fayard, 1989; Cornell, *Beyond Accommodation*, especially pp. 41ff.

cannot treat either world or law as closed:

> to consider rules complete, from Moses' perspective, is to treat them as engravings. To apply rules to cases as if they are already formed bows to rules as idols. Creation is not complete, even if we want to treat it so.[112]

It is not simply a question of the history of contracts being a semiotic endeavour. The history of contracts is a history of a particular tradition of sociality, of a symbolic structure, a particular discipline, a particular culture and its graphic instruments, its inscriptions, its writing: 'But was it not the Judaeo-Christian, rather than the Graeco-Roman, tradition which inserted the question of law in the innermost recess of the question of Being? Only history can get at what this means for us'.[113] At the level of the history of judgment, contracts mean specific assignations of subjectivity, particular constructions of language and of silence, the implication and interpretation or pricing (*inter-pretium*)[114] of certain actions, behaviours and words. At the risk of stating the obvious, the contract is a sign and is subject or party, as Dawson remarked, to a social language or tradition of contracts. Hence the covenant, charter, compact or contract would traditionally begin by invoking the deity (*dei gratia*) and the crown (*fidei defensor*) to indicate both good faith (*bona fide*) and also the universal community of the text (*omnibus christi fidelibus ad quos praesentes literae pervenerint*).[115] The contract is the insignia, effigy or emblem of admission to that community, it is the recognition that the condition of possibility of interpreting the contract in law is the socio-linguistic contract which guarantees our initial access to the law. The contract is not my language but our language, not my law but rather my part – my act, my deed, my confession – before the law. Hence the gender and the sociality of contracts: according to a classical principle of *imitatio imperii*, each subordinate sovereignty – each child of the text – imitates the sovereign constitution and so too each minor contract imitates a sovereign social compact. Such is the order of succession, of contraction,

> the charter is the contract for the following, which quite stupidly one has to believe: Socrates comes *before* Plato, there is between them – and in general – an order of generations, an irreversible sequence of inheritance. Socrates is before, not in front of, but before Plato, therefore behind

112 Jacobson, 'Idolatry of Rules', at p. 1132.
113 Murphy, 'Memorising Politics of Ancient History', at p. 387. See further, P. Legendre, 'Les Maitres de la loi: étude sur la fonction dogmatique en regime industriel', in *idem*, *Ecrits juridiques du moyen age occidental*, London, Variorum, 1988; Murphy, 'The Oldest Social Science?', p. 182. Cf. Rose, *Dialectic of Nihilism*, pp. 77–84.
114 On which fascinating etymology, see Benveniste, *Le Vocabulaire des institutions Indo-Europêenes*, vol. 1.
115 In West, *Symbolaeography*, passim.

him, and the charter binds us to this order: this is how to orient one's thought, this is the left and this is the right, march.[116]

The condition of judgment which critical legal studies has begun to reconstruct is itself a judgment and not a foundation, it is a contract, a social pact, a tradition. It represents us to ourselves, it is our continuity, our identity, our law. It is also our word, our sign, our text.

Finally, how should these ties, these solemn prejudices or articles of faith be transcribed in postmodern conditions? At the very least a critical legal analysis of the history of contract doctrine can build upon deviationist internal analyses. The great failing of deconstruction in America has not been that it was playful, obscure or endlessly interpretative but rather that it uncritically translated and arguably absorbed deconstruction into an existing network of disciplinary practices and their rhetorical forms. When it comes to the demarcation of disciplines, it is the function of critical thought to cross boundaries and to mix genres both in a reflexive political sense and in a stylistic and rhetorical sense of an alternative practice of writing destined to address a future that is not yet formed, neither bound to our existing contract nor subject to the schemata that spell out the conceptual proprieties of its tradition. To 'con-tract' is to do things with texts, to circulate, send and reinvest texts with a reflexive political significance: in an immediate and vital sense, they *are* the locality, the terrain and the community of critical legal thought. In addressing the texts of law, the critic engages with the desire to comprehend the material history, the circulation, interpretation and passing on of the text. Critical thought would also understand the conceptual conditions of possibility of the text and its interpretation. In rethinking the latter issue, the paramount aim is to influence and to change the political community that determines, according to a predefined series of hierarchies and oppositions, both the continuance and the fate of contractual language, its speech and its silence.

The contract, in the words of one recent account, 'is a sexual–social pact, but the story of the sexual contract has been repressed. . . the missing half of the story tells how a specifically modern form of patriarchy is established'.[117] The narrative of contract begins not simply with Hobbes' materialist absolutism grounding law in the violence of monarchy, but similarly with Robert Filmer's *Patriarcha* and with the adoption of a Roman conception of sovereign will and jurisdiction, of the father as legislator, as *Pater patriae*, king and patriarch.[118] The question of who contracts becomes more complex when the legal conception of subject and will is traced to the power – to the name – of the father. Yet even here the boundaries are not discrete or singular. The sexual repression is predicated also upon a

---

116 Derrida, *The Post Card*, p. 20.
117 Pateman, *Sexual Contract*, at p. 1.
118 R. Filmer, *Patriarcha or the Natural Power of Kings*, London, W. Davis, 1680, at p. 20.

specific conception of genealogy as legitimacy and upon succession as passing from father to son. At issue here is not simply a linguistic coincidence, that legitimacy is a familial expression, but a further contract which founds the tradition as history, language, and narrative structure upon these figures of domestic descent: upon what we call power, 'a word derived from Roman law where it originally designated the domestic power of the father'.[119] Our contract, according to Roman law at least, is to obey our parents and our country.[120]

## PAST AS PROLOGUE

The brief excursus above on the possibility of critique in contract law can serve to illustrate three preconditions to the politicisation of critical legal studies. The first consideration is that of the use of history in reconstructing the intellectual development of the doctrinal tradition. Critical legal studies, particularly as a development from some Anglo-American version of historical materialism, has always paid a certain passing due to the power of history.[121] The reconstruction of American law, however, cannot credibly base itself upon the short-term historical journalism of American institutions. Sensitivity to history should face critical legal studies with a series of geopolitical questions as to the destiny and transmission of culturally specific forms of law and of their critique. It would be a history of tradition, of the long time span, of the *longue durée*, of representation, repetition and reproduction.

Second, this historical perspective should force critique to focus upon the systems of classification, the conceptual grids or schemata, whereby doctrine divides, categorises and represents the subject-matter, the disciplines of law. The rewriting of the disciplines, the reformation of what the legal academy does, is a question of a return to epistemic structures, the forms of knowledge that pass as law. It is for this reason that the more radical strands of critical legal studies have chosen to ignore the piecemeal pragmatism of post-realist legal reform and to develop instead novel forms of writing law.[122] Included in the concept of novel doctrinal rhetorics, in biography, the novella, body writing, grammatology or philosophical deconstruction as proper epistolary forms for critical legal scholarship, is a profound change in the object of critical thought in law.

---

119 See particularly Legendre, *L'Inestimable objet de la transmission*, at p. 35.
120 *Digest* 1.1.2.
121 Thus, for example, D. Kennedy, 'The Structure of Blackstone's Commentaries' (1979) 28 *Buffalo Law Review* 205.
122 The list is not a long one, but for dramatic – and perhaps dramatistic – examples, see particularly Hutchinson, *Dwelling on the Threshold*, (particularly 'Indiana Dworkin and Law's Empire'); P. Williams, *The Alchemy of Race and Rights*, Cambridge, Mass., Harvard University Press, 1991; Cornell, *Beyond Accommodation*; P. Schlag, 'Normative and Nowhere to Go' (1991) 43 *Stanford Law Review* 167; and for a remarkable European example, Douzinas, Warrington, and McVeigh, *Postmodern Jurisprudence*, pt. 3.

In one respect the issue returns to the question of identity, but in this instance it is the identity of the intellectual in law that is called into question. It is a matter of the role of a radical scholarship, but it is also a question of the self-definition, the insecurity and the fate of personal investment in or commitment to challenging the established institution and its pedagogy of law. It is a question also of the complicity of the critic in repressive institutional practices, a complicity that extends into a hierarchical programme, an elitist curriculum, an intellectually complacent if not overtly anti-intellectual syllabus and a largely passive relation to the inheritance, transmission and reproduction of the legal tradition. In this respect it will be argued in conclusion that the politics of legal critique are the politics of a particular profession, a questioning of the law of law, but also a questioning of our place within and responsibility for the tradition. The marks of politics in the discourse of critique are neither familiar nor obvious: they do not relate directly to a specific content or programme but rather to an ethics; they do not belong directly to a given tradition but rather to a necessarily ambiguous and potentially subversive place or space in the legal academy; they do not share the organisational framework or umbrella of previous or pluvious movements but rather stand for a critique of organisational or managerial forms of rationality.[123] The politics of reason is not simply a local politics, it is oppositional, fragmentary and frequently obscure. It remains in many respects a politics of style and is in consequence resistant to normative forms of analysis.

The dice are loaded against a politically radical critical legal studies. In sociological terms intellectual radicalism has been the product of institutional insecurity or of externality to the institution.[124] Whatever else the

123 This point has been made in many different ways. M. Foucault, 'Intellectuals and Power', in *idem, Language, Counter-Memory, Practice*; and M. Foucault, *Power/Knowledge*, New York, Pantheon Books, 1980, probably provides one of the more important analyses of a new kind of politics. See also J. Derrida, *Du droit à la philosophie*, Paris, Galilee, 1991, pt. 3. Specifically in relation to the legal tradition, see Derrida, 'Force of Law'; Schlag, 'Le Hors de Texte C'Est Moi'; Cornell, *Philosophy of the Limit*, pp. 170–183; G. Bruns, 'Law and Language' in Leyh (ed.), *Legal Hermeneutics*, pp. 23–40.

124 Bordieu, *Homo Academicus*, at pp. 125–127, associates political radicalism with marginal disciplines or with institutionally threatened individuals. Debray, *Teachers, Writers, Celebrities*, similarly associates the new high intelligentsia with a structurally co-opted clericism; and see also R. Debray, *Modeste contribution aux discours et ceremonies officiels du dixieme anniversaire*, Paris, Maspero, 1978, taking a position close to that of the classic P. Nizan, *Les Chiens de garde*, Paris, Maspero, 1932. In an American context, see Jacoby, *The Last Intellectuals*, at pp. 186 and 190: (discussing the movement of the new left intelligentsia into the universities)

In the United States, however, a dissenting or Marxist culture has never been firmly established; it is diffuse, fragile and frequently lost . . . the influx of left scholars has not changed the picture; reluctantly or enthusiastically they gain respectability at the cost of identity.

For discussion of law and intellectual radicalism, see Goodrich, *Legal Discourse*, at pp. 205–212; P. Fitzpatrick, 'The Abstracts and Brief Chronicles of the Times: Supplementing Jurisprudence', in P. Fitzpatrick (ed.), *Dangerous Supplements*, Durham, NC, Duke University Press, 1991; C. Smart, *Feminism and the Power of Law*, London, Routledge, 1989, ch. 1.

critics may argue, law is the least threatened and one of the best paid of academic disciplines. At most the bulk of critical legal scholars could lay claim to the comfort but insignificance of less privileged law schools. Even here, however, critical scholars have tended to move on, their career trajectories taking them to more privileged schools: the American legal academy can hardly be accused collectively of refusal or inability to 'buy out' or co-opt the radicals where such seemed the easiest course. Second, the history of the western left hardly encourages optimism as to the future of a revolutionary or politically radical institutional tradition. Anderson summarises several histories of western oppositional movements in arguing that

> no matter how otherwise heteroclite, they share one fundamental emblem: a common and latent pessimism. All the major departures or developments of substance within this tradition are distinguished from the classical heritage of historical materialism by the darkness of their implications or conclusions.[125]

This seemingly prescient 'pervasive melancholy' is frequently interpreted as leading from politics to aesthetics – to the 'hyperinflation of aesthetic discourses'[126] – and from activism to passivity if not *ressentiment*.[127] Worse still, the tradition is neither indigenous nor comprehensible to the native intellect. It is taken at best to augur poetry rather than politics, careerism rather than critique, fashion rather than passion.

The question remains, however, as to why a politics of writing, a stylistic radicalism, a purely discursive opposition or subversion should engender such hostility, such grandiloquent rejection from the legal academy. The answer must be linked in some way to the institutional threat that these critics represent. In an important sense the politics of writing brings radicalism home to the academy and challenges, at the very least, the languages of law or in one recent coinage, the 'law of text in the texts of law'.[128] In marked contrast to the disillusion and disfavour with which the traditional left has dismissed 'continental theory' and post-Marxist politics as pretentious, opaque and even dishonest, it is quite possible that the politics of writing will popularise critique both within and without the legal academy. At an immediate level, concern with grammatology, with modes of discourse and with the traditions and mechanisms of transmission, make this particular radicalism well placed to gain access to the

125 Anderson, *Considerations on Western Marxism*, at p. 88; and the later analysis in P. Anderson, 'Modernity and Revolution' (1984) 144 *New Left Review* 96.
126 Baudrillard, *La Transparence du mal*, at pp. 19–21.
127 Jacoby, *The Last Intellectuals*, especially pp. 180–190; Dews, *Logics of Disintegration*, at pp. xiv–xvii. Cf. F. Jameson, *Late Marxism*, London, Verso, 1990, pp. 227–250.
128 See Goodrich, *Languages of Law*; and Douzinas, Warrington and McVeigh, *Postmodern Jurisprudence*, ch. 2.

new media that now dominate cultural life. As a form of hedonism, of writing the body, it is also possible that critical legal studies could not simply oppose but also seduce in the sense of taking the politics of law into the sphere of enjoyment, into the media of representation and reproduction.[129] The question of justice, of the possibility of ethical judgment, is both a question of style or form of representation but equally a politics of inscription, of the link between writing and erasure from the text, between communication and excommunication, freedom and guilt, innocence and bodily sacrifice.

In more directly or at least classically political terms, it can be relatively uncontentiously observed that the politics of the institution, of the academy, revolve around the constitution and policing of sites of enunciation. The institution qualifies, regulates and ordains through patterns of discourse. It establishes rights of speech, jurisdictions, through linguistic examinations, through essays, dissertations, moots, bolts, writing programmes and other verbal performances. It assesses, grades, classifies, marks, assigns, defines, simulates and litigates through the institution of protocols or rhetorics of writing.[130] While it might be argued that threatening the procedures of normalisation within the law school is a far cry from the politics of any genuinely politicised public sphere, it can equally be argued not only that the institution is the last remaining habitus of radicals but that the media of transmission, of teaching and of reproduction, are the site of a new politics, that the educational institution is a fundamental element in the future of radicalism. Whether such a conclusion should be greeted with optimism or pessimism remains an open question. Critical legal studies both represents and transgresses the politics of law: in being an important dimension of a wider legal politics it evidences both the potential and the limitations of that politics, it shows us what politics there is and it show that such a politics is not yet that significant or radical a cultural force. In so doing, it indicates that there is much intellectual space yet to be filled, it indicates that while critical legal studies is a radical force in the legal institution it is not yet radical enough.

129 On the politics of seduction, see particularly J. Baudrillard, *Seduction*, London, Macmillan, 1990; also S. Zizek, *For They Know Not What They Do*. Cf. A. Callinicos, *Against Postmodernism: A Marxist Critique*, London, Polity Press, 1989; also T. Eagleton, *The Ideology of the Aesthetic*, Oxford, Blackwell, 1990. More generally, Kristeva, *Revolution in Poetic Language*; R. Braidotti, *Patterns of Dissonance*, Oxford, Polity Press, 1990; H. Cixous, *Coming to Writing*.
130 In this respect D. Kennedy, *Legal Education as Training for Hierarchy*, Cambridge, Afar, 1982, is perceptive and informative.

# Index

absence 44, 55, 136–7, 148, 155; *see also* nothing
academics 210–13, 216–19
*accessio* 87
Accursius 2, 156
*acheiropoiesis* 155, 157
Act of Supremacy 18, 126
addiction 134, 139–41
Adorno, Theodor 186, 206
aereall signs 23–4
Aeschylus 168, 174
aesthetics 6–7, 52–66, 96–111, 166, 177, 202
Agrippa, Henry 136–7, 146–7
Alciatus, Andreas 41, 91, 95, 97, 132
allegory 128
Allestree, Thomas 148
Alsatia 60
altar 78
America 205–7
amnesia 113, 121–3, 137, 147
*amor fati* 25, 166, 175, 177–8, 183, 203
*amor interruptus* 55–6
*amor matris* 172–4
*amour lointain* 5, 32–44, 54–60, 69–71
analogy 128, 179–81
*anamnesis* 113, 121–4, 127–9, 135
Anderson, Perry 186, 218
Anglicanism 11–15, 90, 134–5
*anima legis* 10, 132
*Antigone* 42
antirrhesis 85, 128, 199
*apertio oris* 84
Aphrodite 42
Apollo 178–9
*apologia* 11–14
*aporia* 8, 52–4, 179–80
apparell 73, 77, 81–2

*apprenticii nobiliores* 78–9
*arcana amoris* 55–8
*arcana iuris* 133
archive 124, 141
Aristotle 132, 168
*ars praedicandi* 119
art: of law 6, 65–6, 96–8, 132–3, 161–4; of love 30, 32, 50–3, 62–71
Astell, Mary 60
Aston, Margaret 12, 98
Atiyah, Patrick 212
augurs 169
autonomy (of law) 136–7, 160–3
autopoiesis 113, 141
Aylmer, Bishop 15

Babel 68, 166, 203
Bachelard, Gaston 167
Bacon, Francis 138, 150–3
Baldus 98
Baldwin, John 36
*Balfour* v *Balfour* 60
Baker, J.H. 75, 94, 107
*Baron and Feme* 150
Baroque 11–14, 53, 147
barristers 79–82
Bataille, G. 78–80, 88–9
Baudrillard, Jean 191–3, 205
Beauvoir, Simone de 167
Behaigne, King of 49
*Bell* v *Lever Bros* 146
Bellapertica, Petrus de 153
Benjamin, Walter 204
Benton, John 36
Benveniste, Emile 100, 188, 214
Bernard of Clairvaux 50
Bernard de Ventadour 54–5
Bishops 152